Jung's Challenge to Contemporary Religion

Edited by
Murray Stein and Robert L. Moore

Murray Stein

Carrin Dunne

David Miller

Nathan Schwartz-Salant

June Singer

Joan Engelsman

Wayne Rollins

William Dols, Jr.

Robert L. Moore

Julia Jewett

David Dalrymple

CHIRON PUBLICATIONS
400 Linden, Wilmette, Illinois 60091

Printed in the United States of America

Edited by Carole Presser

Book design by Elaine M. Hill

Library of Congress Cataloging-in-Publication Data

Jung's challenge to contemporary religion.

Includes bibliographies.
1. Jung, C. G. (Carl Gustav), 1875–1961—Religion.
2. Psychoanalysis and religion. I. Stein, Murray,
1943–   . II. Moore, Robert L.
BF173.J85J9   1987   200'.1'9   86–32703
ISBN 0–933029–09–8

Contents

Editors' Preface   iv

Jung's Green Christ: A Healing Symbol for Christianity
Murray Stein   1

Between Two Thieves: A Response to Jung's Critique of the Christian
Notions of Good and Evil   Carrin Dunne   15

"Attack Upon Christendom!" The Anti-Christianism of Depth Psychology
David L. Miller   27

Patriarchy in Transformation: Judaic, Christian, and Clinical Perspectives
Nathan Schwartz-Salant   41

Jung's Gnosticism and Contemporary Gnosis   June Singer   73

Beyond the Anima: The Female Self in the Image of God
Joan Chamberlain Engelsman   93

Jung's Challenge to Biblical Hermeneutics   Wayne G. Rollins   107

The Church as Crucible for Transformation   William Dols   127

Ritual Process, Initiation, and Contemporary Religion
Robert L. Moore   147

Womansoul: A Feminine Corrective to Christian Imagery
Julia Jewett   161

"Images of Immortality": Jung and the Archetype of Death and Rebirth
David J. Dalrymple   175

Notes About the Contributors   189

Editors' Preface

The psychology of C. G. Jung has by now been used in many ways to enhance the modern person's appreciation of religious experience and symbolism. Unlike other modern psychologists, Jung did not denigrate religion or religious experience but rather believed that religious thought and practice could be authentic expressions of humanity's awareness of the divine. His non-reductive approach to religious image and doctrine has appealed to modern persons who are embued with religious values and tradition but who also seek a new appreciation of what they have. Jung has helped them appropriate their faith within a modern frame of intellectual understandings. Others, who have fallen away from religious traditions, have found in Jung's work a way into religious awareness, in their own styles and using non-collective means. Jung has helped them connect to their life's unique meaning.

What has not been looked at as carefully or taken as seriously are the many ways in which Jung challenged religious traditions, their practices and beliefs. Jung felt that if Christianity, for one, did not change in fundamental ways and evolve, it would become an irrelevant relic. The religions of the West, he argued, must come to terms with their own evil and fashion a new understanding of God; they must drastically revise their patriarchal biases and find new ways of including the feminine within the heart of their symbolic universes; they must open up to new symbols taking form in the collective unconscious; they must change their attitudes toward nature and integrate science into their theological methods; they must open the door to more diversity of belief and practice and honor the individual soul more profoundly; they must stop striving for spiritual perfection and begin struggling for psychological wholeness. Jung felt that the crisis in Western culture was acute. If a way were not found to evolve religiously, which requires fundamental transformations in theology, ethics, everyday religious practice, liturgy, and symbolics, the religious traditions of the West and their cultural expressions were doomed to extinction.

In October 1985, the C. G. Jung Institute of Chicago sponsored a conference on this theme, entitled "Jung's Challenge to Contemporary Religion." The papers included in this volume were first presented in that forum of debate and discussion. The conference was successful because it addressed the concerns of many and discussed them at a deep level of care and sophistication. The tone of the conference was neither hostile toward religion nor congratulatory of it; it was evolutionary, combining both criticism of what is and hints and hopes for future development. The editors participated in this conference and felt it marked a new milestone in the ongoing Jungian contribution to modern culture, as well as the articulation of incisive and balanced criticisms and suggestions for the future of religion in contemporary culture. The editors are delighted to offer these papers to the wider public, in the hope that the discussion begun in Evanston, Illinois, will expand and grow.

Murray Stein and Robert L. Moore

Acknowledgments

The papers included in this volume originated in a conference of the same title sponsored by the C. G. Jung Institute of Chicago in October 1985. This book is made possible in part by the generous support from the Institute and from Mr. and Mrs. James Hemphill.

Jung's Green Christ:
A Healing Symbol
for Christianity

Murray Stein

> History enjoys discrediting
> arbitrarily chosen symbols.
> Arthur Rosenberg

As Christianity opens the pages on its third millennium, it becomes increasingly evident that its symbolic core has begun to undergo a profound process of transformation. New images of God are beginning to appear, new language is being used in the collective prayers, a different sense of the meaning of "God is at work in history" is emerging. Enormous questions remain, however. Are these merely arbitrarily chosen symbols, or are they lasting and genuine? Where is the tradition going? What does all of this change really mean? And how are we to proceed from here?

In the last twenty-five years of his life, Jung addressed himself actively and tirelessly to the issues raised by this evolution in Christian doctrine and symbol. He discusssed these issues at a cognitive level, but, far more importantly, he addressed them with his whole being. His deepest psychic processes became engaged by the dilemma of modern Christianity. The stance he took toward Christianity was that of therapist to patient, and like the therapist who is deeply gripped by the suffering of his patient and takes that suffering into himself for purposes of healing, so Jung took the conflicts of Christianity into himself and sought solutions in the responses that his psyche returned to them.

One of Jung's greatest potential contributions to contemporary consciousness is the discovery, or rather the scientific rediscovery, that "no man is an island entire of itself; every man is a piece of the continent, a part of the main . . ." (John Donne). The great value of this finding lies in its power to overcome the problems of anomie and isolation suffered by so many in our modern age. Jung constructed the term *collective uncon-scious* to discuss this finding.

By collective unconscious, Jung not only means that all humans are deeply connected, but also that no individual's experience is absolutely idiosyncratic and unrelated to the fate of the rest. This concept works in both ways: Individuals are joined to the whole, but also the individual's experiences are not merely personal and individual but may, and often do, have a wider extension of significance. Our experiences are often reflected in the experiences of many others, perhaps even to some extent by all, but we are unaware of these similarities. What we may learn from our ex-periences, therefore, can also be of use more broadly. Naturally, we must begin with ourselves, but we need not limit our horizon of concern and re-flection to personal psychology, even when we are talking about some-thing so ephemeral and seemingly unique and idiosyncratic as a dream or vision. This means that the individual's religious experiences can count toward revising our doctrinal standpoint.

My reflections here are based, then, on the presupposition that what happened to Jung was meaningful not only for him. Likewise, what hap-pens to us is not significant only for us individually. The wider community can benefit. Sometimes it needs to be alerted. Often these signals of tran-scendence, given to the lowly and quite isolated individual, can help the larger community out of an impasse. The community to which I refer throughout this discussion is the contemporary Christian church.

In his autobiography, Jung states that many of his childhood prob-lems, doubts, and struggles with God and Christian belief had their source in the family and in the historical period that surrounded his family (Jung, 1961, p. 90). As a child he was dealing with spiritual and religious prob-lems that his father and his pastor uncles, of whom there were several, his teachers, and the wider Swiss and European cultural world were also suf-fering. One of the key struggles of Jung's early young life was religious.

His fantasy of God the Father on his throne defecating upon Basel's cathedral needs to be placed in this context. The story is familiar. The young boy of ten or twelve comes out of school one day and looks up at the beautiful, gleaming cathedral. Above this cathedral, which was the "residence" of his grandfather, the well-known Basler clergyman Samuel Preiswerk, he imagines God's throne. All seems well with the world. Sud-denly, though, Jung is almost overcome with a sickening completion to his fantasy. He rushes home and for three days tries to control his mind. Finally he gives up and suffers the completion of his thought:

> I gathered all my courage, as though I were about to leap forthwith into hell-fire, and let the thought come. I saw before me the cathedral, the blue sky. God sits on His golden throne, high above the world—and from under the throne an enormous turd falls upon the sparkling new roof, shatters it, and breaks the walls of the cathedral asunder. (Jung, 1961, p. 39)

Completion brought relief in the form of a feeling of grace. He had thought the intolerable thought, and he felt that God Himself had willed that he should think it!

Of course, one could easily speculate about the personal motives for a hostile fantasy of this kind, and that would not miss the point if our purpose were to understand the family dynamics in Jung's early life. But it *would* miss the point that this experience is *also* a reflection of the shattering of a religious container and the radical alteration in the God image that has taken place throughout Western culture over the past several generations, resulting in what we now loosely denominate "modern man." For modern men and women, the gleaming cathedral is smashed. The soothing comfort of containment in an intact Christian tradition is no longer available, and the God who rules over human history has proved to be dangerous and destructive.

As Jung grew older and thought about religious and theological matters at a higher cognitive level, he analyzed the contemporary religious problem in similar but less metaphorical terms. The traditional religious symbols no longer mediate the transcendent factors they once did; they are no longer alive. The modern person reveals an empty space at the center, which was formerly occupied by a God image. Traditional religions no longer adequately represent or contain the souls of modern men and women. The religious imagination has failed to keep up with the rapid changes in human culture during the past several centuries: We no longer know how to imagine God, nor does the modern (i.e., rational, instrumental, ego-centered) person have the means to begin the process of re-imagining and re-perceiving God.

There are many accounts of how this fragmentation of the religious attitude and its collective expression in the Christian West has come to pass. The reformation smashed it; the enlightenment smashed it; the scientific revolution smashed it. A more psychological account says that consciousness smashed it. A critical number of human beings reached a point in the maturation of consciousness that made the traditional stories about God, including even the most exalted and high-minded doctrines, seem childish and mostly anchored in fear and dependency. This expansion of consciousness underlies the manifest historical phenomena: religious reformation, economic and class transformation, cognitive revolution. If we follow the thinking in Jung's childhood fantasy, then God smashed the cathedral, destroying the container in which the God image had been housed and honored for centuries.

What happens when God smashes his own container and its images? This is not only religious iconoclasm; it is catastrophe. But it prepares the way for a new religious event. The God who was once in a box is no longer there. The transference has been broken. The human apprehension of God's character is revealed as false. The true God smashes the frame that humans created. God is no longer held prisoner by orthodoxy and tradition; the traditional God image is revealed as inadequate. For the moment, all definitions—of God as judge, king, creator, etc.—must be scrapped and God left boundless and free, above the church or cathedral, and untied from tribal commitments.

Many hypotheses have been advanced to explain the modern person's religious doubts, emptiness, and confusion. One that has not been greatly stressed but is highly significant is the increasing collective awareness that God is not bound to tribe. The study and appreciation of world religions, in the full sense of the word *religion*, have dealt an enormous blow to the comforts of Christian orthodoxy in the West. The now widespread and still growing awareness that other peoples and tribes also have genuine religions has inflicted a deep narcissistic injury as well. So long as one could say, "yes, but . . ."—"yes, they have religious practices, but they do not know about the one true God as we do"; "yes, they have certain beliefs and superstitions, but those are false and only partially true, as we know with our full revelation"; "yes, they have come close and are genuinely struggling, but the poor benighted devils won't ever get there unless we teach them to read our Bible"—one could maintain the transference illusion that God is our father and has no other children but us. In our times, consciousness has shifted to the point where tribalism in religion is no longer tenable with good conscience. It is now seen as head-in-the-sand transference, pure and simple.

A modern man's dream illustrates the emotional impact of having this realization:

I'm with my family, and my father is confronted with the rumor that he has been married before. He hesitates replying, and then changes character and tells us that not only has he been married many times, but he also has other children and other families. We can't believe it! We're in shock. I question him, but he is no longer at all like my father. I feel he has betrayed us, has led a secret life, is not at all what I thought he was. I am terribly upset, angry, hurt, and worried that the other children will arrive to claim their inheritance when my father dies. I don't want to share, and am afraid I'll lose what's coming to me.

While this dream has personal significance for the dreamer, it also reaches beyond his own psychology. God's smashing of the Basel cathedral in Jung's fantasy and this man's dream both point to God the betrayer, out of character, not a "good father" figure at all, and wildly free of conventions. It should be added that this dreamer's father was also, like Jung's father, a Protestant minister, for some years dead at the time of the dream.

I think the awareness that tribalism in religion is no longer honest and legitimate permeates modern culture and consciousness, particularly in a highly pluralistic society. Of course tribalism continues to exist in all traditional religions, and indeed it has won a new lease on life in the various fundamentalisms throughout the world. But modern means of communication that are available practically everywhere, as well as the sophisticated articulations of differing religious and theological viewpoints in schools and libraries, plus the constant exposure to anthropological studies and findings in contemporary education, make it nearly impossible to maintain the tribalistic assumptions without creating serious splitting in the psyche. Jung's experience and thought points to the sense of God as a non-transference object. Theologians like Paul Tillich, who spoke of the God beyond the God image, have expressed a similar viewpoint in theological circles.

The modern breakdown in transference to God and the consequent, or accompanying, impossibility of tribalism in religion have yielded what Jung termed the "modern man in search of his soul." With the passing of active tribalism, there has come the modern experience of anomie and lack of kinship with the universe. The sense of specialness that comes with feeling singled out and chosen by God, bound to Him by a sacred covenant, redeemed through faith and belief in certain doctrines, has been lost. Today one is still born a Jew, a Christian, or a Buddhist, but one usually remains such out of custom or convenience. Many who feel themselves to be religious, not to mention all in the completely secular fold, are no longer emotionally and intellectually contained in a tribal or traditional religion. If you realize that God doesn't care whether you're Baptist of Buddhist, what do you do?

This so-called "modern person" has developed several options to satisfy the religious need. One is to shop around and be syncretistic: a little Zen, some Sufi, a bit of *I Ching*, astrology and Tarot symbols, etc., are mixed into a religious cocktail. The American Indians are "in" this year, so how about a little Native American? Or one could get more serious and pick one of these novel pathways and take it some steps further: become a Zen master, a Sufi dervish, or an American Indian shaman(ess). I remember being seized by laughter once when a professor of mine characterized Jung's 18th volume in the *Collected Works*, "The Symbolic Life," as consisting of short essays on the order of "Why I am not a Catholic!" Why not go on with the exercise and have a whole series: "Why I am not a dancing dervish," "Why I am not a practising alchemist," "Why I am not an Islamic fundamentalist." The problem with this option is that each of these "other" religious paths has a long history of its own, is tribal in its own way, and can't be simply put on and off again like a pair of pants. One can *study* all of these religious phenomena with great profit, but once consciousness has reached beyond the transference God, one is not able to join another tribalism with much depth of conviction. It's like exchanging your father for someone else's: You become an orphan, or at best a stepchild. And how can you believe in *their* picture of God if you can't believe your own?

Other options are available for consideration: resolute secularism; any number of causes and ideologies (Marxism, socialism, capitalism, Jungianism, etc.); head-in-the-sand tribalism; or regression to religious fundamentalism. I will not discuss these further here, but will instead turn to another related question: What about the tradition that has been left behind?

Is there perhaps a way for a tribal religious tradition—Christianity, for our purposes here—to transform its patterns to meet the challenge of the modern person who no longer has a transference to the tribal God, whose cathedral is smashed, whose father has shown his unfaithfulness to his own family and spawned other families? Can one be a religious Christian and *not* believe that Jesus Christ is the *only* way, the *only* answer, the *Only-begotten Son* of the once-and-for-all covenanted and faithful Father? Can Christianity be brought into the world of other religions as a co-equal, without needing to assume superiority, and yet survive as a soul-restoring, soul-healing, soul-containing religious tradition? I believe the continuing existence of Christianity as a viable religious option, given the direction of consciousness over the last several centuries, will depend upon its making a transformation that can answer these questions affirmatively.

I shall now consider a vision of Jung's from his later life, and his *method* of being a religious person, as a means for Christianity to open itself to the possibilities of the future. Jung's life was deeply oriented by religious experience and thinking, perhaps not to the extent indicated by his autobiography, but still, to an extraordinary degree for a modern man. In the book *Jung's Treatment of Christianity*, I try to show how and why he was so engrossed with his own religious tradition, Christianity. I do not believe he was a "haunted prophet" (Stern) who was trying to preach a new gospel to Christians or to modern persons, but I do believe, and I think made clear in my book, that he was deeply and personally engaged by the problems facing Christianity in modern times. This engagement was much like what happens in psychotherapy, when the analyst/doctor becomes involved with the psychic material of a patient. The doctor's psyche responds to the suffering of the patient, and by reading this response (i.e., by using the countertransference) the doctor's own inner reactions become the tool for guiding the healing process in the patient. The doctor's dreams, fantasies, thoughts, and feelings about the patient, as they develop in the presence of the patient and in the sphere of mutuality that emerges between them, have a bearing on the healing process.

Jung, I have argued, was engaged in this kind of activity with Christianity, which became his "patient," and the dreams and other unconscious products of his later years had largely to do with this patient. It is in this light that I want to consider a significant vision he experienced in 1939, when he was about 65 years of age. He reports this vision in *Memories, Dreams, Reflections*:

> In 1939 I gave a seminar on the *Spiritual Exercises* of Ignatius Loyola. At the same time I was occupied on the studies for *Psychology and Alchemy*. One night I awoke and saw, bathed in bright light at the foot of my bed, the figure of Christ on the Cross. It was not quite life-size, but extremely distinct; and I saw that his body was made of greenish gold. The vision was marvelously beautiful, and yet I was profoundly shaken by it. . . . I had been thinking a great deal about the *Anima Christi*, one of the meditations from the *Spiritual Exercises*. The vision came to me as if to point out that I had overlooked something in my reflections: the analogy of Christ with the *aurum non vulgi* and the *viriditas*

of the alchemists. When I realized that the vision pointed to this central alchemical symbol, and that I had had an essentially alchemical vision of Christ,
I felt comforted.

The green gold is the living quality which the alchemists saw not only in man
but also in inorganic nature. It is an expression of the life-spirit, the *anima
mundi* or *filius macrocosmi*, the Anthropos who animates the whole cosmos.
This spirit has poured himself out into everything, even into inorganic matter;
he is present in metal and stone. My vision was thus a union of the Christ-
image with his analogue in matter, the *filius macrocosmi*. If I had not been so
struck by the greenish-gold, I would have been tempted to assume that something essential was missing from my "Christian" view. . . . The emphasis
on the metal, however, showed me the undisguised alchemical conception of
Christ as a union of spiritually alive and physically dead matter. (Jung 1961,
pp. 210–211)

My comments on this vision will converge, I hope, upon the point of a
suggestion for transformation within Christianity. The first comment has
to do with Jung himself. It is most certainly the case that Jung's consciousness, by the age of 65, was well beyond the bounds of a need for the
transference God. One can, of course, be deceived, but I believe it's fairly
safe to say that, at least with respect to the need for a transference object
in the form of a tribal doctrine of God, Jung was beyond it. So the point I
want to make firmly here is that there *is* religion and religious experience
beyond personal transference needs. This point is important because of the
rather widespread psychoanalytic view that once the transference need is
"analyzed" and "worked through," religion loses its *raison d'être* and becomes untenable. It cannot any longer exist, because the unconscious reason for it has been destroyed. Jung disagrees, of course, and argues that
there is something like an "instinct" for religion, that religion is *essentially*
(i.e., archetypally) human and not based on unresolved, infantile needs
and the repetition compulsion. The larger point is, therefore, that religion
is still a live option for modern men and women, even after they have analyzed the transference and outgrown the need for a "parent in heaven."

The second point stems from the observation that in his later years,
after about the age of 65 and just about the time of this vision, Jung
turned intensively to the study and "therapy," as I call it, of his religious
tradition. Throughout his lifetime he had studied all major world religions
and most of their heretical offshoots; he had unearthed Gnosticism and alchemy; he had delved deeply into such out-of-the-way religious texts as
The Tibetan Book of the Dead and the *I Ching*; he had visited the American

Indian, the Elgoni African, the Moor and the East Indian; he had studied anthropology. Now in his 60s he was returning to Christianity, where he had started, and he would dedicate his last two decades to this work. His return to what he had rejected earlier, to his own tradition, in order to let the psyche be activated and to respond to it anew, is an important fact to consider in this reflection on the potential value of this vision for Christianity's transformation. The transformation of Christianity is going to require the modern psyche to incubate its traditional images and doctrines, and then to respond to them in its own new way. This is the way of individuation: an evolution of history, whether personal or traditional/collective—not a new tradition, not the step-child route, not a syncretism, but a new outgrowth of the former tribal tradition.

The third point pertains to the nature of revelation. The tribal traditions have fixed revelation in the past: "Our Fathers said . . .". After the words of the authoritative figures have been recorded and codified, the resultant tradition may add only commentary and clarification. There may be some extensions and further amplifications of doctrine, but there are not new revelations on the same footing as the old. From the tribalistic viewpoint, of course, this safeguard is necessary, otherwise anyone could speak with the authority of the Fathers. Everyone has a different opinion, dream, or vision, and the cacaphony of voices would soon become deafening. This fear of opening the doors to new revelation is the collective equivalent of the repression barrier in the individual psyche. And as personal analysis does, the treatment of Christianity in Jung's hands would dismember the repression barrier and allow the unconscious once more to speak as it did of old.

Jung's openness to revelation, however, does not mean simply being ready to accept at face value every notion or image that might flash into consciousness. These psychic contents need to be interpreted; their meaning is not self-evident. And interpretation is both a learned skill and an art. One thing is certain: There can be no satisfying interpretation without some reference to the past, to the tradition, to the "complexes." In the instance of Jung's Green Christ vision, one sees that he first tested his interpretation against his own personal psychology and its attainments; then he related the image to what he had been studying in the recent past and to what his consciousness had been occupied with; finally, and most importantly for our purposes, he set his psychic image, his revelation, into the context of the tradition of thought and doctrine to which it most deeply belonged, namely the Christian tradition and its chronic habit of splitting the world of spirit from the world of matter. The psychic image is interpreted as a healing symbol for the most central split within the Christian tradition, that between spirit and matter. Naturally, Jung the man was as subject to this split as are the rest of us who are heirs to the same spiritual tradition, so the symbol was a specific healing symbol for him, but also for the wider tradition which he was studying and in which he lived.

These first three points establish Jung's credentials. One wants to know something about the dreamer or visionary who is claiming, and for whom one claims, revelatory authority. Jung was personally beyond the need for a transference God; he was genuinely engaged with the tradition, having returned to it after a long period of rejection; and he was able to discriminate the personal issues involved from the symbolic, general ones.

What, then, about the actual content of the vision? I follow Jung's thought and associations into alchemy. The greenish-gold Christ on the Cross at the foot of his bed is the traditional symbol of Christianity, but with a difference: He is an image of the *filius philosophorum* of the alchemists, but this figure has been assimilated to, or takes the form of, the Christ of Christian tradition. Who is this other figure, the *filius philosophorum*? He is the son of the Mother, of matter, in contradistinction to the son of the Father, of spirit. This image represents the response of the unconscious to the conscious attitude of the Christian dominant. The Christian dominant expresses itself in the structure of patriarchal values and thought-patterns. This is symbolized in the Trinity, which excludes matter, earth, the feminine, the chthonic, the dark, the instinctual, and the body from the doctrine of God. The *filius philosophorum*, on the other hand, represents the psyche's compensatory response to the patriarchal development of the last two millennia. In his more frequent form, he is *Mercurius duplex*, a highly problematical agent, the spirit of the earth and the unconscious, of instinctuality and impulse, of tricksterism and deception. This Mercurius is precisely one who will not be committed and tied down, crucified, nailed to the cross for the sake of anyone. He is, if anything, the spoiled child of the mother, the second son, the willful spirit of the rejected mother who is not to be tamed or fettered to authority's structures.

It was the perennial concern of the alchemists to redeem this spirit, to bring it to consciousness and to hold it there. This would require violating the prohibition that patriarchal Christianity had placed upon matter, the body, nature, and instinct. Their intuition was that body and nature were not altogether corrupt and evil, but rather that they contained a spark of divinity, a bit of God, and this value needed to be redeemed. This would appear as gold, upon which was projected the kernel of divine substance in matter. On a psychological level, Jung felt compelled to release the treasure within the unconscious, below the repression of tradition, which would lead to a personal experience of the God within, a revelation of the Self.

This numinosity within, the spark of gold within the realm of matter and nature, appear in Jung's vision of the green Christ. This vision was the response of the unconscious to Jung's shamanic incubation of the problems of Christianity. The *filius philosophorum*, the child of nature, but in the image of the son of the Heavenly Father, was similarly sacrificing himself upon the cross of wholeness. This is a sign, or symbol, of nature's cooperation, finally, with the Judeo-Christian line of development: The unconscious may be prepared to come along *if* given its due.

For Jung the vision of the green Christ symbolized healing the split between spirit and nature that had plagued his own life, as it had the lives of his father and his other Christian forebears. In this vision, the spirit of nature and the son of the heavenly Father are brought together in a single image. Father and Mother are uniting and cooperating. This image also shows us, who are Jung's readers and students, that his soul was, finally, Christian, and not European "pagan." His unconscious showed its character in the figure of the green Christ, and this figure is surprisingly close to being identical to the Christ of Christian tradition.

To get to this point, however, Jung had had to suffer the trials of modernity: The cathedral was smashed; he had experienced disillusionment with the traditional images and understandings of God; and he had been forced to mature beyond the need for the transference God of traditional Christianity. But he had gone further, and for this reason we must consider him to be a post-modern man. After opening himself to the chaos of the unconscious and to years of stumbling in the dark in search of a new center of religious existence, he found it. And this places him beyond the wasteland of modernity. One of the points of resolution for him came in the figure of the green Christ, the return of a traditional image, but with an essential difference: The figure was of greenish gold; it was the son of nature.

If we take Jung's life as having collective significance, we must now ask: Of what possible therapeutic value for Christianity is the resolution that Jung found to the problem of modernity? How can the panacea pro-duced by this physician, Jung, be of use to this patient, Christianity? How can Jung's individuation speak to the healing of Christianity and to its transformative evolution? On the supposition that no man is an island, I think we can at least say, modestly, that the *way* in which Jung resolved the problem of modernity and traditional religion could point to a possible way for others. But beyond that, can we see how the Christian tradition *itself* might benefit? If the Christian tradition were to look to Jung as a possible healer of its ailments, could it find something there, perhaps not so much in his words as in his life, that would stimulate a transformational process? Let me speculate and imagine a little.

If we personify Christianity and imagine it as a patient who needs in-ner healing to overcome its age-old splits and prepare itself for the next phase of its development, I think it would come away from Doctor Jung with a clear message, spoken or unspoken. The message to Christianity would be:

> Open yourself to the unconscious. Honor the dream. Allow the unconscious to smash the cathedral and to show you a larger image of God, because your God is too small and too confined in the boxes of dogma and habit. Recognize that your tribalism is based on wish and projection and has very little or nothing to do with reality, and is very distorted. Allow yourself to consider all the other paths to God as equally valid and legitimate, and possibly equally tribal and limited, but do not abandon your history, and do not think the other tra-ditions can bail you out if you will just learn some new tricks from them. In-stead, concentrate yourself on your own symbols and on your own history, and let your unconscious respond, trusting that the God who revealed himself in the beginning will respond with symbols of transformation and renewal. But you must be prepared to take responsibility for these new revelations, to test them by your very best means of interpretation and discernment, not according to what you have already known, but according to what you know you need and have not yet found. And be ready to be surprised. Above all, be prepared to let God be whole. This is a great risk, but your life depends on it.

There is a set of famous church windows in Zurich that were designed by the Russian-Jewish artist, Marc Chagall. Chagall's Christ is green. The central window is named "Christ glorified." Green is, of course, the color of springtime, of verdant earth, of hope and new life, of the earth reborn. This is the Christ of the resurrection and ascension, having been crucified and now reborn. In this image we can also see the green and golden elements that were found in Jung's vision. As far as I have been able to determine, this window was designed completely independently of any knowledge of Jung's vision.

The windows were completed in 1970, some thirty years after Jung beheld his vision in his house in Küsnacht. They are located in the Fraumuenster Church (the "women's cloister") in the oldest section of Zurich, about five miles up the lake from Jung's home. I consider this falling together of images to be synchronistic and not merely fortuitous. Having occurred in the consciousness of two creative individuals in our time at that place, it may be a "sign of the times" that the split between spirit and nature is being healed within Christianity and that the *filius philosophorum*, the son of nature, is being assimilated to the tradition, also that the spiritual tradition is being transformed by nature. Surely Chagall could not have intended, consciously, to smuggle the alchemical Christ into the very heart of Christian tradition through the door of the windows, in the church of the women, in Zürich! Yet that's what he did.

What the concrete outcomes and implications of this new development may be for a future Christianity will take decades, or centuries, to become evident. But the movement toward healing the rift between spiritual and physical/material realms is certainly under way, and Jung's Green Christ vision is a harbinger of it.

References

Donne, J. *Devotions Upon Emergent Occasions*, ed. John Sparrow (Cambridge: Cambridge University Press, 1923).

Jung, C. G. 1961. *Memories, Dreams, Reflections*. New York: Random House.

Stein, M. 1985. *Jung's Treatment of Christianity*. Wilmette, Ill.: Chiron Publications.

Stern, P. 1976. *C. G. Jung: The Haunted Prophet*. New York: George Braziller.

Tillich, P. 1973. *Systematic Theology*, vol. III. Chicago: University of Chicago Press.

Between Two Thieves:
A Response to Jung's
Critique of the Christian
Notions of Good and Evil

Carrin Dunne

When I first began to consider Jung's challenge to the Christian notion of evil, I knew right away that I was in over my head. It took a while longer to realize that "over my head" is the better place to be vis-à-vis the question of good and evil. Throughout the Christian centuries, the problem of evil has been both a scandal and a stumbling-block for the rational mind, the stumbling-block being that if God is good, then God is not God, the scandal being that if God is God, then God is not good.[1] The question underlying the logical dilemma might be formulated thus: Given the ongoing presence and power of evil in this world, what are we to think of God? It is a disturbing question. It may even become a grievous question, as the words 'scandal' and 'stumbling-block' suggest. We know that in Jung's experience, at least one important friendship (his friendship with Victor White)[2] came to grief over it. How then am I to deal with such a question?

I would like to avoid a logical impasse; I would especially like to avoid coming to grief over the question. The likelihood of falling on the horns of a dilemma by following a purely rational approach suggests that help might be found by following the hints of the irrational mind such as dreams, images, hunches, and feelings. The danger of coming to grief warns me to pay close attention to the disturbance produced within me as I ponder the question of evil, to follow the track of that disturbance, and to employ all the powers of my conscious mind and heart to understand it. I am also minded, like Job, to seek God's help against God, for to approach the Mystery is to run the risk of perishing, and we know from

Saint Paul, if we do not know from our own experience and from a contemplation of human history, that evil is part of the Mystery, the *mysterium iniquitatis* of which he speaks in the second letter to the Thessalonians.[3]

Let me begin with my initial question: Given the ongoing presence and power of evil in the world, what are we to think of God? According to Jung, the Christian notion of God as "light, and in him is no darkness at all" (I John 1:15) does not tally with such a state of affairs. Nor does he accept the axiom "all good from God, all evil from man," the earliest sources of which he found in Tatian (2nd c. A.D.) and in Saint Basil the Great's *Hexaemeron*.[4] Even more unacceptable is the kind of philosophical casuistry which argues that evil is neither a presence nor a power but a non-being, a lack of presence and a lack of power. All these objections are aimed at the Christian notion of God as the *Summum Bonum* (the highest or absolute, unqualified Good) and its corollary, evil as *privatio boni* (a privation or absence of goodness).

It must be said for Jung that he fights fire with fire. He appeals not so much to philosophical reasoning as he does to Scripture itself, and in particular to the Book of Job, to make his point against God and for man. He takes the Scriptural revelation seriously and he takes God seriously, which should mean that he comes down on the side of scandal ("If God is God, then God is not good"). But Jung is not so naive as merely to switch the Christian axiom to read "all evil from God, all good from man." God is rather a totality, being both good and evil or, to intensify the paradox, all-good and all-evil. Such a notion of God corresponds better to the composite picture of the Old Testament, where, according to Deuteronomy 32:4, he is "a God of truth and without iniquity," and, according to Isaiah 45:7, he is the creator of darkness and evil as well as of light and peace.

Is the paradoxical God of the Old Testament still the God of the New? Or has God undergone a sea change corresponding to the developing consciousness of man? In the words of Nicolaus Caussinus, has the raging rhinoceros of the Old Testament, overcome by the love of a pure virgin, transformed in her lap into a God of love?[5] Whatever the differences between the Old and New Testaments, it seems to me that the early Church, by affirming the continuing validity of the Old Testament writings, implied that one and the same God is to be found in both Testaments.[6] You will notice that I prefer to call the nature of God paradoxical rather than contradictory. A contradiction brings mind and heart to a full stop; a paradox invites us beyond the either/or of logic and even of morality.

But if the Christian God is none other than the God of Job and the God of Psalm 88 (89), why is it that Christian tradition emphasizes only the bright aspects: goodness, light, love? How can the God whom Jung describes as an "amoral phenomenon" (in *Answer to Job*) be the *Summum Bonum?*[7] First of all, both Jung and Christian tradition agree that in the ultimate or absolute sense we do not know what is good and what is evil.[8] We call something good or evil within the context of a particular situation as we perceive it. There are two qualifiers at work here: the timeframe, and our understanding of what is good or bad for us. We do not have the "big picture," a total view of history, so what may appear to be evil in the short run may turn out to be a greater good in the long run. Also, we have but a limited understanding of what is best for us. The Christian affirmation of the *Summum Bonum* is a reaching beyond understanding; it is the expression of a belief that in the long run and in the fullness of understanding "all shall be well and all manner of thing shall be well."[9]

While Jung had very little personal sympathy for the notion of God as the *Summum Bonum*, in a letter to Victor White dated 9 to 14 April 1952, he concedes that the doctrine of the *Summum Bonum* and its consequence, the *privatio boni*, is a truly religious statement, archetypally motivated. He writes: "Empirically we are unable to confirm the existence of anything absolute, i.e., there are no logical means to establish an absolute truth, except a tautology. *Yet we are moved* (by archetypal motifs) *to make such statements.*"[10] And again: "I only deny that the *privatio boni* is a logical statement, but I admit the obvious truth that it is a 'metaphysical' truth based upon an archetypal 'motif.'"[11] In the same letter he goes on to say: "The supreme powers are assumed to be either indifferent or more often good than evil. There is an archetypal accent upon the good aspect, but only slightly so."[12]

Jung's terms *archetypal motif* and *archetypal motive* have to do, I think, with what the Christian tradition calls *belief* and *believing*. It is difficult to talk about such things intelligibly, because we are dealing with something quite near what Meister Eckhart calls the "core" of the soul. Not with the core itself, which can only be characterized in negative terms as the place of silence and peace where none of the powers of the soul are in operation as such, but with what may be called its first expression: the form of the forms of feeling, the form of the forms of imagination, the form of the forms of thought, and the form of the forms of action.[13] *Form* here refers not only to the shape of the feeling, image, thought or action (the motif), but to its inherent dynamism (the motive) as well. It follows that a belief like the *Summum Bonum*, that "all shall be well and all manner of thing shall be well," is supremely holy and "wholifying," if I may use such a term, for those who are shaped and moved by it. But the fact that the supreme powers may also be believed to be indifferent, and that this thought may also be holy and "wholifying," is a further indication that with belief (hence, with the archetypes) we are not yet at the human essence itself, even if we have reached the boundaries of language. I think of the famous line from St. Augustine's *Confessions*, "Our hearts are restless until they rest in Thee,"[14] and realize that it holds true not only for those who find repose in the goodness of God, but also for those who find repose in supreme detachment.

A second reason for the accent on goodness in the Christian tradition may be as an internal counterpoise to the direness of the external Christian event. The death and failure of the Messiah, the excommunication of the early Christians from the synagogue, the disappointing delay of the Lord's return and the coming of his kingdom, and the likelihood of martyrdom would all be contributing factors. Whereas the original Exodus as the shaping event of Old Testament religion was full of earthly promise and joy, as was Mohammed's victory at Mecca as the shaping event of Islam, the Christian event was in human terms a tragedy of the first magnitude. It had to call forth a leap into extreme spiritualization on the one hand, with a paradoxical understanding of good and evil on the other.

The religious reasons for the *Summum Bonum/privatio boni* doctrine are not the really disturbing factors for Jung, however. Nor is the illogicality of an imbalance between good and evil, despite what he says to Victor White in the letter of 9 April 1952. He even gives a certain approval to the polarization of good and evil in the Christian era, coincident with the Age of Pisces, as a necessary stage in the individuation process,[15] though we who belong to the end of that age are particularly aware of the tension and conflict involved as the two fish move farther and farther apart. What bothers Jung are the negative psychological effects of the "all good from God, all evil from man" axiom, which tends to create in man a negative inflation, a kind of "Luciferian vanity,"[16] the pinpointing of the human soul as the seat of evil despite the (religious) fact that the serpent pre-exists man.[17] At the same time, it leads us to downplay evil as a non-being (read absence of presence and absence of power), which gives man the perfect excuse to avoid taking his shadow or dark side seriously.[18]

What we have here is an extremely odd situation in which the human soul is given an exaggerated importance as the cause of evil, elevated to the position of a dark God, and at the same time devalued, reduced to a nothingness and an impotence, since the dark God is not. A doctrine that has its roots in Origen and St. Basil the Great reaches full expression with St. Augustine and his struggle to deliver himself from Manichaeism. Since God is the creator of all things, in order to preserve both the unity and the goodness of God (as opposed to the Manichaean doctrine of two ultimate principles, one good, the other evil), an ingenious solution is hit upon by interpreting evil as non-being, not part of the creation at all but, as it were, a hole in creation. The philosophical expression of the doctrine would be: Everything which is, insofar as it is, is good.

But what about the unhappy fate of the human soul? In order to save God, have we sacrificed the soul as a scapegoat? The tension of the question produced in me the following dream.

> A woman with long dark hair and in a bright red dress has a huge, gaping hole in the upper half of her torso. It is as though it has been blasted away by a cannon shot so that her entire chest cavity is missing. She moves into the embrace of another human being and the wound is instantly healed. She asks: "Is this it?" and a voice answers: "No, that is not it." The scene repeats itself twice more. Each time she asks: "Is this it?" and the voice answers: "No, that is not it."

> In a darkened movie theatre a small boy dressed in knickers, knee socks, and a touring cap is scrambling around beneath the seats, looking for a bit of film. The curl of film which he has not yet found is about twelve to fifteen inches long.

I cannot attempt a complete analysis of the dream in the space of a short paper; in addition, the dream remains opaque to me. But I can share with you some impressions. First of all, the dream strikes me as being profoundly archetypal. There is the woman, the man, and the child. The child dressed as he is reminds me of photographs of my own father as a child, so the boy is at once the father and the child of the woman, in other words, a divine child. He also reminds me of early movie stars like Jackie Coogan and Mickey Rooney. The dream as a whole has a feeling of the great Osiris myth, but in reverse: instead of Isis healing (re-membering) Osiris, it is Osiris who heals the wounded Isis; the child groping for a lost image (a filmmaker friend of mine explained that a piece of film twelve to fifteen inches long would in all probability contain but one im-

age) is somewhat reminiscent of Horus, who lost an eye. The missing
chest cavity means that almost all of the vital organs have been blasted
away. The wounded woman is an image of the predicament of the soul,
and as woman, her own soul (the soul as the life [= vital organs] of the
body) has been lost. Several titles to the dream occurred to me one after
the other. First, *"Privatio Boni,"* since I made a definite association between the dream and the question that plagued me; then "Behold
Woman," corresponding to the *Ecce Homo* of the Gospel; and finally
"Does Woman Have A Soul?," a poignant echo to the contemptuous
question debated in medieval seminaries and often quoted by Jung, *"Habet
mulier animam?"*

What remains opaque in the dream is the thrice-repeated question,
"Is this it?" and the answer given by a disembodied voice, "No, that is not
it." What is the *it* about which the woman asks? She may be asking, "Is
this the *privatio boni?,"* *this* referring to her great wound, and the answer
may imply that the *privatio boni* is more inclusive, involving the darkened
theatre and the lost image as well. Or she may be asking, "Is this the
Summum Bonum?," *this* referring to the healing embrace, and the answer
may imply that the *Summum Bonum* involves not only her healing, but
also the birth of the child and what is still to come, the recovery of the
lost vision. Or it may be that both readings are correct, and that there is a
strange and marvelous reason why *it* may be both *privatio boni* and *Summum Bonum.*[19]

I think it was my dream of the wounded woman, with the secret
pathways and connections made by dreams, which caused me to fasten
upon the image of Christ crucified between two thieves as I was pursuing
the problem of the *privatio boni* through certain passages in *Aion.* There
Jung writes:

> Christ is our nearest analogy of the self and its meaning. . . . Yet, although the
> attributes of Christ (consubstantiality with the Father, coeternity, filiation, par-
> thenogenesis, crucifixion, Lamb sacrificed between opposites, One divided into
> Many, etc.) undoubtedly mark him out as an embodiment of the self, looked at
> from the psychological angle he corresponds to only one half of the archetype.
> The other half appears in the Antichrist. The latter is just as much a manifes-
> tation of the self, except that he consists of its dark aspect. Both are Christian
> symbols, and they have the same meaning as the image of the Saviour crucified
> between two thieves.[20]

I must confess that I am puzzled by Jung's claim that the Christ-Antichrist
opposition has the same meaning as the image of the Saviour crucified be-

tween two thieves. On the one hand, there is the opposition between good and evil, bright and dark; on the other hand, there is the image of the Crucified as the mysterious "third" or uniting symbol "between" good and evil. It seems to me, too, that in paintings of the Crucifixion, I remember the thieves depicted through a trick of perspective as smaller than the figure of Christ, as though the opposition between good and evil occurs on a lesser plane of reality than does the great uniting Mystery of the middle.

The image continued to haunt me and began to fix on the notion of the sacred wounds, the obvious connection between my dream and the holy Mystery. There were differences, of course. The woman's head is not bound with thorns; her hair flows long, dark, and free. Her hands and feet are not pinioned. But there is a connection in what we might call the Great Wound: the pierced heart of Christ, the gaping hole in her chest. It is the Great Wound not only because of its physical centrality, but because it has been so long and so thoroughly contemplated throughout the Christian centuries, beginning with the connection made through sacred art to John 7:37–39.

> In the last day, that great day of the feast, Jesus stood and cried, saying, If any man thirst, let him come unto me, and drink.
>
> He that believeth on me, as the scripture hath said, out of his belly shall flow rivers of living water.
>
> But this he spake of the Spirit, which they that believe on him should receive: for the Holy Ghost was not yet given; because that Jesus was not yet glorified.

The promise "out of his belly (RSV: "heart," NEB: "from within him") shall flow rivers of living water," is not an exact quote from Scripture but a condensation of a whole tissue of texts from Isaiah, Ezekiel, and Zechariah.[21] The *his* of "his belly" is also ambiguous; it refers both to Christ (Christian art having clearly identified it as the Great Wound in Christ's side) and to the believer. But to what does it refer in the believer if not to a comparable wound? I began to realize that the *privatio boni*, so aptly symbolized in our time of black holes and white holes in space by a gaping wound,[22] is not just the opposite of the *Summum Bonum*, but *is* the *Summum Bonum*.

Another point of fascination in the image of Christ crucified between two thieves is the paradoxical notion of the good thief. The good thief is called "good" in the tradition because he recognized the Messiah in that defeated man, and even *in extremis* had confidence in the coming of his kingdom.[23] We realize that a thief may be good, but do we also realize that good may be a thief? And if so, of what does it rob us?

Again a dream came to my assistance. I called it "Waters Above, Waters Below."

> *I am working on a toilet or water closet, working in the middle range, and trying to work out a connection between the waters above in the tank and the waters below in the toilet. Between the two there is a box, which is like a mouth with teeth. I keep trying to make more room in the middle by prying the jaws apart, so that I can fit together the copper tubing inside the box, connecting the waters above and below. The jaws want to snap shut in a dangerous way. It requires all my strength and care to keep them open and carry on my work.*

I believe that the dream gives a fairly clear picture of both the work and the plight of the soul. Here she struggles to make more space in the middle, to extend the human region or to humanize the opposites by making a connection between the Great Above and the Great Below. The connecting factor is human love, symbolized by the copper tubing (copper being sacred to Venus). The opposites as such have a divine character, pure goodness and unmitigated evil being extremes beyond our fathoming. As such they are inimical to us, symbolized in the dream by a double row of teeth ready to snap shut. They endanger the soul in that she runs the risk of losing her hands as she works to make the connection.

I think of the Eskimo sea goddess, who once was a human girl whose father threw her out of the boat, perhaps as a sacrificial appeasement. When she tried to save herself by grasping the side of the boat, he chopped off her fingers, which became the food animals of the sea. She, however, sank to the bottom and became a goddess. Goddess that she was, she could no longer do for herself. Her hair would become tangled and matted and she would fall into a brown study and refuse to send up the food animals, until the shaman would come and comb her hair for her and soothe her with his words.

And I think of the Brothers Grimm tale of "The Girl Without Hands." The girl's impoverished father foolishly promised the Devil whatever was standing behind his mill in exchange for a fortune. When the Devil came to claim the daughter, she had washed herself and drawn a circle around herself with white chalk, and he could not come near. The second time the Devil came she was forbidden to wash, but she had wept on her hands and he still could not claim her. The father was then made to promise to cut off her hands or be taken himself. He did as he was told, but when the Devil came for her the third time, she had wept on the stumps and he had no more power over her. She left her father's house and wandered into a forest, where an Angel befriended her, enabling her to enter the King's garden and eat. There the King found her and loved her and had silver hands fashioned for her. Later, the Devil intervened again, disrupting communication between the King, who was off on a journey, and the King's mother, by substituting false messages and ordering the death of the Queen and her child. The Queen fled deeper into the forest to the house where "all dwell free," where the Angel once again took care of her. There in the house where "all dwell free" her natural hands grew back. Finally, she and her son, Sorrowful, were reunited with the King, who had sought them for seven years.

In my dream the opposites appear as two sides of one reality, a double row of teeth hinged by a single jaw. It casts a certain light on the roles of the Devil and the Angel in the story of "The Girl Without Hands," while in that story it is perhaps clearer than in the dream that the opposites are working for her as well as against her. Without the malefic/benefic work of the opposites she would not have been maimed, but there would have been no love story, either; there would have been no separation of the lovers, but then she would not have found the house where "all dwell free." Whereas in the Eskimo myth the soul is reabsorbed into the divine, in the story of "The Girl Without Hands" the human world of action and passion maintains itself over against and by means of the divine. My dream even suggests that the human work of making a connection of love between the waters above and the waters below is an assist to the divine.

What is it that occurs in the middle? When I contemplate the image of Christ crucified between two thieves, it seems to me that the opposites of good and evil represented by the thieves are the lesser (human) reality and that the *coincidentia oppositorum* in the sacred wounds is divine, but when I contemplate my dreams and the related stories, it seems to me that the opposition of good and evil is a struggle occurring within the divine reality, and that the work of uniting them is a work and a suffering which are profoundly human. Whichever perspective I take—whether the opposition of good and evil is writ small, as in the image of the Crucified between two thieves, or writ large, as in the image of the girl without hands between Devil and Angel—it differs from the perspective of rational theology and morality in which there is no middle.

Again I am compelled to ask, what is it that occurs in the middle? If the conflict is writ small, what occurs in the middle is the suffering of God and the healing of the human soul. If the conflict is writ large, what occurs in the middle is the suffering of the soul and the healing of God. One way of perceiving it feels religious; the other way of perceiving it feels presumptuous and sacrilegious. The one thought is a revered expression of medieval Christian piety; the other thought is a slowly and reluctantly formed expression of modern "impiety," one that receives what is perhaps its sharpest and most virulent expression to date in C. G. Jung's *Answer to Job.*

It is not difficult to point out the unfairness of the presentation of God (and of Christ) in *Answer to Job.* While Jung does stick to Biblical evidence, he clearly makes a choice of those texts that suit his purpose. What interests me is what I sense to be his purpose. I think it can best be grasped on the basis of an analogy with an experience Jung underwent as a boy which he describes in his autobiography.

> One fine summer day that same year I came out of school at noon and went to the cathedral square. The sky was gloriously blue, the day one of radiant sunshine. The roof of the cathedral glittered, the sun sparkling from the new, brightly glazed tiles. I was overwhelmed by the beauty of the sight, and thought: "The world is beautiful and the church is beautiful, and God made all this and sits above it far away in the blue sky on a golden throne and. . . ." Here came a great hole in my thoughts, and a choking sensation. I felt numbed, and knew only: "Don't go on thinking now! Something terrible is coming, something I do not want to think, something I dare not even approach. Why not? Because I would be committing the most frightful of sins. . . . "[24]

The boy struggled against the compelling thought for three days and three nights, finally concluding that God himself was forcing upon him the unwelcome thought. Summoning up his courage, he let it come. The scene repeated itself.

> I saw before me the cathedral, the blue sky. God sits on his golden throne, high above the world—and from under the throne an enormous turd falls upon the sparkling new roof, shatters it, and breaks the walls of the cathedral asunder.[25]

Amusing as the image may be, there are serious implications both for the dignity of God and the future of the Church. But what concerns me at the moment is the effect it had on Jung himself. He describes it.

So that was it! I felt an enormous, an indescribable relief. Instead of the expected damnation, grace had come upon me, and with it an unutterable bliss such as I had never known. I wept for happiness and gratitude. The wisdom and goodness of God had been revealed to me now that I had yielded to his inexorable command. It was as though I had experienced an illumination. A great many things I had not previously understood became clear to me. That was what my father had not understood, I thought; he had failed to experience the will of God, had opposed it for the best of reasons and out of the deepest faith. And that was why he had never experienced the miracle of grace which heals all and makes all comprehensible.[26]

Suppose we expand this experience, putting modern irreligious man over against his medieval religious father in place of the youthful Jung over against his parson father. I believe Jung saw modern man caught in the sweat of his three-night struggle against the blasphemous thought. In *Answer to Job*, which he begins with the telling words from II Samuel 1:26, "I am distressed for thee, my brother . . . ," Jung is encouraging us to go ahead and think what is wanting to come to thought. If it is God's own will that we perceive the drama of good and evil as a divine struggle of monstrous proportions that we (and only we) can make human, if God is calling out to us for help, who are we to cry blasphemy?[27]

In closing, let me propose some future considerations. What if, once we allowed the other thought to think itself through to fruition,[28] we were able to hold both thoughts together? What if the conflict of good and evil were experienced at once as a human sundering healed by the suffering of God and as a divine sundering healed by the suffering of mankind? If full credence were given to both perspectives, the dilemma of God (his power versus his goodness) and the dilemma of the soul (her guilt versus her helplessness) would be resolved, not by being neutralized after the fashion of the rational mind, but through a true marriage of God and the soul, for better and for worse.

Notes

1. Archibald MacLeish's succinct formulation of the problem in *J.B.*, *A Play in Verse* (Boston: Houghton Mifflin, 1958), p. 14.

2. The course of the friendship may be traced, at least from Jung's point of view, in C. G. Jung, *Letters*, vols. 1 and 2 (Princeton: Princeton University Press, 1953).

3. In recent New Testament exegesis, the following comment has been made with regard to the *mysterium iniquitatis*: "In Pauline literature *mystery* refers to 'a thing, a person or a doctrine which is hidden and inaccessible to human consciousness because it is the secret of the divine plan or the secret of the divine act at the Parousia' (Rigaux). Iniquity is *mystery* because it enters, in a manner which is for us both disconcerting and difficult to understand,

into the plan of God." My translation from the *Traduction Oecuménique de la Bible: Nouveau Testament* (édition intégrale) (Paris: les Editions du Cerf, 1972), II Thessalonians 2:7, notes.

4. C. G. Jung. *Aion: Researches into the Phenomenology of the Self* in *Collected Works*, vol. 9, part ii (Princeton University Press, 1959), para. 81 ff. Origen is the first Christian theologian to put forward the *privatio boni* theory (para. 74).

5. C. G. Jung, *Letters*, vol. 2, pp. 153 and 240.

6. Even more to the point is the Christian rejection of the Gnostic claim that the Creator God of the Old Testament is a cruel, inferior demiurge.

7. C. G. Jung. *Answer to Job* in *Collected Works*, vol. 11 (Princeton: Princeton University Press, 1958), pars. 560, 600, and 605.

8. See St. Thomas Aquinas' careful discussion of human knowledge of the divine mystery in *Summa Theologica*, Ia., questions 12 and 13. There (especially Ia., q. 13, articles 2, 3, and 6) he distinguishes between what is said of God in revelation and what we are able to understand in that saying. As a judgment, 'God is good' is true absolutely, truer of God than it is of creatures, but in terms of meaning, we understand goodness only as it exists in creatures. We thus find ourselves in the strange situation of being able to say (truly) more than we know.

9. Blessed Julian of Norwich, *Revelations of Divine Love Shewed to a Devout Ankress* (Westminster: Newman Press, 1952), p. 48, and quoted by T. S. Eliot in "Little Gidding." The exact quoation (from Brit. Mus. MS Sloane 2499) is "Synne is behovabil, but al shal be wel & al shal be wel & al manner of thyng shal be wele."

10. *Letters*, II, p. 52 (Jung's italics).

11. *Ibid.*

12. Ibid., p. 53. The slight accent on the good is due, I think, to a difference of meaning carried by the term 'good' when applied to God. It is not good as opposed to evil, but the good we experience in a unification of opposites as opposed to sin in their sundering. Cf. the German *Sunde* (sin) and its affinity to the English 'sunder.'

13. I make a distinction between belief (the form of the forms) and faith, which refers to the act of the core itself and is not the act of a particular faculty of soul, nor does it have a characterizable form. In other words, it cannot be "spelled out" as a belief can (to some extent).

14. Book I, chapter 1.

15. See *Aion*, pars. 125 and 126.

16. *Ibid.*, pars. 114, and *Letters*, I, p. 540.

17. *Letters*, II, p. 60.

18. *Letters*, I, p. 541.

19. Cf. the notion of *it* in Bruno Bettelheim's *Freud and Man's Soul* (New York: Knopf, 1983).

20. *Aion*, para. 79.

21. See Isaiah 12:3; 43:20; 44:3; 55:1; 58:11; Ezekiel 44:1–12; Zechariah 13:1; 14:8.

22. Keep in mind the double meaning of *gape*: to yawn, and to stare wonderingly.

23. Luke 23:42.

24. C. G. Jung. *Memories, Dreams, Reflections* (New York: Random House, 1961), p. 36.

25. *Ibid.*, p. 39.

26. *Ibid.*, p. 40.

27. It would be well to keep in mind that Christianity was born amid charges of blasphemy (Matthew 26:65).

28. The vision of the suffering of God and of the healing of the human soul has been as thoroughly worked out in mystical literature as has the axiom "all good from God, all evil from man" in rational philosophy and theology. A major reason why the complementary perspective appears impious is that it has not yet been so fully worked out in mind and heart. Despite Plato's efforts in the Socratic *Apology* to point to a deeper meaning of piety, it remains firmly entangled with the familiar.

"Attack Upon Christendom!" The Anti-Christianism of Depth Psychology

David L. Miller

> I have come to debase the coinage.
> Diogenes
> To make light of philosophy
> is true philosophy.
> Pascal
> Opposition is true friendship.
> Blake

Two years before Freud was born, Søren Kierkegaard wrote the last of a series of essays which, precisely on behalf of Christianity, railed against Christian theology and practice. Gathered under the appropriate title, *Attack Upon Christendom* (1854–55), the iconoclastic thrust of these writings was never unclear, though the style was sometimes indirect, wounding from behind, as the author himself observed. The following parable is typical, and it will serve as a representative anecdote for the reflections which come after it.

> Think of a hospital. The patients are dying like flies. The methods are altered in one way and another. It's no use. What does it come from? It comes from the building, the whole building is full of poison. That the patients are registered as dead, one of this disease, and that one of another, is not true; for they are all dead from the poison that is in the building.

> So it is in the religious sphere. That the religious situation is lamentable, that religiously men are in a pitiable state, nothing is more certain. So one man

---

*Portions of this chapter are reprinted with the permission of Fordham University Press from David L. Miller, "'Attack Upon Christendom!,'" *Thought* 61:56–67 (March 1986).

thinks that it would help to get a new hymnal, another a new altar-book, another a musical service, etc., etc.

In vain, for it comes from the building. The whole edifice . . . has developed poison. For this reason the religious life is sick or has died out. (1956 pp. 139f)

More than half a century after Kierkegaard penned these words, in a letter to Freud in June of 1910, C. G. Jung continued the "attack upon christendom," now from the side of psychology rather than theology, shifting Kierkegaard's metaphor only slightly from "contaminated hospital" to "misery institute." Jung wrote:

I think we must give it [psychoanalysis] time to infiltrate into people from many centres, to revivify among the intellectuals a feeling for symbol and myth, ever so gently to transform Christ back into the sooth-saying god of the vine, which he was, and in this way absorb those ecstatic instinctual forces of Christianity for the *one* purpose of making the cult and the sacred myth what they once were—a drunken feast of joy where man regained the ethos and holiness of an animal. That indeed was the beauty and purpose of classical religion, which· from God knows what temporary biological needs has turned into a Misery Institute. (*Letters* 1:18)[1]

Freud was not a little supportive of Jung's sentiment in his response of a few days later (McGuire, ed., 1974, p. 295), which, in light of the fact that Kierkegaard's perspective has by and large been abandoned in twentieth-century theology,[2] invites a query: Could the view be entertained that an iconoclastic perspective in *theology* is being carried in post-modern times by depth *psychology*? Such is the idea of this article's exploration.

The Anti-Christianism of Depth Psychology

From Freud to the neo-Freudian, Lacan, and from Jung to the neo-Jungian, Hillman, depth psychology in the twentieth century has been permeated with an anti-Christianism. This is a hard fact which many attempts to soften in the name of humanism or spiritualism have not managed to obscure. As we review this psychologically iconoclastic tradition briefly, attempting to discover its sensibility by way of an overview, it may be well not to forget that these therapists are angry. People have come to them in pain and torment, and the sufferings occasionally result, not from personal histories, but from cultural ideas and habits, some of which are carried by a nominally Christian Western culture. They are wounded by an unconscious theology rather than by an individual psychology alone. Freud and Jung, Lacan and Hillman, are therapists. They feel for these persons. So it is not surprising if, on behalf of their patients, they are outraged against religion, at least against religion as it has been conceived and practiced.

FREUD

The argument is well known and often rehearsed.[3] The human animal is ill-equipped, especially when compared with other animals, to endure in nature and history. Man and women have therefore invented civilization in order to have a way of coping. But the solution has been bought at a high price to the individual: namely, loss of sensual pleasure and instinctual renunciation. Furthermore, the repression involved in the strategy of adjusting to the demands of reality may only result later in the outbreak of neurosis. Civilization's discontented souls are psychologically fragile.

One aspect of the social strategy of dwelling in nature and history by banding together is the institutionalization of religion. If a person feels like a child in the face of the forces of reality, it would be natural to wish for a father to take care of one. The beliefs and rituals of religion are the acting-out of this wish: Daddy-in-Heaven will look after me! To the suggestion that people may well need some defenses, some as-if structures for living, some affirmation of the irrationality of things (*Credo quia absurdum est*), Freud responds that, not only does the religious way keep the individual childish, feeling shame, guilt, and anxiety by projecting all power outside of oneself onto god, gods, or some other, but also this strategy, tried for several millenia, has not worked. People are as frightened and sick as ever, perhaps more so, and there are wars and rumours of wars with no end in sight. As far as religion goes, it is time to give it up. Religion is a universal obsessional neurosis (Freud 1961, pp. 5–45).

In spite of his psychotherapeutic judgment, Freud himself did not give religion up. At least, its *fascinosum* did not let go of him. Indeed, before one draws the conclusion decisively that Freud's critique of religion is hostile to religion, that his identification of theology and piety as childish wish-fulfillment works not in the service of faith, it would be well to recall two complicating factors. (1) In a postscript to the autobiography written in 1935, Freud referred to his work in medicine, science, and psychoanalysis as a detour. He said that in the years after 1912 he returned to matters which had interested him as a child when he was "scarcely old enough for thinking" (Freud 1961, p. 3). These matters had to do with religion and culture. (2) Further, it is not altogether clear that the work, *Moses and Monotheism*, published posthumously in the same year that Freud died (1939), is against religion. At least, it could hardly be conceived as being psychologically resistant to religion's symbols and images. That Freud is theologically iconoclastic is incontrovertible. But whether his iconoclasm serves faith or not, and what his life-long fascination with religion means, may be less obvious matters, matters that are complex and overdetermined. We shall return to the complexity in a moment.

JUNG

The usual view, to be sure, is that Jung is as soft on religion as Freud is hard against it. But it is not any more clear that Jung's positive views on religious image and symbol are friendly to actual theology and piety, than it is clear that Freud's negative views are unfriendly.

Of course Jung affirmed that "Christ is a symbol of the self" (Jung 1959, pp. 36–71). But which Christ? It is not the Christ of orthodox theology or usual pious practice; rather, Jung's affirmation was a Christ of so-called "gnostic" (i.e., heretical) Christianity. Again, Jung identified the importance of the Christian eucharist as crucial for occidental women and men as a symbol of the process of psychological individuation. But what Mass? It was the Holy Communion interpreted from the point of view of barbarous pagan rites (the Aztec Teoqualo) and seen through a prism of gnostic alchemy (the visions of Zosimos)! (Jung 1942, pp. 201–46)

The typical course Jung's writing traverses when speaking about Christianity is as follows: he affirms the inevitability of the influence of the patterns and paradigms of Christian image and symbol on Western modes of behavior and patterns of consciousness (which may be largely unconscious), not to mention the important transpersonal carrying power for personal messes of religion's symbolic vessels, but then he quickly adds that these imaginal and symbolic vessels are not functioning because they have "lost their thrilling power" (Jung 1968, p. 301), and they have lost their power because they have been construed theologically and practically in one-sided ways (e.g., neglecting the shadow-side, the feminine side, the physical side, etc.). Nowhere is this sort of argument stated more passionately than when Jung speaks about the Christian theological explanation of the existence of evil in a monotheistic universe as *privatio bono* (e.g., Jung 1959, pp. 41–62; Jung 1952, pp. 357ff).

Jung's passionate plea for patients goes like this. If one imagines, prompted by Christian orthodoxy, that evil is not objective in itself, i.e., if it is only the "privation of (God-given) good" by women and men, then *omne bonum a deo et omne malum ab homine*, "all good is of God and all evil is from people." This theological fantasy about the nature of things is, from Jung's therapeutic perspective, too optimistic about evil, since it denies evil any objective status, and it is too pessimistic about persons, since it blames all suffering on them. Thus, a religious viewpoint, logically necessitated by a monotheistic God who is *Summum Bonum*, is responsible for human feelings of shame, guilt, and anxiety, not to mention inferiority, worthlessness, and depression. At least in part, Jung's clients suffer from an unconscious Christian theology rather than from a conscious personal history.

The sentiment of Jung's argumentative strategy is not unlike that of Franz Overbeck, who writes that "one can call theology the Satan of religion" (1961, p. 13), and it is very near to the view of the historian of religion, Henry Corbin, who wrote of "the fateful complicity of theology in the problem of the West" (1979, p. 13). Did not Jorge Luis Borges write, "God is not a theologian!" And Michelet, "Theology is the art of befuddling oneself methodically!"

Just as certain Freudian revisionists (e.g., Fromm) attempt to soften Freud's "attack upon christendom," so some Jungian interpreters obscure the negative aspect of Jung's argument. For example, both Victor White and Edward Edinger have written extensively about the therapeutic possibilities in Christian archetypes.[4] And there are others, too, who highlight Jung's affirmation of Christian image and symbol (see Stein, *Jung's Treatment of Christianity* [1985] for an excellent review of this literature). But on the other hand, such sober and authoritative interpreters of Jung as Marie-Louise von Franz and Aniela Jaffé stress the tension between traditional versions of Christian symbolic image and the authentic images which well up from the individual depths (Von Franz 1964, p. 226; Jaffé 1969, pp. 245, 255, 267). Jaffé goes so far as to compare Jung's view to Nietzsche's "death of God," to DeChirico's "metaphysical void," and to Kandinsky's "heaven is empty"!

LACAN

Just as it takes time for the light of a distant star to strike our earthly perception, so it has taken nearly half a century for the psychotherapeutic "attack upon christendom" by Freud and Jung to make full impact. The truly radical dimensions of the critique perpetrated on behalf of those who suffer life in a Christian (?) culture turn on seeing that the neurosis of religion-as-practiced (Freud) and the imbalance of religion-as-interpreted-theologically (Jung) were antecedently implicit in the Christian images themselves. *Von den Göttern die Schatten fällt,* wrote Rilke (1962, p. 28). "Gods cast shadows." There is a dark side secretly resident in the language and logic of Christianity's "good news," even when the piety is not acted out in childish ways and even when the theology is not intellectualistically and patriarchally one-sided.

On the Freudian side, it has been Jacques Lacan who, already in 1936, but especially in his seminars after 1953, has mounted the "attack." Though he told his followers that he was "neither for nor against any particular religion" (1968, p. 316), he also reported to them that a Christian is *inanalyzable.* And again, he observed that "the triumph of religion would mean the defeat of psychotherapy" (quoted in Hillman 1985). Why?

The essence of therapy is the re-attainment of "the dialectics of desire" whose abode is the order of *l'imaginaire.* The crux of the construction and the destruction of this order comes early in a person's life. It comes at the *stade de miroir* during which an individual learns to identify herself or himself with an image which is other than ego. The desire is in the relation between ego and image; the dialectic is in the "mirror-play" (Lacan 1968, pp. xii–xiii).

The dialectic of desire is "foreclosed" (Freud's *Verwerfung*), however, as a person's psychological life shifts from the order of *l'imaginaire* to that of the "real" and to that of the "symbolic," where attempts are made in the direction of self-identification literalistically (fantasies of the real, i.e., signification behind signifiers) and/or discursively (fantasies of meaning, i.e., signifiers which signify). Such foreclosures of the "imaginal" and its dialectic of desire are supported by a religious ambience, like that of the Christian West, in which it is insisted that the locus of human meaning is history, because the realm of ego and its history (individual or collective) is precisely the place of "mighty acts of God," i.e., history is the realm of the really real because it is really symbolic of the trans-historical.

The foreclosing on the "imaginal" in the name of the "real" and its "symbolic" ordering is, in Lacan's lexicon, performed in the "name of the father" which paternalistically carries "the law of the father" over against the *jouissance* of the dialectic of desire (Lacan 1968, p. 67). Concerning

Freud's fundamental discovery that the real is the imaginal and the imaginal is (for the psychology of an individual) the real, Lacan wrote: "And what is his [Freud's] self-analysis, if not the brilliant mapping of the law of desire suspended in the Name-of-the-father" (1978, p. 48). A Christian (wittingly or unwittingly) is, on these terms, *inanalyzable*. The triumph of religion (the name of the father) would mean the defeat of psychotherapy (*jouissance* whose locus is *l'imaginaire*).

Lacan is clear about this. Fantasies of the "real" or "symbolic" make "dia-logos," with its play of meanings, as in a mirror, impossible. And without this play, "without dialectic," meanings are schizophrenic, "anchored to paternal *points de caption*" (1968, pp. 129ff). "The absence of *jouissance*," Lacan tells his seminar, "makes the universe vain" (1977, p. 317). "The will to castration (the loss of *jouissance*) inscribed in the paternal) Other . . . culminates in the supreme narcissism of the Lost Cause (this is the way of Greek tragedy, which Claudel rediscovers in a Christianity of despair)" (1977, p. 324).

HILLMAN

The radical Freudian, Norman O. Brown, writing in *Love's Body*, saw the Lacanian point independently of Lacan. He saw that the psychological problem, which Western religion supports and with which it is complicit, "is that of the relations between speech and language in the subject" (Lacan 1977, p. 68), and, like Lacan, stressing the fundamental importance of eros and play in linguistic meanings, Brown wrote that "the real deceivers are the literalists. Literal meaning is conscious meaning, in the upright Protestant way" (1966, p. 245).

On this matter of literalism and religion, radical Freudians and radical Jungians conspire. James Hillman, in the Terry Lectures at Yale University during 1972, announced that he wanted to join "Owen Barfield and Norman Brown in a mafia of metaphor to protect plain men from literalism" (1975 *b*, p. 149). And, again and again, for Hillman, as for Lacan and Brown, the attack upon literalism is at base an attack upon what Hillman calls "chistianism" (1975 *a*, pp. 85–90).[5]

Hillman's patients—like those of Freud, Jung, and Lacan—often suffer from unconscious theology not of their own making. In 1969, at the Eranos Conference in Switzerland, in a lecture entitled "First Adam, then Eve," Hillman protested, in the name of the soul, the inferiority of psychological femininity in the dominant Christian mythos (1972, pp. 215–87). In his lectures in New Haven three years later, he railed against the one-sided lack of pagan Mediterranean feeling in Northern European Protestant sensibility (1975b, pp. 104, 217, 219, 221, 228). In 1975, his book, *Dream and the Underworld,* argued that the psychological depressions of guilt and anxiety and shame are often a product of the implicit message from Christianity that one should not have to descend to the depths because a savior has done this for all women and men, conquering once for all a person's hells. So, if I feel "down," I must be bad (1975a, pp. 85ff). In 1982, Hillman had lost patience on another score which made losers of his clients and their feelings. This time it was the proscription of the animal and animality in the Christian theological tradition (1983), pp. 305–10). In an article on alchemical symbolism, Hillman spoke directly: "The border between fundamentalism in religion and delusional literalism is subtle indeed" (1981b, pp. 25, 56). And, most recently, in his Eranos lecture of 1985, Hillman argued that the fundamental notion of "revelation" in the Christian West has contaminated psychological consciousness so that a differentiation between revelation and paranoia is impossible for people to sense and for theorists to map ("On Paranoia"). Psychopathology is built into the language of Christianity and into the logic of its theology (see Hillman, "Psychology: Monotheistic or Polytheistic?" [1981a])

Though some Jungians in the past have attempted to soften the "attack upon christendom" which joins Hillman and Lacan (see footnote 4), more recent Jungian writings in the psychology of religion lean in the more radical direction. Murray Stein's *Jung's Treatment of Christianity* (1985) (the pun in the title suggesting that the religious tradition is the sick patient), and Elie Humbert's article, "Jung and the Question of Religion" (1985), are important cases in point. But even closer to Hillman's therapeutic worries are those of the Roman Catholic priest, Professor of Religion, and Jungian analyst, John P. Dourley, the subtitle of whose book, *The Illness That We Are,* would more appropriately have been "Jung's Critique of Christianity," rather than "A Jungian Critique of Christianity." Dourley observes: "Jung's writings, which can be so admiring of the Christian tradition, its symbols and its rites, yet also accuse it of currently making people ill" (1984, p. 12). ". . . theologians and their followers too often need professional and so-called secular help to recover from the consequences of their theology" (*ibid.,* p. 88). Dourley wonders: "How can we avoid the faith that kills?" (*ibid.,* p. 75).

The Anti-Christianism of Christianity

Before one concludes that the anti-christianism of twentieth-century depth psychology functions negatively for Christian religiousity and theologism, it may be well to recall the iconoclastic temper of this very tradition in relation to itself. Indeed, the angry, prophetic railing of psychologists should come as no surprise to the Christian. Kierkegaard has been invoked at the outset. But before Kierkegaard or Bonhöffer or Tillich or Vahanian or Hamilton or Hopper . . . there is already Jesus, as well as the prophetic Jewish tradition in which he stood.

> Beware of practicing your piety before men in order to be seen by them; for then you will have no reward from your Father who is in heaven. Thus, when you give alms, sound no trumpet before you, as the hypocrites do in the synagogues and in the streets, that they may be praised by men. . . . And when you pray, you must not be like the hypocrites; for they love to stand and pray in the synagogues and at the street corners, that they may be seen by men. (Matthew 6:1–2,5)

> And in his teaching he said, "Beware of the scribes, who like to go about in long robes, and to have salutations in the market places and the best seats in the synagogues and the places of honor at feasts, who devour widow's houses and for a pretense make long prayers. They will receive the greater condemnation." (Mark 12:38–40)

> Jesus said, "For judgment I came into this world, that those who do not see may see, and that those who see may become blind." (John 9:39)

> "I hate, I despise your feasts, and I take no delight in your solemn assemblies. . . . Take away from me the noise of your songs; to the melody of your harps I will not listen." (Amos 5:21, 23)

> ". . . [T]he high places of Isaac shall be made desolate, and the sanctuaries of Israel shall be laid waste, and I will rise against the house of Jeroboam." (Amos 7:9)

> "My anger is hot against the shepherds [religious and political leaders], and I will punish [them]." (Zechariah 10:3)

Indeed, think of those who have spoken out against religion in the interest of a deep religious meaning for the people: Paul and Luther, the Buddha and Nagarjuna, Lao Tzu and Dogen. Does not the Zen tradition say: "If you meet the Buddha on the road, kill him!" and "Miso (bean paste) that smells like miso is not good miso. Religion that smells like religion is not good religion." So, the German Protestant theologian, Jürgen Moltmann, not too long ago cited the Marxist philosopher, Ernst Bloch, who said: "Only an atheist can be a good Christian." And then Moltmann went on to explain: "An atheist for God's sake . . . destroys all images, traditions, and religious feelings of his own that unite him with God in an illusive fashion; and he does so for the sake of the inexpressibly living, wholly different God. His atheism is negative theology" (1970, p. 28). As the poet Hölderlin wrote: ". . . *bis Gottes Fehl hilft.*"—"Sometimes God's absence helps" (1961, p. 138).

Depth Psychology as Post-Modern Theology

Perhaps depth psychology can help. Perhaps it can help religion as much as it does individuals, by providing a new (old) theology, one that Murray Stein calls "psycho-theologizing" (1985, p. 150). This, at least, was the argument of Will Herberg.

Herberg was arguing as a theologian when, in 1957, he supported Freud's anti-religious stance against pro-religious views of Freudian (he could have mentioned Jungian) revisionists (e.g., Jules Masserman, Erich Fromm, and others). Herberg affirmed Freud's telling of the truth about the self, a truth which Freud tells "with deep earnestness and conviction."

> What he tells us about ourselves is not always pleasant to hear, but it is of vital importance since it challenges our many devices of self-exculpation. Freud will not permit us to see ourselves as blameless innocents victimized by history, society, or culture. . . . Freud's teaching reinforces the Jewish-Christian conviction of the dubiousness of all human virtue and the ambiguity of all human achievements. . . . Grateful we [theologians and religious persons] may be for Freud's stubborn integrity, his refusal to conciliate, his indignant rejection of sham. (1957, p. 160)

Herberg's words could apply as well to Jung, and they could be repeated with emphasis for Lacan and Hillman.

But Herberg also turns his iconoclastic theological rhetoric against the psychology, whether Freudian or Jungian, that would attempt to compromise an anti-christianism. "Is that all to the good (theologically)?" Herberg asks. "What kind of religion does he (Masserman in this case) vincidate?" And Herberg answers forthrightly:

> Any one at all acquainted with the Bible and the structure of biblical faith will be struck by the strange fact that the very beliefs Dr. Masserman strives to vindicate as the essentials of religion because they are the Ur-defenses of man, are the beliefs that biblical faith is especially concerned to question and reject. Surely it is obvious that in biblical faith man is *not* immortal and invulnerable; he is as the grass that withereth, here today and gone tomorrow . . . The Bible warns repeatedly against illusions about man's goodwill: "The heart [of man] is

deceitful above all things, and desperately wicked; who can understand it?" (Jer. 17:9). (1957, p. 162)

And then Herberg concludes:

> Incredible as it may seem, Freud with his *rejection* of religion, was closer to, or at least less distant from, the biblical position than Dr. Masserman with his vindication of it . . . in Freud's iconoclasm there is an aspect of God's truth almost completely lost in the "pro-religionism" of our time. Freud was hostile to religion, but much of what he took for religion was sham and deserved his hostility. Above all, he hated sham. He had nothing but contempt for those who were trying to win favor for religion by presenting it under false colors so as to deprive it of its "scandal" and challenge. (1957, pp. 162–63)

So it is, too, with Jung's hatred (on behalf of the suffering souls) of *imitatio Christi* and one-sided theology, not to mention Lacan's impatience with the Law of the Father or Hillman's raillery against a Protestant literalism that does not protest or re-form.

Which religion is depth psychology against? It is against the religion of false piety, the religion used as human wish- or need-fulfilment, a crutch or opiate, the religion of spiritual pride (worst of all sins). *Personal* (i.e., egoic) Lord and Savior, indeed! Psychology is against a religion shoring up defensive and narcissistic ego against Other, Id, Collective Archetypal *Imago, Jouissance,* Pagan Gods still living our lives, the Little People of the Unconscious. It is against attempts to shore up ego against the perduring Trans-Personal, i.e., it is against religion which is against Religion. Depth psychology is against the religion religion is against, or should be.

In a pro-religious time, a time of religious retrenchment in the face of post-modern possibility, religion may need depth psychology's assistance in recovering its own deep insight. At least one can imagine that Kierkegaard would have welcomed psychology's depriving religion of an implicit understanding of itself as crutch or opiate. On April 10, 1855, Kierkegaard wrote: "This is the shocking thing. Perhaps too it is without an analogy in history that a religion has died by flourishing. But note that in saying 'flourishing,' Christianity is understood as the opposite of what the New Testament understands as Christianity. The religion of suffering has become the religion of not-suffering, of overcoming suffering . . ." (1956, p. 142). Concerning this Kierkegaard told a parable:

> They tell a ludicrous story about an innkeeper. It is said that he sold his beer by the bottle for a cent less than he paid for it; and when a certain man said to

him, "How does that balance the account?" he replied, "It's the volume that does it." . . . There can be no doubt [Kierkegaard muses] that this innkeeper knew very well that one bottle of beer which he sold for 3 cents meant a loss of 1 cent when it cost him 4 cents. Also, with regard to ten bottles the inn-keeper will be able to hold fast to that it is a loss. But 100,000 bottles! Here the big number stirs the imagination, the round number runs away with it, and the inkeeper becomes dazed—it's a profit, says he, for the volume does it. So also with the calculation which arrives at a Christian nation by adding up units which are not Christian, getting the result by means of the notion that the big number does it. For true Christianity this is the most dangerous of all illusions. (*Ibid.*, pp. 30ff)

And Kierkegaard lived a century before evangelism by television!

In Walker Percy's novel *The Last Gentlemen* an item from Sutter's journal resonates with Kierkegaard's parable and with the theological importance of depth psychology's "attack upon christendom." The entry reads:

Christ should leave us. He is too much with us and I don't like his friends. We have no hope of recovering Christ until Christ leaves us. There is after all something worse than being God-forsaken. It is when God overstays his wel-come and takes up with the wrong people. (1966, p. 372)

In post-modernity it may be that religion could do much worse than tak-ing up with its apparent enemy, depth psychology. It may, thereby, re-cover its own deepest insight. At least, depth psychology *in its most radical form* does not smell like religion. And—whether in psychotherapy or in religion—bean paste that smells like bean paste is not.

Notes

1. A footnote to this letter, added by the editor, seems to imply that Jung later (in a letter of April 9, 1959, never released) repudiated his strong critique with words like "incred-ible folly that filled the days of my youth." But this is by no means clear. At a Christmas cel-ebration with his family in 1957, he is still referring to the "lost" sense of Christianity as a drinking feast (1979, pp. 143ff), and, when he was 70, Jung complained of religious ideas having lost "the numinosity, i.e., their thrilling power" (1968, p. 301).

2. The words "by and large" are used in this sentence so as to permit a remembering that there have been notable exceptions in the twentieth century to the lost iconoclasm in theology. Suffice it to mention the names of Dietrich Bonhöffer, Paul Tillich, William Ham-ilton, Gabriel Vahanian, and Stanley R. Hopper. Others will come to the mind of the reader. But the work of these courageous thinkers has not seemed to have carried the day in a time of the "return of religion to the secular city."

3. The allusion here is to the writings by Freud that are listed below in the References.

4. The allusion here is especially to White's work, *God and the Unconscious*, (1953), and to Edinger's articles on alchemy in the journal, *Quadrant*, in addition to three privately dis-tributed tape-series: "Jahweh and Individuation" (4 tapes) and "The Blood of Christ" (2 tapes), both from The Centerpoint Foundation, Nashua, Hew Hampshire; and, "The Chris-

tian Archetype" (4 tapes), from C. G. Jung Institute, San Francisco, California. The work by Murray Stein, *Jung's Treatment of Christianity* (1985), lists other sources of this sort.

5. I have written elsewhere in regard to rapprochement in the works of Lacan and Hillman (see Miller 1983, pp. 330ff).

6. More recently, the work, *Erring*, by Mark Taylor, (1984) is to this point.

References

Brown, N. O. 1966. *Love's body.* New York: Random House.

Corbin, H. 1979. Time of Eranos. *Eranos and its meaning.* Ascona: Eranos Foundation.

Dourley, J. P. 1984. *The illness that we are: A Jungian critique of Christianity.* Toronto: Inner City Books.

Edinger, E. 1973. *Ego and archetype.* Baltimore: Penguin Books.

Franz, M.-L. von. 1964. The Process of Individuation. In C. G. Jung, ed., *Man and his symbols,* pp. 158-229. Garden City: Doubleday & Company, Inc.: 1964.

Freud, S. 1924-50. Obsessional acts and religious practices. In *Collected papers,* vols. 1-5, pp. 2, 25. London: International Psychoanalytic Press.

_____. 1930. *Civilization and its discontents,* J. Strachey, tr. New York: W. W. Norton & Co.

_____. 1961. *The future of an illusion,* J. Stachey, tr. New York: W. W. Norton & Co.

_____. 1967. *Moses and monotheism,* K. Jones, tr. New York: Vintage Books.

_____. 1980. *Totem and taboo,* J. Strachey, tr. New York: W. W. Norton & Co.

Herberg, W. 1957. Freud and the revisionists. In B. Nelson, ed., *Freud and the twentieth century.* New York: Meridian Books.

Hillman, J. 1972. *The myth of analysis.* New York: Harper and Row.

_____. 1975a. *Dream and the underworld.* New York: Harper and Row.

_____. 1975b. *Re-visioning psychology.* New York: Harper and Row.

_____. 1981a. Psychology: Monotheistic or polytheistic? In D. L. Miller, ed., *The new polytheism: Rebirth of the gods and goddesses,* pp. 109–142. Dallas: Spring Publications.

_____. 1981b. Silver and white earth. *Spring 1981:* 21–66. Dallas: Spring Publications.

_____. 1983. The animal kingdom in the human dream. *Eranos Jahrbuch 51-1982.* Frankfurt: Insel Verlag.

_____. 1985. On paranoia. *Eranos Jahrbuch 54-1985.* Frankfurt: Insel Verlag, forthcoming.

Hölderlin, F. 1961. Dichterberuf (The poet's vocation). In M. Hamburger, ed., *Selected verse.* Baltimore: Penguin.

Humbert, E. 1985. Jung and the question of religion. *Spring 1985.* Dallas: Spring Publications.

Jaffé, A. 1969. Symbolism in the visual arts. In C. G. Jung, ed., *Man and his symbols,* pp. 230–71. Garden City: Doubleday & Company, Inc.

Jung, C. G. 1942. Transformation symbolism in the mass. In *Collected works,* 11:201-98. Princeton: Princeton University Press, 1958.

_____. 1952. *Answer to Job.* In *Collected works,* 11:355-474. Princeton: Princeton University Press, 1969.

_____. 1959. *Aion: Researches into the phenomenology of the self.* In *Collected works,* 9, ii. Princeton: Princeton University Press.

_____. 1968. *Alchemical studies.* In *Collected works,* vol. 13. Princeton: Princeton University Press.

_____. 1974. *Letters,* vols 1-2. Princeton: Princeton University Press.

_____. 1979. *Word and image.* K. Winston, tr. Princeton: Princeton University Press.

Kierkegaard, S. 1956. *Attack upon Christendom*, W. Lowrie, tr. Boston: Beacon Press.

Lacan, J. 1968. *The language of the self*, A. Wilden, tr. Baltimore: Johns Hopkins Press.

—————. 1977. *Ecrits: A selection*, A. Sheridan, tr. New York: W. W. Norton and Co., Inc.

—————. 1978. *The four fundamental concepts of psycho-analysis*, A. Sheridan, tr. New York: W. W. Norton and Co., Inc.

McGuire, W. ed. 1974. *The Freud-Jung letters*, R. Manheim and R. Hull, tr. Princeton: Princeton University Press.

Miller, D. The Holy Ghost and the grateful dead. *Eranos Jahrbuch* 52-1983: 277–346. Frankfurt: Insel Verlag.

Moltmann, J. 1970. Introduction. In Ernst Bloch, ed., *Man on his own*, E. B. Ashton, tr. New York: Herder and Herder.

Overbeck, F. 1961. *Christentum und kultur*, C. A. Bernouli, ed. Darmstadt: Wissenschftliche Buchgesellschaft.

Percy, W. 1966. *The last gentleman*. New York: Farrar, Straus and Giroux.

Rilke, R. M. 1962. *Sonnets to Orpheus*, M. D. H. Norton, tr. New York: W. W. Norton & Co.

Stein, M. 1985. *Jung's treatment of Christianity: The psychotherapy of a religious tradition*. Wilmette, Il.: Chiron Publications.

Taylor, M. 1984. *Erring: A postmodern a/theology*. Chicago: University of Chicago Press.

White, V. 1953. *God and the unconscious*. Chicago: H. Regnery.

Patriarchy in Transformation: Judaic, Christian, and Clinical Perspectives

Nathan Schwartz-Salant

> *Incarnation (on) the human level*
> *appears as individuation.*
> C. G. Jung (1942, p. 171)

Introduction: Pleromatic Processes
and the Clinical Relevance of Jung's Writings on Religion

How does a person's internal world come into existence? Does it stem from something larger, originally whole? Is this *object* numinous and transcendent? Or is this a romantic hypothesis that is easily undone by observations of infant development? Is the far more adequate and scientific answer that the inner world is built up through pleasurable and unpleasurable stimuli, modified somewhat by internal processes but largely by an external mothering figure? Is the pain and suffering of early individuation a result, then, of the intense abandonment anxieties a child suffers, an absence of a "good-enough mother" (Winnicott 1971, p. 10), and is this to be our model for the vicissitudes of all later development? Or is this pain a result, *in the child as in later adult forms of individuation,* of a far greater Wholeness, *ineffable* to normal consensus consciousness, incarnating into space-time reality?

For most object relations and ego-psychological clinicians, the anxieties of developmental processes are to a degree both natural and functional, serving, for example, to transform omnipotence and the tendency to cling to hallucinatory wish fulfillment. But some clinicians, such as Wilfred Bion, who are usually not considered in the mainstream of thinking about psychic processes, take a more radical view of the intense persecutory anxieties that can exist in infancy and adult life, and consider that they can perform the function of dissolving psychic containers so that new forms can come into existence (Eigen 1985, pp. 322–23).

Jung's approach corresponds to this attitude. Using the terminology of the religious systems he was studying, Jung would say that it was evil that led to the incarnation of the *numinosum,* or that evil was the driving force that made the *numinosum* an actual rather than a potential factor (Jung 1942, p. 196). This positive valuation of the destructive aspects of human and divine nature is not found only as a major thesis of Manicheism and Zoroastrian thinking, but is also found in Freud's idea that the ego seeks out objects to love in order not to be destroyed by the death instinct, and in Bion's positive evaluation of Melanie Klein's paranoid-schizoid position. Bion regards it not only as a stage that must be outgrown in a moral development that grasps the destructive nature of rage, hate, envy, and lies, but as one that can also dissolve the psychic structures or containers formed by processes of inner union, notably the depressive position. There the infant's perceptions of the good and and bad breast cease to be in terms of separate part-objects, and instead are of a whole object which becomes an inner psychic container.

Bion's idea corresponds to the kind of alchemical thinking Jung uncovered in his many years of research. For example in the most famous alchemical text, the *Rosarium Philosophorum,* there is a stage of the union of opposites, known in alchemy as the *coniunctio,* which is followed by states akin to the Kleinian paranoid-schizoid position and severe depressive anxieties of loss, all to the end of transforming bodily rigidities and the consciousness of the soul so that it can descend into a new container, the transformed body-soul union known as the *lapis* (Jung 1946, pp. 465–70). The "bad trip" is valued; it is recognized that it contains the power to dissolve the containers that are inadequate to receive the soul's new experiences, especially experiences that unmask falseness through contact with those domains called God, or the *numinosum.* The key, of course, is to have a "good trip" to incarnate. The intense persecutory anxieties, or affecto-motor storms of early infant life, must be parts of a process, not dominants in themselves, as is often the case in borderline personality disorders.

In Jung's thought, what incarnates is not primarily a universe of introjects of interpersonal relations. Rather, his emphasis is on archetypal processes that, while projecting onto outer human object relations as part of the process of their coming into actual, affective reality in the subject, are nevertheless in no way reducible to introjections of *these* objects. One often gets the impression that Jung was extremely wary of the way in which object relations could distort one's truth, and in this he has a kinship with Lacan's distrust of mirroring (Eigen 1981, pp. 421–22). Also, Jung places little value on the process of identification, which is so critical to object-relations approaches in which inner structure is heavily dependent upon outer objects.

In most object-relational approaches, the goal is to gain a real perception of the outer object, unclouded by denial, envy, idealization, and magical omnipotence, and to gain a perception of a realistic inner world as well, unfettered by grandiose self objects that can never be realized in reality. But for Jung the goal is to have an inner world that is a link to the *numinosum*, to states of mind that, while not distorting outer object relations, transcend space-time perceptions.

Jung's research into the transformation of the patriarchal God-image was a central way in which he dealt with the *numinosum* as it entered into man. This incarnation is never complete, and was thought about by Jung in terms of the idea of the continual incarnation of the Holy Ghost, which "On the human level appears as 'individuation'" (1942, p. 157; 1952, p. 457). In object-relations approaches, the creation of an inner world is also a major goal. Are we dealing with similar items in different ways, one mythical and the other scientifically based, in observing infant development?

The following quotation from Jung will help us begin to address this question.

> Although the birth of Christ is an event that occurred but once in history, it has always existed in eternity. For the layman in these matters, the identity of a nontemporal, eternal event with a unique historical occurrence is something that is extremely difficult to conceive. He must, however, accustom himself to the idea that "time" is a relative concept and needs to be complemented by that of the "simultaneous" existence, in the Bardo or pleroma, of all historical processes. What exists in the pleroma as an eternal process appears in time as an aperiodic sequence, that is to say, it is repeated many times in an irregular pattern. . . . *When these things occur in modern variants, therefore, they should not be regarded merely as personal episodes, moods, or chance idiosyncrasies in people, but as fragments of the pleromatic process itself, which, broken up into individual events occurring in time, is an essential component or aspect of the divine drama.* (1952, pp. 400–401; italics added)

Jung thus differentiates what he calls eternal processes existing in the pleroma from the fragments of this process that we see in individual events in time. It is this differentiation of events in space-time—for example, as stages in an infant's development—from its larger process in what Jung calls the pleroma, that separates Jungian approaches to clinical material from all others.

> The causalism that underlies our scientific view of the world breaks everything down into individual processes which it punctiliously tries to isolate from all other parallel processes. This tendency is absolutely necessary if we are to gain reliable knowledge of the world, but philosophically it has the disadvantage of breaking up, or obscuring, the universal interrelationship of events so that a recognition of the greater relationship, i.e., of the unity of the world, becomes more and more difficult. Everything that happens, however, happens in the same "one world" and is a part of it. For this reason, events must possess an *a priori* aspect of unity . . . . (1955, p. 464)

Jung's approach and model is precisely the same as David Bohm's in modern physics (1980). His idea of an *implicate order*, or Jung's of the pleroma, out of which fragments, the discreet events we witness in space-time, fall and return, is based upon the same ancient Hermetic wisdom (Bamford 1981, pp. 5–25). Bohm writes:

> Physics has become almost totally committed to the notion that the order of the universe is basically mechanistic. The most common form of this notion is that the world is assumed to be constituted by a set of separately existent, indivisible and unchangeable "elementary particles," which are the fundamental "building blocks" of the entire universe. Originally, these were thought to be atoms . . . but then, these were in turn found to be subject to transformation into hundreds of different kinds of unstable particles, and now even smaller particles called "quarks" and "partons" have been postulated to explain these transformations. Though these have not yet been isolated there appears to be an unshakable faith among physicists that either such particles, or some other kind yet to be discovered, will eventually (explain) everything. (1980, p. 173)

Bohm, like Jung, recognizes the necessity for beginning with a state of wholeness. His *implicate order* is what Jung called the pleroma, the Bardo, the Unus Mundus (1955, pp. 462ff), or the alchemical god Mercurius (1955, p. 465). For Bohm, processes here are characterized by their Oneness, just as they are for Jung. But in our normal space-time world, characterized by Bohm as the explicate order, events are seen as discreet, and their underlying wholeness vanishes from view.

> In terms of the implicate order one may say that everything is enfolded into everything. This contrasts with the explicate order now dominant in phys-

ics in which things are unfolded in the sense that each thing lies only in its own particular region of space (and time) and outside the regions belonging to other things. . . . What distinguishes the explicate order (is) a set or recurrent and relatively stable elements that are outside of each other. . . . In the prevailing mechanistic approach . . . these elements are taken as constituting the basic reality. . . . When one works in terms of the implicate order, one begins with the undivided wholeness of the universe, and the task of science is to derive the parts through abstraction from the whole. (1980, pp. 178–79)

Clinical concepts today generally stem from observations of infant and child development, along with other inferences made from transference/countertransference interactions with adult patients. From this data, clinicians have deduced seminal concepts such as the depressive position or the rapprochement subphase of separation-individuation, and they have grasped psychic reality in terms of internal objects, part-objects, complexes, and so forth. These are all conceptualizations within the confines of the explicate order. In Jung's approach, they must further be seen as fragments of a larger pleromatic process, just as Bohm insists that the quarks and partons and other elementary particles must be seen as fragments of a far larger implicate order. Thus Jung's emphasis is that healing depends upon a linking to the larger world of the pleroma, and consequently one must be able to grasp processes such as the depressive position not only in their space-time matrix, but as aspects of a divine drama.

Many developmental approaches begin with some conception of oneness. Out of the stages Erich Neumann calls the maternal uroboros, followed by paternal or patriarchal uroboros (1954, pp. 17–19; 1955, pp. 317–19), the ego is gradually to develop, and the internal world to differentiate. But now Neumann's conceptions leave the realm of oneness, and the *parts* of this foundation become the main focus. This is a method that is nowadays common to all developmental approaches. Many may not elevate the initial state of oneness to any high order, and like Mahler may see it primarily as an autistic state that precludes meaningful contact (symbiosis, in her terms) with a mothering-figure. Other clinicians, such as Michael Fordham, would disagree with this position on the earliest life of the infant, but would still see an initial state of Oneness, not characterized by notions of symbiosis (Fordham 1985) or common boundaries between a mother and her infant. Rather, the child is reckoned to have a uniqueness and process that can be observed without reference to a mothering figure, and without undervaluing the mother-child interaction in the least. For Fordham, the starting point is a *nuclear self* that eventually must "deintegrate" (Fordham 1967, p. 16), wherein parts of this unity continually manifest as new psychic structure. Another differing viewpoint is found in the influential work of Ronald Fairbairn, who posited an initial state that he called the original ego. Out of this state, internal structure develops into parts such as the central ego and the so-called libidinal and anti-libidinal egos, along with the superego. Fairbairn's theory has a mysterious twist to it for many other object-relations theorists, for he insisted that this initial original ego was not a part-object, but was whole and also subject to repression, something generally assumed to be a developmental acquisition (Rinsley 1982, p. 85).

Whether one begins with a notion of transcendent oneness as cast by Neumann in a maternal or paternal uroboros, Mahler's autistic stage of the first month of life, Fordham's nuclear self, or Fairbairn's original ego—to mention a few examples—the general tendency is to see how the parts of psychic structure then develop. There is a wide variety of approaches to the development of an individual self. But even an approach such as Neumann's, that respects an initial state of oneness out of which psychic structures unfold, soon leaves off touch with this basic background order. It would seem to be a value to lose touch with it, and to heroically become involved in daily life in a space-time matrix. In almost all these developmental approaches, the essential line of thinking is along classical scientific approaches. The parts that develop, or the parts out of which inner structures are conceived of forming, are not dealt with from the point of view of sensing their living relationship to a background oneness. They become like grains of sand that are parts of the personality, not grains of sand that each contain the whole.

Jung's approach is different. His orientation to healing embodied the need to bring our fragmentary space-time life back to its origins in the oneness of existence. This is a fuller statement of his approach than is carried by the idea that healing stems from the *numinosum*. Rather, healing depends upon linking to the background source of existence as we can know it, ineffable experiences that lead to symbolic manifestations of the Unus Mundus. "Everything that happens, however, happens in the same 'one world' and is part of it. For this reason, events must possess an *a priori* aspect of unity" (1955, p. 414).

This emphasis upon turning to oneness could appear to be a mystical, if not a wish-fulfilling approach to therapy. What does such a viewpoint have to do with ill patients? Are not most people injured in the early years of childhood, and does not their cure depend upon "working through" the associated developmental failures? Would not an analyst who sees a borderline patient's failure to negotiate rapprochement issues as something linked to a religious issue of the incarnation of the *numinosum* into space-time existence be aligning with the patient's delusional and primary-process thinking? Certainly the analyst who avoids such developmental issues and the way that they repeat in the transference/countertransference will be very ineffective, at best. Yet, the age-old wisdom of the Hermetic tradition (Bamford 1981), which Jung has followed, holds that healing depends upon a return to origins. This does not mean a return to images and experiences of the personal mother, for example in a process of therapeutic regression, but the *eternal return* to an experience of the pleroma, which is the matrix of life.

A Clinical Example

A patient has been seeing me for several years suffering from a severe rapprochement failure. Her initial dream showed this issue by repeated sequences of being with me, separating, and then having great difficulty in finding me again. In the transference, this pattern eventually became repetitious, but did not immediately manifest. For approximately six months our therapeutic connection was based on a positive transference, and after the session she would leave feeling me with her and she sustained an internal connection to me until the next session. But as soon as negative transference elements appeared, she quickly lost this object constancy, and after six months I began to disappear from her mind and memory between sessions. When she returned to the next session, she had little memory of our past session, and entertained thoughts of terminating because "after analysis we would have no relationship, so what's the point?"

This is a very characteristic scenario in borderline patients suffering from a severe rapprochement crisis. We could, after some time, begin to reconstruct the early childhood traumas that undermined her development. Her mother's depression and tendency to withdraw from her toddler's exuberance was clear from memories and dreams, and was especially replicated in my countertransference reactions, many of which seemed to be induced. This, along with experiences of healthy affective union in the analytical setting, was the working substance of at least two years of analysis, with the experiences of union always then lost to her rapprochement trauma. The following session(s) would then be devoted to analyzing her splitting defenses, mind-body dissociations, and her painful states of feeling ugly. In turn, a harmonious contact could then be established, perhaps taking several weeks to achieve, and then the familiar pattern would repeat wherein it would appear that nothing had transpired that had any structural significance.

The nature of the experiences that I am calling *union* or *harmonious contact* were themselves genuine, but were also achieved at the expense of sidestepping or going beyond persecutory affects of abandonment. The nature of the contact I am describing is akin to the alchemical image called the *coniunctio*, or *union*, in Winnicott's sense, as an experience that was neither a state of fusion nor separation (1971, pp. 97–98). These union experiences were partial and not intense. They never led to an experience of a genuine "third thing" between us and in which we both participated. (I have described such unions elsewhere [1984, 1986].) But there was something of this, and with it a genuine sense of kinship emerged, enough to allow her to suffer the pain of loss of union over and over again. Considering that well over twenty years of previous analyses had never touched her abandonment feelings in a contained and integrating way, this was no mean accomplishment.

Thus her rapprochement could be dealt with over and over, in the manner of the alchemical motto of *dissolve and coagulate*. But how was this central failure part of a divine drama? Up to now it had been conceived of strictly in terms of her developmental issues and their replay in the transference-countertransference process. Its larger significance emerged quite significantly after she had gone to a yoga retreat and had had a mild religious experience, a sense of inner light.

When she returned to analysis the following day, I felt tendencies toward withdrawal and depression, affects I had to wrestle with in myself. She was split from them, and instead connected to the positive experience she had had. She was also now not split from me. It was as if her experience or psyche was layered, with her recent uplifting experience in the foreground, and the previous rapprochement issues in the background. Both were palpable, the rapprochement issues through induction into me of depressed, dead feelings, and her light, which I could perceive through imaginal sight.

After sometime in the session I could bring out what I was experiencing, carefully noting both states, having been aware of the fact that there was also an expectancy of envious spoiling at hand. In this manner she could soon see her abandonment expectancies, *but now she could see them in the face of her daring to bring her true power derived from the* numinosum *into space-time life.* Before, she had always split her life into a secular and a religious part, a careful understanding of issues of psychotherapy, and a separate life devoted to meditation and healing practices. Now the two had met, and it was possible to understand her pain and suffering of rapprochement as part of the larger drama of the incarnation of the *numinosum.* Like many borderline patients, she had known this level as an outer, transcendent fact, but it had never incarnated into immanence, and thus had left her with an inner emptiness and absence of self.

Thus this patient's tortuous history of abandonment could be seen as a replay of the second and third year of life with her mother. But it could also be seen as a fragment of a larger process of the incarnation of the *numinosum* into her psyche, and her terrors of abandonment if she dared allow this process to occur. If she dared take the power it yields—the power that is known not through feeling powerful but, paradoxically, through feeling an open heart to others and the larger source that had gracefully entered her being—then to her mind nobody would be there for her. For, in fact, she would then be faced with the aloneness endemic to the individuation process. Rapprochement in these terms means a link with the *numinosum* and suffering of the torment of bringing that awareness and experience back into space-time reality. And her rapprochement failures in early life could be seen as fragmentary aspects of this divine process, cast within the vicissitudes of her early mother and father relationship.

Pleromatic Processes and Their Space-Time Restrictions

Understanding developmental issues in the larger framework of a "divine process" is especially important in understanding creativity, which is a special instance of linking to pleromatic processes. The creative person's efforts to embody an inner vision always meets with limitation and incompleteness. The restrictions of space-time reality cannot perfectly mirror the sense of wholeness that can be known in contact with the pleroma. One's product never perfectly mirrors the vision one hopes can be produced. The creative act itself thus destroys something, and it creates an object that fails to fully reflect one's deepest self and its perceptions. These states are similar to those felt in developmental struggles in the depressive position or in rapprochement issues. Yet, if reduced to these developmental issues, the creative act itself becomes only an exercise in sublimation of persecutory and depressive anxieties, which is surely a caricature of no value.

If one recognizes a larger dimension of existence such as Jung described with the ancient term *pleroma,* and further recognizes that an individual may contact it and its processes through creative, imaginal efforts, then developmental stages that we have been discussing can be seen as effects of a process of union between the ascending imagination and its link to the material life of the body, a canvas, a piece of stone—a union of matter and spirit. This process, the alchemical *coniunctio,* is the larger issue, and the stages known to theories of infant development are fragments of the *entrance* of the *coniunctio* into space-time reality.

Jung's alchemical studies localize his finest efforts to bring pleromatic levels into relationship with space-time experiences. The processes that the alchemists describe, especially the *coniunctio* and its associated states as depicted in the *Rosarium Philosophorum* (1946), deal with transformations of spirit into matter and matter into spirit. *Materialize the spirit and spiritualize matter* is a refrain running throughout alchemy. It is beyond the confines of this paper to discuss this in greater detail, but it is important to note that *where* the union takes place is a critical concern of the alchemists. It is an important question, for if we are dealing with processes that are atemporal, how can we think of their union with personality elements and modes of perception that orient to outer, space-time fragments and distinctions?

There are at least several possibilities. We can posit the existence of *the unconscious* and insist that it contains both personal, which is to say historical and time-related repressed contents, as well as archetypal, atemporal ones that have never been conscious to the individual. Then, one can make use of a model of projection, and work with the hypothesis that both of these levels can project onto another person, and that these projections can be taken back, thus forming inner structures of varying complexity and subtlety. One thus works with a model based upon categories of *inside* and *outside,* even though such distinctions do not hold for pleromatic processes *per se,* save those that are integrated into a human being, the drama pointed to in its fullness in the Incarnation.

This approach is useful for personal unconscious elements, or contents that were known in space-time existence and then were lost to awareness. We can assume that in some sense these contents are *inside*. But does it also follow that archetypal levels that structure pleromatic processes can also ever get *inside*? We know this can happen to a degree, but it is never fully accomplished, and most likely it is only ever accomplished in a very minimal way. Generally, archetypal experiences are felt within a space that is not compatible with spatial distinctions such as inside or outside.

I believe that Jung's use of a projection model, "taking back anima and animus projections," distorts his study of the transference. One never "takes back" projections of this sort. One may "take back" partial aspects of these archetypes, but always the major qualities stay closer to their pleromatic source and have to be met halfway, in their mystery of union in a space of relations that is neither inside nor outside anyone.

When Jung finds that the death of the patriarchal God-image leads to the appearance of symbolic forms such as the mandala centered by the *coniunctio* (1937, p. 94), he is pointing to a transformation of consciousness. But to think of this change in the Cartesian categories of space and time—inside and outside a person—limits the goal of relating the fragments of our existence back to their roots as part of a divine, pleromatic drama.

In the *Rosarium Philosophorum*, the alchemical text that Jung took as a thread through the complexities of the transference and countertransference, the stage the alchemists call the *nigredo* follows the *coniunctio* or union of male and female, spirit and matter. The experiences known as the depressive position or the rapprochement subphase are experiences of union—mother and child, the good and bad breast—but unions that are fragments of their fuller, pleromatic form. They are unions, however, that represent that larger process as it meets space and time, and consequently these developmental stages are crucial ones. What is generally emphasized, however, are the accompanying affects of these stages, not the union itself. The result of such a union is always stages such as the *nigredo* and its abandonment anxieties and depressions. But experiencing the imaginal union state and *then* experiencing the associated depressive and schizoid patterns is a way of healing that both relates these fragments to a larger sphere of union and more directly partakes of that union. The divine drama thus inextricably mixes with space-time, personal existence, lends it meaning, and itself becomes realized.

The Patriarchal God-Image

Jung's starting point or image whereby he grasps wholeness incarnating into the explicate space-time world is the motif of the death of the Patriarchal God-image, the Father with a capital "F." He orients the development of internal human structures and the Self both culturally and historically, back to its roots in the Old Testament. This does not mean that he does not take far more general "origins" or images of Oneness into consideration, images such as the alchemical Mercurius or the Unus Mundus, but in his writings on religion, the Old Testament God image is usually the starting point, for that is the way our Western heritage initially grasped wholeness.

The psychological condition that Jung called the rule of the Father is a state in which "Man, world, and God form a whole, a unity unclouded by criticism" (1942, p. 134). "The world of the Father typifies an age which is characterized by a pristine oneness with the whole of Nature, no matter whether this oneness be beautiful or ugly or awe inspiring." (*ibid.*). "It is a passive unreflecting condition, a mere awareness of what is given, without intellectual or moral judgment. This is true both individually and collectively" (*ibid.*, p. 181). "Yahweh is not split but is an *antimony*—a totality of inner opposites" (1952, p. 369). He is a *complexio oppositorum*, a numinous whole.

In this state there is little sense of an interior world, of an inner self that has goals that we can choose to follow or discard. There is no sense of individuation as a growing awareness of an inner center. The inner world is still largely projected onto this particular God-image, a condition of identity between a single archetype and the unconscious. But this stage, in which the God-image is outside of a person, believed in or experienced as a state of archaic identity or projective identification, can be followed by one in which there is an indwelling of this Spirit such that a psychic center, a Self is formed. This is especially the result of an *experience* of its *numinosum*. A person may experience this new center as being inside or interior to his or her personality, a source of wisdom and orientation, which acts like a symbolic compass. It feels like an immanent aspect of the larger experience of the *numinosum*, which was only known as something outside the individual. It is a background object that yields a sense of assurance and direction to life, but often is a source of seemingly irrational choices as viewed by the person's family and friends. *Its will* is often followed by the person with a faith that is based upon contact with the *numinosum.* But the inner experience of the Self is also felt to be an aspect of the larger, outer experience of the *numinosum,* for example through the soul's contact with God, the *unio mystica.*

There is an awareness of a substantial sameness (the experience that leads to the doctrine of the *homoousia*) between them, the inner Self being felt to be an indwelling of the substance of the previous experience. But it is also felt to be of a vastly different scale. In this link between the two qualities of the *numinosum,* the categories of inside and outside blur and become meaningless. Yes, immanence is an inner experience, but it is also an outer one in the sense that the deeper it is experienced, the more we are inside of it, and at the same time the more it is remembered as being outside of us. It is a gross simplification to attempt to think about the Self in space-time categories, and if someone is not a poet, paradoxes are often the only possible language of communication.

In this crucial development from the patriarchal God-image toward the dimension of inwardness, there is still little sense of symbolism, little sense of a differentiated inner or outer world. At best a single symbol of light or order reigns, a reminder of the primal experience of God.

The state of consciousness rooting in a patriarchal God-image can exist without direct illumination. It can be carried by religious dogma, and as such can still be very healthy (Jung 1937, p. 9). A patriarchal orientation that no longer has a living illumination, having lost its numinous link—out of fear, for example, or as Jung notes, out of being fascinated and emptied out by the creative process itself (1952, p. 412)—can still function in the same manner as one truly illumined. It can operate out of a faith in a divine order that is outside its mortal frame, as happens as a result of the positive effect of dogma. The individual can act as if he or she were connected to the vast energy sea known through more direct contact with the oneness of God, with the ground from which one feels chosen. Chosenness can be an experience of someone whose soul has met its divine origins. Without direct illumination, chosenness becomes a part of the dogma.

Pathologies of the Quest for the Patriarchal God

Linking with an outer object that is felt as numinous, whole, and caring, richly complex, full of meaning and depth, even if it also has negative characteristics, is a hallmark of a live patriarchal God-image. It represents a developmental stage, in both phylogenetic and an ontogenetic sense. Perhaps to some degree everyone knows this experience of the *numinosum* at birth, a thought carried in the age-old notion that *the child is a child of God*. There certainly are individuals for whom the loss of this relationship to the *numinosum* is a primal loss of *union* and a trauma that then clouds their development, lingering on as a search for the sacred link and as pathological attempts to re-create it. This pathology lies in the unconscious and delusional identification of a human being with this image. A person may employ idealization, splitting, and repression for the purpose of creating someone in the image of the archetype.

The patriarchal God-image projected onto a real person often caricatures a relationship of people to the God of the Old Testament. The caricature can be obvious to other people, who cannot understand how the person keeps it up. Except in a limited range of behavior, the object of the archetypal projection is unsuited to carry the God-projection. The projection often needs to be energized over and over again. For example, a woman maintained a Father-God projection onto a man only by making him potent through the energy of her own sexuality. Once she departed from this behavior, and waited for his sexuality to function without her seductive arousal of it, he was impotent and then not a very good hook for her projection. This was the beginning of her eventual awareness of the nature of her projection. In other cases, the hope for potency and change tends to go on in the face of the most glaring contradictions between reality and the God-projection, and only eventually dissolves with years of analytical work. Of course, one usually does not know that this is the delusion working behind the scenes, for the person who is possessed by it can be very realistic about his or her seemingly hopeless relationship. Yet, it goes on.

It is vital to recognize that this quest goes on in a deeply unconscious manner. Splitting in borderline states into all-good and all-bad objects, as in Fairbairn's notion of libidinal and anti-libidinal egos, or rewarding and withholding part-objects in the Masterson-Rinsley approach, is a more conscious level. The quest for a patriarchal oneness is deeper, pertaining to a schizoid and hidden level. It is a fantasy that attempts to enforce itself with a delusional strength. As I have said, a person will often stay in relationship with someone that he or she recognizes to be negative in numerous ways. The person may also recognize realistic, good aspects. But the scales, as they appear to an observer and even to the person when in a rational frame of mind, can be weighted toward how destructive the relationship is. Yet the person stays in it, and often stays for a very long time. This bond is not broken up by experiencing and coming to terms with abandonment fears. Defenses against abandonment by real outer people, replicating severe rapprochement traumas of Mahler's separation-individuation process, do not sufficiently explain the resistance to change, in spite of their central importance. Instead, a deeply unconscious delusion is at work, one that really believes the person *is* the patriarchal God-experience fervently desired.

If someone has never sufficiently had the experience of the patriarchal God-image, he or she cannot give it up. This leads to the kind of unconscious schizoid fantasy life I mentioned. But another detail is important here. Very often, people will have had a father who lacked the energy and spirit that could make him a suitable carrier of the patriarchal-God projection. *This leads to the child's fantasy of energizing the father, usually through sexuality.* For example, a young man reports a dream from early childhood of riding on the back of a flying superman, and having anal intercourse with him. It would seem that he had to keep superman going!

Archetypal Processes
in the Transformation of the Patriarchal God-Image

Jung emphasizes the function of human reflection and consciousness in the process whereby this God-image transforms. He thus differentiates between a natural, largely unconscious model of individuation, and a conscious one. The difference is enormous (1952, p. 468). In Jung's model, which follows the path of the unfolding of the oneness of the Father into its forms in Christianity, the key issue is the awareness of the shadow in religious terms of evil (1942, pp. 134–136). A developmental shift can occur when a person begins to reflect upon the inequities of life and the grave issues of moral injustice, especially his or her own immorality. When this occurs, in distinction to consciously or unconsciously focusing upon a God-image that contains all possibilities and will eventually set things right, this state of oneness gives way to what Jung calls the Son. This is a new Self experience characterized by its immanence, and it is associated with individual discrimination between the opposites of good and evil (1942, p. 181).

Jung's emphasis upon morality should not be misunderstood. It certainly concerns evil as a substantial reality, but he says:

One of the toughest roots of evil is unconsciousness. . . . I could wish that the saying of Jesus, "Man, if thou knowest what thou doest, thou art blessed, but if thou knowest not, thou art accursed, and a transgressor of the law," were still in the gospels. . . . It might well be the motto for a new morality. (1942, p. 197)

Jung's sense of morality can be seen as concerned with truth as against lies achieved through unconsciousness. In actual clinical work, especially with borderline disorders or that sector in anyone, the *lie* is the refusal to stand for what one actually *sees*, for the perceptions that register the behavior of others and oneself, yet also denies it. This is the lie that leads to falseness and the false-self personality. It is the lie that is only dethroned by facing the truth of one's long-dismissed perceptions. Often these perceptions were distorted in infancy by an infant's denials of its parents' hatred and envy of it, for such affects could not be tolerated and the denial was a life-saving device. It takes courage to recover such perceptions in adult life, and to face them in the transference and countertransference process, especially as new versions of them are created by the analyst's behavior.

The lie that must be uncovered in dealing with the delusional projection of the patriarchal God-image is the unconscious resistance to *seeing* that such a projection exists. The person has denied his or her capacity to see this, and reclaiming it is always a shock. For years this capacity to perceive things as they are has been hidden away with the schizoid layer that thrives upon the delusional belief system. When a patient recently said, "Finally I see that I have always wanted him to be my father, but something more as well, to be the protector and source of harmony I never had," she was *seeing* in a way she had avoided for her entire adult life.

As a result of the transformation of the God-image through man's greater consciousness (Jung 1952, p. 406), the initial patriarchal image of oneness first changed into a trinity (Jung 1942, p. 174) and then into a quaternity, the spirit completing the Trinity (*ibid.*, p. 175). Jung shows how this spirit as the Holy Ghost has always had feminine aspects (*ibid.*, p. 161). This feminine archetypal quality primarily functions in the unfolding of the God-image, through the image of the *hieros gamos* or the *coniunctio*, as an image of order through *union*, not through the heroic act of *overcoming* disorder. The mystery of union, the *coniunctio*, is thought of by Jung as a stage along a path that results in a new image of oneness (1946, pp. 92, 94 n.56). We shall see the truth of Jung's remarkable reconstructions in clinical material.

Clinical Example of the Delusional Quest
for the Patriarchal Experience of Oneness

A woman reports the following dream:

> She is with a man, her current boyfriend. Her father is small and on a shelf some distance away. A chicken lies next to her. She takes her boyfriend's penis off his body and inserts it into the backside of the chicken. Then she worries the penis will now be poisoned. She hurries to put it into a refrigerator.

The chicken could be seen as a maternal image, and the act of taking the penis as linked to primal-scene envy, in which she takes the place of the father. Her envy, in this way of thinking, spoils her introject of the father's phallus, and she is left persecuted and in need of strong splitting defenses. One could readily see a so-called inverted Oedipal complex. Such interpretations, especially of her deep-seated hatred of the father for his emotional absence, had little effect until a far deeper fantasy was uncovered.

Only when this woman came to the startling realization that she was living a deeply delusional belief that the man (in her dream) was someone she could have a relationship of harmony with—of fullness and concern, one in which God the Father was experienced—only then could change begin to occur. And we could then also realize that the dream had a much deeper meaning. The penis she takes represents the drive to re-energize the father, for the chicken turned out to be not primarily a mother symbol, but represented her father's "chicken anima." He was afraid of the world, and in spite of a good spiritual makeup, he could never bring his values into reality. He was "on the shelf." She unconsciously attempted to energize him so that he could carry the projection of the Father.

This was an act that was fueled by incestuous fantasies. Also, it was contaminated by envy, a source of the destructive belief that she could never have what she really wanted. The incestuous element primarily acted as a barrier to the incarnation of the patriarchal God-image, of it becoming an inner Self experience. For years prior to the analysis, this woman had numerous dreams of special objects such as spaceships or marvelous birds coming down from heaven, but when they approached her they were poisonous. The God-image has been poisoned by the incest. That is how the unconscious saw it. A cruel result of this situation is that a person seeking the God-image in another person cannot employ his creative gifts for his own purpose. At best the person becomes a beacon of light and value for others.

The discovery of the delusion in this case followed upon discovering and working with the imagery of an inner couple, taking the form of her mother and father in a delusionally created state of harmony. This was pieced together in many ways. It was especially highlighted by a dream in which her mother, with a broken leg, was dragging herself to bring her husband breakfast in bed. Apparently, the mother's need to create the delusion of harmony had no limit! The discovery of her inner couple, which was an image that also affected our interaction, was a door to discovering her patriarchal delusion. *As Jung has shown* (1952, p. 397), *the image of a male-female union, the* coniunctio, *becomes a dominant image of the Self after the death of the patriarchal God-image.* In clinical practice the awareness of such inner couples and their relationship to the transference/countertransference process can in turn lead to the demise of the delusional-patriarchal orientation to the *numinosum.*

The nature of the archetypal God-projection is not clarified by considering it to be a narcissistic, idealized transference. Rather, idealization can exist to serve a deeper, archetypal process, a fundamentally religious problem of a person and the God not sufficiently known in a positive way. The nature of the archetypal transference is far deeper, and often does not unfold through the analysis of narcissistic transferences. If anything, this is a precondition for deeper uncovering of a schizoid dynamic hiding the archetypal material. This should not be twisted about to again be thought of as a defense against an idealized transference.

Once the delusional nature of the quest for a patriarchal God-image and its wholeness is faced, a severe, even schizoid, depression can set in. Life is then felt as not worth living. The death animus or anima becomes the true lover, and perhaps always has been. Just as Yahweh, in a Kaballistic myth, has a demon lover, Lilith, while his bride, the Shekinah, is in exile, so too someone seeking his or her God in such delusional fashion often winds up with a demon lover instead. My experience has been that imaginally *seeing* this as a background quality or a "waking dream"—as in active imagination, but in the here and now of the analytic session—is at times an important part of the process of uncovering the delusional God-projection.

If the loss can be sustained, a new phase can begin, one in which an inner Self begins to grow. For example, in the case of the woman whose Self-images were poisonous, the painful process of realizing that her quest for harmony had been based upon delusions led to a dream of a beautiful copper mandala behind a tombstone. Copper, as the patient knew, is associated with the Goddess Venus. The death of the old god would thus reveal the rejected feminine, the goddess, just as Jung's archetypal researches show (1937, p. 82, 94).

When her delusion finally dissolved, the analysis centered upon a depressive position with her father, something she had never lived through. Prior to this, the patient had always secretly scanned me for any emotional absences, however slight or large, but now this activity could become focused. Previously her delusional quest prevented focusing upon her intense hatred of any emotional absence that she perceived. Her fear of loss of her archetypal projection, which was also onto me in the transference, precluded this. But now her intense negative feelings could emerge, which was absolutely essential.

Jung makes a special point of emphasizing the importance of the realization of the shadow for the actualization of psychic potentials (1942, p. 196). In this case, after the delusional archetypal fantasy was deconstructed, the *nigredo* which followed brought intense negative feelings toward her father that were focused in the transference. It is usually not possible to reduce imagery such as "poison" in her dream to a single emotion, but certainly hatred of her father played a strong role, a hatred rooted in his emotional absence. Prior to uncovering her delusional system, this was split off in despair and rage with God, as was the negative transference. Not unlike many patients with a borderline disposition, she held a deep-seated rage at God for His abandonment of her. Now her abandonment issue could also be focused in interpersonal relations.

It must also be recognized that her depressive position was also with the Father with a capital "F." On the one hand, she suffered from her intensely negative affects aimed at me in the transference, but she also suffered from her loss of the God-image. Entering into levels of the personal, space-time unconscious in the transference and countertransference meant a loss of her previous God-image, even if it was delusionally constructed. In a sense, she entered a state of loss and mourning for what was lost so early and then experienced as never truly there. As in the previous clinical material, it is necessary to think in terms of a personal and archetypal aspect to the depressive position. In a sense it is a door between personal and archetypal levels, and opens on both.

It is easy to reduce an authentic level of religious experience or its quest to a pathological delusion or to an idealized defense against persecutory anxieties. (The latter are imaged by poison in the above dream.) But this reduction is the kind of analytical maneuver *that patients will all too readily accept,* for the *numinosum* is a threat and challenge that few want to take up. One must work back and forth between the personal and the archetypal as the two levels of the depressive position, and also as the two qualities of idealization, on the one hand defensive, and on the other, an attempt to re-link with a sacred object.

A Comparison of Jung's View of Internal Structure with Developmental Theories

What is extremely interesting is that no matter how an initial unitary state is thought of, many and surely the most influential theories all follow the same pattern concerning the way the unitary state unfolds into an inner life: *It splits up into three or four internal structures.* This is the archetypal pattern that Jung discussed in "A Psychological Approach to the Dogma of the Trinity" (1942), and in *Answer to Job* (1952). Theories differ regarding the nature of the three or four parts of psychic structure or stages of individuation and their healthy or pathological development. Like all theoretical structures, they are arrived at through projecting inner structural forms onto the data obtained through observation, carefully assessing the fit of theory and data along the way. The inner structural forms that are projected are the archetypal processes that Jung has mapped out that characterize the incarnation of pleromatic structures into the world of space-time.

Could this lead to a rapprochement between Jungian-pleromatic conceptions and the structures and processes characterized from the viewpoint of the ego and its development through interacting with outer object relations? In one sense it is like digging through a mountain from both sides and seeing if and where the tunnels meet. One can in this way find areas of convergence and of divergence, the latter being especially prominent when origins and the function of the *numinosum* is considered. But is this kind of meeting really what is desired? Comparing similarities between Jung's researches into psychic structures and their pleromatic roots with developmental approaches may serve more to highlight a seductive potential in these approaches. While they hold out important clinical insights and are definitely useful, they also have the shadow side of reducing the Self to the ego, and the feminine or the goddess to the personal mother.

In Mahler's approach, for example, we find four stages, with the fourth subphase, Consolidation of Individuality and the Beginning of Emotional Object Constancy, being different from the other three, "since it is open-ended at the older end" (Mahler *et al.* 1975, p. 112). The fourth stage is ongoing throughout life, and thus also differs from the previous three. Otto Kernberg also postulates four stages in normal development (1972, pp. 233–47). A fourfold model that contains an exceptional quality to the "fourth" is found in Federn's work in his distinction between active, passive, and reflective *ego feelings*, and *medial ego feelings*, which, as Donald Rinsley notes, signify the most basic awareness of one's existence, and lie close to the core of the ego (Rinsley 1982, p. 5). In Fairbairn's approach, an original whole object splits up into a libidinal ego and an anti-libidinal ego, and also into a central (or reality) ego. To these three parts there is added a fourth, the superego, which may have harsh forms, stemming from the sadistic, anti-libidinal ego, but also Ideal ones stemming from the original whole object (*ibid.*, pp. 85, 90). Fairbairn's schema was extended by Harry Guntrip (1969, pp. 73–74), so that a piece of the original pristine oneness further splits off from where it was hidden, in the libidinal ego and its masochistic behavior, to form a fourth part, the so-called "regressed ego," also called the true self (*ibid.*, p. 77). Fairbairn's model can be seen in the Masterson-Rinsley model of borderline structure, in which a rejecting part-object and a withdrawing one are analogous to Fairbairn's libidinal and anti-libidinal egos, along with a reality ego, severely depleted by its need for delusionally denying abandonment (Rinsley 1982, p. 41).

Developmental theories that take note of infant observation will model through the same archetypal process as the one Jung observed in terms of an incarnating God-image. But these theories focus on the ego as the carrier of wholeness. This in itself is also part of the unfolding of the archetypal process of the Incarnation, finding form in the metaphor of Christ or the Messiah as the Son of Man. The existence of the Self, man's relation to a sense of his oneness and wholeness, is thus a function of man's consciousness. But theories that conceive of the process of individuation developmentally do not reckon with the process of union as the *coniunctio*, an archetypal process that structures the space between two people and is far more complex and rich than a simple notion of a good and bad breast-image uniting, as in Klein's approach to the depressive position. While *there are a shadow issue and a union* here, which are the same ingredients Jung found to underpin the Incarnation of the *numinosum* into inner structures, such theories do not contain conscious considerations of evil leading to a new kind of union whose central image is the *coniunctio*, nor do they lead toward a state of wholeness, *an inner Self as a numinous center of personality.* The internalized whole breast-object is not the same as this inner object.

Archetypal patterns will appear in a healthy or an intellectually distorted way, as in object-relations approaches that devalue the Fourth as the Transcendent Other. While the same fourfold structure may be found in Jung's and in these other approaches, there is a vast difference in Jung's emphasis upon the Fourth. This is found especially in his approach to the feminine and in general to the psychic reality of the *numinosum* as it incarnates in man.

The formation of an inner structure as a quaternity, or the model of the individuation process unfolding in four stages, with the fourth in both instances often having an unusual quality, underlies various approaches to object relations. But the similarity in structural approaches soon diminishes when we look to the quality and goals of the quaternity structure. Object-relations approaches are derived from the vicissitudes of outer relationships, which then have a strong determining influence upon inner structure, while Jung's view of the Self and its unfolding is largely rooted in the autonomy of the archetypes (1952, pp. 469–70). The object relations approach points to the consolidation of an ego and object constancy; the Jungian goal points to outer adaptation, but not at the cost of linking to the inner world of psychic reality. The object-relational emphasis stresses a "reality ego," and with it objectivity. Jung's emphasis is different. Rather, the quality of consciousness that can appreciate and be guided by the symbol, by a mythical or imaginal consciousness, is aimed at. With this comes a relativizing of what can be called objective (von Franz 1974, p. 122). The nature of the quality of consciousness that enters when the "fourth" is dealt with in Jung's sense is not an extension of a third phase or structure, but is a genuinely different structure that includes subjectivity, the body, the feminine, the reality of evil—all with a link to the oneness of existence (von Franz 1974, pp. 128–31).

In most approaches to object relations, notions of innate destructiveness, conceptualized by Freud and Klein as the death instinct, are not popular and never had much influence. Destructive impulses are generally taken to be a result of too much frustration, a lack of "good enough mothering." This is a throwback to the doctrine of the *privatio boni* view of evil, which Jung finds to be nonsense (1952, p. 383 n. 13). For Jung, the dark side of the psyche, mythologically the Devil, is a substantial reality. Furthermore, "the shadow and the opposing will is the necessary condition for all actualization" (1942, p. 196). In many object-relations theories, the Kleinian view being an exception, the strong emphasis is not upon the integration of one's dark aspects, whether they be greed, envy, rage, ruthlessness, and so forth, but upon mirroring and empathy. A prevalence of destructive affects are often seen as a result of a mothering figure's empathic failure.

Another difference is that in object relations and developmental approaches, the feminine hardly appears except as the outer mother and the processes by which the breast-mother becomes internalized. The feminine as a quality of psyche, *per se,* is found to a marginal degree in Winnicott's notion of *being* in distinction to *doing,* and was elaborated upon by Guntrip (1969, pp. 257–63), but is otherwise rarely mentioned. Separation from the mother and her internalization is the goal, so that in life new separations and the capacity for union may emerge. While Winnicott is one of several important exceptions, the goal of these theories is to exist as an ego in time and space. The internal world is undervalued and is often conceived of as a place in which to hide (*ibid.,* p. 75).

These theories regard such splitting as pathological, without awareness that the resultant pathological structures, which are devoted to defense and denial, only overlay a potentially positive archetypal pattern. Libidinal and anti-libidinal egos, rewarding and withholding part-objects, are all pathological forms of oppositions such as Christ and Satan, or Osiris and Seth in Egyptian myth. Without such oppositions, based upon the reality of the struggle between the light, life-giving and the dark, destructive sides of life, there is no incarnation of the *numinosum.* The Self one deals with is something obscure and pale, such as "self-feeling," not a numinous center of psyche that is also a content of the ego, nor a center that has both a masculine and feminine root.

The feminine is the essence of the quaternity structure. This not only means the best qualities of object relations, such as the emphasis found there upon relatedness, empathy, and *being* in distinction to *doing,* but also implies a different approach to consciousness and the body. The heart becomes more central than the head. The *imaginal,* as active imagination (Jung 1916) but also as a here and now act of *embodied seeing* as an entrance into the processes of the *coniunctio,* is also a key aspect of the re-

covery of the feminine. Most crucially, the orientation to pleromatic processes, as in the subtle body imaginally perceived between two people
(Schwartz-Salant, 1986), is a central feature of feminine logos. And all of
this follows from the death and transformation of the patriarchal
God-image.

Moral Awareness and Vision as Paths to the Incarnation: Reflections on Jung's *Answer to Job*

The *Book of Job* shows the patriarchal God-image in its most negative
form. The phenomenon of Yahweh in this late book of the Old Testament
was particularly gripping for Jung, and his *Answer to Job* was the only work
that he found totally satisfying, an outpouring of his soul's wisdom. "If
there is anything like the spirit seizing one by the scruff of the neck, it is
the way this book came into being" (Jung 1975, p. 20).

While there is little explicit about clinical practice in this book, *Answer to Job* has a good deal to say about psychotherapy, especially with the
borderline patient. The person lives in a psyche that can at any time be
devastated by what feels to him or her like a natural catastrophe, so far
are these "Yahweh-affects" beyond control. Healing can only begin when
this devastating phenomenon is somehow tamed, somehow calmed.

> The Book of Job serves as a paradigm for a certain experience of God which
> has a special significance for us today. These experiences come upon man from
> inside as well as from outside, and it is useless to interpret them rationalistically
> and thus weaken them by apotropaic means. It is far better to admit the affect
> and submit to its violence than try to escape it by all sorts of intellectual tricks
> or by emotional value-judgments. Although, by giving way to the affect, one
> imitates all the bad qualities of the outrageous act that provoked it and thus
> makes oneself guilty of the same fault, that is precisely the point of the whole
> preceding: the violence is meant to penetrate a man's vitals, and he to suc-
> cumb to its action. He must be affected by it, otherwise its full effect will not
> reach him. But he should know, or learn to know, what has affected him, for
> in this way he transforms the blindness of the violence on the one hand and of
> the affect on the other into knowledge. (1952, p. 366)

These affects are part of the numinous, archetypal contents that af-
flict the borderline patient. Jung would appear to counsel a kind of acting-
out of the transference, "giving way to the affect [and] imitating all the
bad qualities of the outrageous act that provoked it . . . thus mak[ing]
oneself guilty of the same fault." Jung insists that only in this way, by being affected by the affects, can the analyst come to know them and trans-

form them. Could there be a fuller prescription for "wild analysis," in which technique and a sense of process is abandoned in favor of focusing on whatever strong affects and intuitions emerge within the analytical encounter?

If only things were so simple, so easily dismissed! The borderline individual is ravished by Yahweh-affects, *but he or she also fails to learn from the experience.* These affects devastate the soul and force it to live on the brink of nothingness and within a constant fog of despair, yet he or she also is capable of the most blatant forms of denial and splitting from inner affective states, so that they are not sufficiently experienced. The borderline individual is the "as-if" patient. An analyst is often left in the position of experiencing and reflecting upon Yahweh-affects *for the patient.* We may not want to act them out, but to a degree we always will. Even if we carefully contain these devastating affect-fields, the patient will *see* that they exist as part of our inner attitude. If the patient fails to *see* this, he or she fails to *see* intense negative feelings toward him or her. In this the patient colludes with us, for no one wants to experience these levels, whatever their source, whether they stem from induction or from one's own borderline sectors. This lack of *sight* will exist in the patient because he or she has denied his or her *vision,* and that denial is in large measure the cause of his or her proneness to being emotionally overwhelmed.

If the borderline patient is helped to recover what he or she actually *sees,* then what he or she *sees* is often that we have acted as badly or worse than the patient has in identification with an inner, persecutory violence! We always succumb, but do we also learn to know what has affected us? That is the crucial issue Jung raises. What is often surprising about the borderline patient is that no matter how ruthless he or she is, he or she will often value this kind of awareness. The patient will not stop short of anything but an exhaustive understanding of the analyst's errors in empathy and ill will toward him or her, appearing through inappropriate interventions and emotions. Thus tenacity is something that may be all too easily passed off by the analyst as yet more of the *patient's* ruthlessness.

To recognize the value of Jung's study for clinical practice, we can imagine the Job-Yahweh encounter as a dyad that structures the unconscious aspect of the transference. This dyad is a phenomenon of the pleromatic or archetypal world as it intersects space-time. When it constellates—that is to say, when the the Job story is actualized, a condition that is chronic with the borderline patient but potential for everyone—

either the analyst or the patient tends to unconsciously take on either the role of Job or Yahweh. Often these alternate with uncomfortable rapidity.

The "Yahweh-affects" can be withering to the analyst as they sweep through the person and affect the analyst through projective identification, participation mystique, psychic infection—all a host of names for the fact that these affects exist still in contact with the oneness of the pleroma. They are still capable of jumping time-space laws and structures, affecting one psyche as well as another. These affects ravish the soul, and consequently they pose a severe moral problem. Yet the borderline individual is incapable of meeting this moral challenge. What can our moral stance be in all of this? And is the moral stance sufficient?

We must first recognize the nature of the attack we experience. It is a mixture of the Yahweh-affects and a kind of *vision* that *sees* us in ways that can be very painful. We are always some what open to the penetration of the patient's *imaginal sight,* for amidst the affect fields that can be so destructive there is also some truth. We always do have a moral deficiency, either as a Job-like righteousness when we are afflicted by "the patient's" Yahweh-affects—"Who, me? What have I done wrong?"—or as we unconsciously identify with the Yahweh aspect of the unconscious dyad, and through its tyrannical affects court a secret lack of concern, if not hatred, for our patient. The borderline individual *sees* this, but through a vengeful eye. It is a kind of vision that latches on to not only gross injustice, but to small things as well. For example, he or she fixes upon unconscious mood shifts in another person, a turn of phrase or a careless action, any of which could easily be allowed to pass with the result that the person *seen*—the better phrase may be *scanned*—would then find an equilibrium, come back to relatedness. The person's fall into unconscious behavior could have been transitory, but this grace is usually not allowed by the borderline individual unless he or she is in a masochist phase. The patient feels these acts by another person to be extremely dangerous. If the patient splits from his or her *vision,* he or she then becomes inwardly persecuted by what he or she has *seen,* albeit *seen* in a severely dramatized and often distorted manner. Or the patient may attack us with his or her *vision,* thinking he or she is only pointing something out for our elucidation or discussion, and is oblivious to the acid-like affects that accompany his or her *sight,* like the vision of the untamed Egyptian eye goddess. In the process, we often find ourselves confronted by a perception of "how bad we are" that contains painful strands of truth, and often more than mere strands.

This complicates matters, for a soul's vulnerable state cannot take the intense affects that accompany this kind of *penetration*. We may find ourselves in a position of submitting rather masochistically, just to get the person to stop, or we may tend to resort to narcissistic-power defenses through which we match the person's knowledge with our own, which is always a shabby display that the patient sees through. But, in distinction to such defenses, we may find *concern for ourselves* and stop the battle. We may think something like: "No matter how bad I am, no matter what I have done to this person in my unconsciousness, no matter how right he is, my soul is being attacked and I cannot allow that to happen." But we must also experience the affects. Imaginally, we may grasp the fact that a young part of ourselves feels terrified and unprotected, and *seeing* this, we may become *its* ally, empathic with its state of abandonment and emotional flooding. In acting in this way, the patient ceases to become the enemy; we stand for our soul and not against the patient. As a consequence of this imaginal act, we will also *see* the patient differently, not as Yahweh withering us with affects that are unbearable, but as someone possessed by this archetype. The patient's own soul is being ravished by its affects, and he or she is in terror that we will not see this, but will instead identify him or her with a power that is not the patient's at all, but is killing him or her.

Job seems to represent an attitude that is soul-centered, concerned with this state of one's inner being, no matter how powerful and *right* the afflicting outer forces may be. A moral position comes into being, one that judges ruthlessness as unacceptable even if it be also correct, even as it may contain a deep-seated wisdom of Job's shadow quality of self-righteousness.

It is well known from clinical practice that it often makes sense to recognize that we often feel overwhelmed as an inductive effect of the patient's transference. The purpose of this process is to help us empathize with the patient's own helplessness, something that can be easily overlooked, as he or she seems powerful while actually being possessed by the torrent of Yahweh-like states. This is always an important of view. But in Jung's stance, there is a different inherent ontology: One remains aware of the soul-killing quality of what afflicts us, and especially aware of how powerless we are in the face of it—as long as we do not flee into identifications with the same tyranny! In the Middle Ages one held the Cross up to the Devil, the meaning being that only an awareness of overwhelming demonic power drives, felt in profound vulnerability with an eye and heart open toward the Eros of Christ, could defeat Satan. The ego stands aside. Two powers battle. This is far from a masochistic stance.

In this position we recognize and imaginally add a "third thing." There is an afflicting Job-Yahweh dyad, but also a sense of something else, an Eros for the soul: in Jung's analysis, the image of Christ. It is the awareness of the soul-killing quality of the Yahweh-affects, an awareness that cannot come into existence so long as we identify ourselves or the patient with these contents, but only emerges when we recognize that *it* is persecuting both of us; that in turn opens us to the love of soul. Clearly, an act of faith is involved in this process, for we have no assurance that the "third thing" will enter, only a steadfast awareness that without it we are lost as souls, and reduced to power drives that possess our egos and yield the delusion that we are in control.

We are never certain that we will survive the Yahweh-Job dyad, especially the patient's identification with a withering demonic vision. Michael Eigen writes that "It is [the] intersection of profound vulnerability and saving indestructibility that brings the paradox of faith to a new level" (1981, p. 416). He then quotes what he refers to as Winnicott's "most memorable expression of faith":

> The subject says to the object. "I destroyed you," and the object is there to receive the communication. From now on the subject says: "Hello object!" "I destroyed you." "I love you" "You have value for me because of your survival of my destruction of you." "While I am loving you I am all the time destroying you in (unconscious) *fantasy.*" (Winnicott 1971, p. 90)

The "object" survives the attacks of the "subject" just as Job survives Yahweh's attack (Jung 1952, p. 383). But Jung's approach goes beyond Winnicott's. One is not only in a position of surviving another *person's* destructiveness, but the destructiveness of a God, of numinous energies. These can be dealt with apotropaically, rationally reduced to a developmental stage, as a failure in passage through the depressive position or some issue of maternal abandonment. This approach, while often an important point of view, also represses and diminishes the *numinosum* involved. In doing this one *sees* differently from the way Jung does, one does not *see* the nature of what one is confronting. "Yahweh is a phenomenon and, as Job says, 'not a man'" (*ibid.*, p. 383).

"The unconscious mind of man *sees* correctly even when conscious reason is blind and impotent" (Jung 1952, p. 386). Job's unconscious has *seen* Yahweh, *seen* "Yahweh's dual nature" (*ibid.*). It is this quality of *vision* that Jung emphasizes. It is difficult to stand for this kind of perception, for it is often dim and readily overruled by other forces such as are seen in Job's "comforters," the inner voices that would have us instead focus upon our own shortcomings. That is the scapegoat shadow quality of a patriarchal God-image: "We must have done something wrong; how else can it be so bad?"

William Blake, as Kathleen Raine tells us, points out that Job is only released when he *sees* God (Raine 1982, p. 289). This is more than *unconscious sight* leading to a moral position.

> I knew you then only by hearsay;
> but now, having seen you with my own eyes,
> I retract all I have said,
> and in dust and ashes I repent. (Job 42:5–6)

Jung not only pays little attention to Job's *conscious vision*, but he demeans it. "Shrewdly," Jung says, "Job takes up Yahweh's aggressive words and prostrates himself at his feet as if he were indeed the defeated antagonist" (1952, p. 382). And, "The therapeutic measure of unresisting acceptance had proved its value yet again" (*ibid.*, p. 383). For Jung it is Job's moral victory over the immoral affect fields, represented by Yahweh, not Job's regained *vision*, that is the decisive transformative factor leading to the incarnation.

Job's attitude is that of someone who has *experienced* the transcendent energies of his God. He recognizes the falseness of his previous "empty-headed words" (Job 42:5–6). He becomes aware of his narcissism, and knows that he also knew his falseness all along, but denied it, perhaps out of power needs and fears of abandonment. To someone now hearing Job, it could appear that he has gone into a masochistic regression, a kind of painful humility, at best: "In dust and ashes I repent." But this would surely surprise Job, for he has these humbled feelings against a background of joy, of having *seen* God. This vision gives him a new-found attitude, a right to question Yahweh: "Now it is my turn to ask questions and yours to inform me." This is hardly a regression.

Many a borderline patient has had a transcendent vision, either as a central religious experience, an out of the body death-bed *vision*, or simply because of a propensity to experience the *numinosum* as a result of a highly creative unconscious combined with weak ego boundaries. These patients know the level of the transcendent self. *What is not known is its immanence, for it has never incarnated.* Often *seeing* this level of light in the patient, an act like active imagination in the here and now, and mentioning it, even though it may be a fleeing instant that could be easily ignored, has an important outcome. This kind of *seeing* of the patient's own numinous connection, often long abandoned, has the same kind of restorative effect as Job's *vision* of Yahweh. It is also a main factor in *its* Incarnation, once again as is Job's *vision*.

But this does not mean we preach mystical experiences, only that we register that many people know this level and have split it off. And it also points us to the question of the difference between an unconscious and a conscious kind of *vision*. For we may suffer what appear to be the patient's attacks without *seeing* in the patient anything like his or her soul suffering amidst an affect storm, teetering upon a brink of despair. And we may hear everything the patient tells us as having some value, but not as carrying anything like true *sight*. We must help the borderline patient to gain his or her own *sight* in a conscious way, perhaps from a compulsive activity of scanning other people, or else we must arouse it from its condition of *absence*, that opposite state of imaginal inertness we also meet in these patients.

Vision heals. *Embodied vision* is a gift of the archetypal feminine. The *imaginal sight* and the experience of her sacred mystery, the *coniunctio*, is a path of healing, strongly constellated in the pleroma in our historical time, and awaiting Incarnation into individual lives.

References

Bamford, C. 1981. Introduction: Homage to Pythagoras. *Lindisfarne Letter* 14. West Stockbridge, Mass.: Lindisfarne Press.

Bohm, D. 1980. *Wholeness and the implicate order.* London: Routledge & Kegan Paul.

Eigen, M. 1981. The area of faith in Winnicott, Lacan and Bion. *International Journal of Psycho-analysis,* vol. 62.

_____. Toward Bion's starting point: Between catastrophe and faith. *International J. Psycho-Analysis,* vol. 66.

Fordham, M. 1967. *The self and autism.* London: William Heinemann Medical Books, Ltd.

_____. 1985. Abandonment in infancy. *Chiron: A Review of Jungian Analysis* 1985: 1–21.

Franz, M.-L. von. 1974. *Number and time.* Evanston, Il.: Northwestern University Press.

Guntrip, H. 1969. *Schizoid phenomena, object relations and the self.* New York: International Universities Press.

Jung, C. G. 1942. A psychological approach to the dogma of the trinity. In *Collected Works,* 11:107–200. Princeton: Princeton University Press, 1969.

_____. 1946. The psychology of the transference. In *Collected Works,* 16:163–323. Princeton: Princeton University Press, 1966.

_____. 1952. *Answer to Job.* In *Collected Works,* 11:355–470. Princeton: Princeton University Press, 1969.

_____. 1955. *Mysterium coniunctionis*. In *Collected Works*, vol. 14. Princeton: Princeton University Press, 1970.

_____. 1975. *Letters*, vol. 2, G. Adler, ed. Princeton: Princeton University Press.

Kernberg, O. 1972. Early ego integration and object relations. *Annals of the New York Academy of Sciences* 193:233–47.

Mahler, M. 1980. Rapprochement subphase of the separation-individuation process. In *Rapprochement*, Lax et al., eds. New York: Jason Aronson.

_____ et al. 1975. *The psychological birth of the human infant*. New York: Basic Books.

Masterson, J. 1981. *The narcissistic and borderline disorders*. New York: Brunner/Mazel.

Neumann, E. 1954. *The origins and history of consciousness*. London: Routledge & Kegan Paul.

_____. 1955. *The great mother*. London: Routledge & Kegan Paul.

Rinsley, D. 1982. *Borderline and other self disorders*. New York: Jason Aronson.

Segal, H. 1980. *Melanie Klein*. New York: Viking.

Schwartz-Salant, N. 1984. Archetypal factors underlying sexual acting-out in the transference/countertransference process. *Chiron: A Review of Jungian Analysis* 1984:1–30.

_____. 1986. On the subtle-body concept in clinical practice. In *The body in analysis*, N. Schwartz-Salant & M. Stein, eds., Wilmette, Ill.: Chiron Publications, pp. 19–58.

Winnicott, D. W. 1971. *Playing and reality*. London: Tavistock.

Jung's Gnosticism and Contemporary Gnosis

June Singer

I

My interest in Gnosticism, and particularly in Jung's Gnosticism, is fairly recent, and yet I am able to trace its roots back through my own writings from the perspective of an age that has as one of its advantages the possibility of a long view. I recall that in my first book, written about the work of William Blake (Singer 1970), I was preoccupied with Gnostic ideas. Blake's work, peopled with angels who are devils and devils who are angels, turns orthodox theology upside down. Indeed, Blake called the corpus of his work "the Bible of Hell, which the world shall have it whether they will or no!" (Blake 1957). He dealt with the fall of man from his divine status, and the separation of the masculine principle from the feminine principle, leading to a one-sided involvement with law and machinery and other evils of this temporal world.

I then moved on to write about Jung's psychology (Singer 1972), and found myself wondering what the archetypes were and whether they were really necessary. An archetypal world that is superordinate to this world and influences the world we know in ways about which we are unconscious is also a Gnostic concept, but I did not realize it then. It was only when I began to concern myself with the problem of androgyny (Singer 1976) that I became aware that the anima described by Jung is an aspect of the World Soul, Anima Mundi. In her higher aspect she is the feminine aspect or consort of the Divine Essence. As I studied the various myths surrounding the Divine Syzygy, the "Two in One," I found myself intrigued by the possibility of another dimension of reality beyond the one

73

we know and call "our world." In the other dimension, unity and order would prevail, unlike in this dimension, which is characterized by the splitting of opposites, fragmentation, and disorder.

From the point of view of Christianity, Gnosticism is a nearly forgotten "faith" or, rather, a "heresy" that was fairly common in the first two centuries of the Christian era. It was marked by strange rituals and practices that were usually carried on in secret by an esoteric cult or a number of esoteric cults. It espoused dualistic philosophies, served an alien God, and had an elaborate system of angels and demons. We will discuss a little later what the Gnostics themselves had to say about their understanding of the nature of things.

Gnosis means *knowing*, knowing from the observation of one's own inner process, as well as from a perception of the world without. Jung was fond of quoting Bishop Clement of Alexandria, who was strongly influenced by Gnosticism: "He who knows himself knows God." To know oneself and to thereby know God means to know all that there is to know, since for the Gnostic everything that lives in this manifest world exists because it carries a spark of life, or light, which emanates from the Divine Light or energy that empowers the universe and all that lies within it. This is the meaning of William Blake's statement, "For everything that lives is holy." Gnosis also means knowing that the Divine Spark has been lost or covered over in this material world, that it has been overcome by the powers of this world. For the Gnostic, the task is to find that spark and care for it and to redeem it. In this sense, Jung worked in the spirit of gnosis.

Often I have asked myself what was the essential difference between Jung and Freud. I knew about their personality clashes, the complications of their relationships, the issue of fatherhood and sonship. I also knew about Jung's disagreement with Freud on questions about the role of sexuality in neurosis. And I knew that Jung's creative and somewhat rebellious side could not tolerate what he saw as Freud's dogmatism. But I felt that these "reasons" were only partial, that there must be a more fundamental difference underlying all these reasons, something so crucial that it split asunder the relationship that was so precious to both Freud and Jung. Finally it came to me what that crucial issue was.

For Freud, the fundamental aspect of the human psyche was the ego, and the unconscious was mostly derivative of the ego. The Freudian unconscious, what Jung called "the personal unconscious," contained mostly the flotsam and jetsam of life's experiences that had been rejected, forgotten, or repressed. Freud saw as his task the recapturing of these experiences, bringing them up into consciousness and thereby widening the ego as it accommodated the contents of the unconscious.

For Jung, it was the unconscious that was fundamental. The ego derived from the unconscious. Jung saw human existence as beginning in the unconscious matrix of the maternal sea, and only gradually emerging from it. Jung agreed with Freud that personal repressions took place in the process of ego development, and that these could, and probably should, be recovered from the personal unconscious. But above and below this personal unconscious, there existed for Jung a collective unconscious so vast that one could not even imagine it. For Jung, the unconscious was primary, and the ego was secondary to his concern.

If we consider Jung's early history, we may be able to get some idea of how he came to be so involved with the deepest of life's mysteries. We recall the earliest dream that Jung remembered, probably before he was five years old. In an underground temple, he sees a huge phallus standing erect upon a huge golden throne. He is paralyzed with terror, and just at that moment his mother calls out to him, "Yes, just look at him. That is the man-eater!" Jung never forgot the image of this fearful subterranean god, and associated it in his mind with Jesus whenever the name of Jesus came up in his household. Good and evil were confused and confusing to him. There was no authority to whom he could turn for help to find meaning for this dream or for the many dreams and fantasies that would become so much a part of his life. He turned inward, to his own intuitive wisdom, which he later would understand to be a channel to the collective wisdom of the collective unconscious.

It is not difficult to understand how Jung became attracted to Gnosticism. All through his school years Jung, the pastor's son, wondered about the nature of God. His father's god was cold and unfeeling; he was responsible for many restrictions and prohibitions and the images of Jesuits clothed in black. In Memories, Dreams, Reflections, Jung said, "Church gradually became a place of torment to me." It often seemed to him that religious precepts were being put in the place of the will of God, solely for the purpose of sparing people the necessity of personally understanding God's will. "I grew more and more skeptical, and my father's sermons. . . became acutely embarrassing to me. . . . Does he really know what he is talking about? Could he have me, his son, put to the knife as a human sacrifice, like Isaac, or deliver him to an unjust court which would have him crucified, like Jesus?" (Jung 1963, p. 47). As a boy, Jung concluded, "Obviously we do not know the will of God at all, for if we did we would treat this central problem with awe. . . . And who posed the problem? Nobody ever answered me that. I knew that I had to find the answer out of my deepest self, that I was alone before God . . ." (Jung 1963, p. 47).

Jung's unwillingness to accept unthinkingly the precepts handed down to him may have prepared him to confront the mysterious realm beyond the stars—which, he taught, exists also in the human soul. He was to name this mystery "the collective unconscious," and to use a new kind of psychology to probe its depths. As he read in the Gnostic literature, he learned that the Gnostics saw the world as a product of divine tragedy, a disharmony in the Realm of God, a baleful destiny in which man is entangled and from which he must be set free (Rudolph 1985, p. 66). The Gnostics, too, found much to condemn in the Old Testament images of the creator-god of Genesis.

The subject of Gnosticism occupied Jung during the period from 1916 to 1926, according to Aniela Jaffé (1984, p. 48), and there are indications that he had some knowledge of it before that time. When I sought to gain some understanding of what was so important to him, I soon found myself immersed in a huge body of esoteric literature. Much of it came to light in the Gnostic treatises of the first two centuries that were discovered in 1945 in earthenware jars buried in a field at Nag Hammadi in Egypt. The 52 scriptures of the *Nag Hammadi Library* were written in Coptic, having been translated from the Greek. Previously most of our information about Gnosticism had come from the early Church fathers, who were extremely critical of it. The books found at Nag Hammadi at last gave us the actual words of the Gnostics.

Ancient Gnosticism had as a very strong element an apparently dualistic character. This dualism is seen in the distinction between God and the Creator, or between God and the World. It is not between God and the Devil. There is in Gnosticism an unequivocally negative valuation of the visible world together with its creator. This is a shocking statement to most people who were reared in any of the currently practiced traditional religions. The world is evil! The creator-god made a mess of things! He produced a kingdom of evil, ignorance, and darkness! The identification of "evil" with the "creator-god" and "matter" is embedded in Gnosis as a fundamental conception. With such a point of view, the Gnostics posed a very serious threat to any kind of orthodoxy. Orthodoxy can only be sustained if people believe that their faith is valid and that their god will be good, at least to them.

But over and against this negative conception is a still more fundamental one, which is that there is an Other, who stands above all the gods of all tribes and all nations. That which is "beyond the stars" refers to an unknown alien presence that cannot be described, because it cannot be known by those with the limited vision that is born of faith and reason. In the Gnostic text, the Secret Book of John, there is the statement by the exalted Christ:

> Concerning him, the Spirit, it is not fitting to think of him as a God, or that he is of a (particular) sort. For he is more excellent than the gods: he is a dominion (arche) over which none rules; for there is none before him, nor does he need them (the gods); he does not even need life, for he is eternal. . . . He is light. He is illimitable, since there is none before him to limit him. [He is] not subject to judgment, since there is none before him to judge him. He is not corporeal, he is not incorporeal. He is not great, he is not small. He is nothing at all that exists, but something more excellent than that. (Rudolph, p. 66)

The description which is not a description continues on and on.

Awareness of this unknown entity is not limited to those who are called Gnostics. It exists in Taoism, where it is said, "The Tao that can be told is not the eternal Tao. The name that can be named is not the eternal name" (Tao Te Ching 1972). And in the Kabbalah, which is said by Jewish mystics to have preceded creation, there is the "En Sof," the limitless or boundless, which symbolizes total unity beyond comprehension. "In the minds of the Kabbalists, the En-Sof is no-thing, does not exist, is not fathomable and cannot be discussed in terms of Being or Non-Being" (Ponce 1972, pp. 94–95).

Speaking of the Gnostics, Plotinus said, "For of all earthly things nothing is of value to them, but only an Other after which they will at some time strive" (Rudolph, p. 61). This other-worldly and unknown God who dwells beyond all visible creation is for the Gnostic the real lord of the universe. The world in which we live is not the work of the true God, but that of a subordinate being. Nevertheless, the higher God exercises influence in varying ways for the well-being of human beings through "providence" (pronoia), which comes to expression on earth. This conception of God in Gnosis stands in marked contrast to all the world's gods that are known, who "in their limitation—there is even reference to their folly

—do not know the true God and therefore act as if he did not exist" (Rudolph, p. 61). The higher God, remote from the world, is properly described only negatively, that is, in terms of what he is not, or in images that express his inimitable status, free from any kind of relation to the world.

After the canon of the Old Testament was closed, and before the canonizing of the New Testament, inspired authors continued to write sacred scriptures. They were Jews, Christians, Gnostics, and pagans. Except for the texts that found their way into the New Testament, most of these other writings were rejected, suppressed, and forgotten. Yet many of them contain a richness and beauty that is aesthetically equal or superior to what was included in the New Testament. They also contain much vital information on such matters as, for example, the infancy of Jesus, and alternate versions of the major biblical stories, such as the creation of the world and the events surrounding Adam and Eve.

What were the reasons for the exclusion of this material from the canon? Some say that it was excluded because of its later origin; however, there is reason to believe that this is not necessarily so, that in fact some of the earlier documents derive from the Jewish oral tradition that predates Christianity, and some reflect the Zoroastrian tradition that goes back even further. Others attribute the rejection to the fierce political and religious rivalry between various sects, between Christian, Jew, and Gnostic. But as we begin to penetrate the implications of these writings, we can recognize that it is likely they were suppressed because of their gnosticizing tendencies, which threatened the authority of orthodox Christianity. The politics of religion could not be hospitable to a faith that proclaims that all your gods are mere distortions created by your own minds or your own interests, that the real God is higher than your gods and cannot be appropriated by you. Wisely, the Gnostics of those days went underground.

Let us remember that Jesus never proclaimed himself to be the founder of a new religion. He was a Jew, and did not regard himself as anything else. However, like many Jewish reformers before him and many after him, he was critical of some of the more tribalisitic aspects of Judaism such as, for example, animal sacrifice, the emphasis on legalism, the policy of destroying the enemy, and exclusion of the gentile from Jewish society. He sought a more liberal and universal emphasis in the faith. Jesus' vision of God was closer to the prophetic tradition within Judaism than it was to that of the Pharisees, with their excessive legalisms. Consequently, like prophets and reformers in any age, he had serious problems with those who supported the status quo. For Jesus, the adversaries were Rome, and those Jews who found it advantageous to pay tribute to Rome in exchange for tolerance of their religious differences. They lived under the *pax Romana*, in which many religions could coexist so long as they did not threaten the power of Caesar.

The first followers of Jesus were Jews. Christianity as a religion separate from Judaism came later, when the Church fathers could interpret what Jesus meant without having to confront him and find out whether their interpretations of his words accurately represented what he had intended. Those followers of Jesus who saw things differently from the orthodox Church were branded as heretics. They were deprived of their authority and even of their religious freedom. Many of them went into the desert, where they could seek God in their own way.

The Gnostics of those days denied any validity to the orthodox Church. In fact, they had a quite different concept of the nature of the world, one that of necessity rejected the authority of the Church—indeed, any authority that was imposed upon them from without. For them, authority stemmed from a divine spark that emanated from an unknown source beyond this world and imbued each human being with life. Gnostic rituals were designed to evoke this spark in the human soul; it was a process that could not be institutionalized. When they were persecuted and threatened with extinction by the nascent Church, Gnostics continued their rituals and practices in secret. They preserved at least some of their manuscripts. The visibility of the Gnostics in the prevailing culture decreased, but somehow they remained as an "antibody in the bloodstream of Christianity."[1]

Jung must have read with great interest the Gnostic "Anonymous Treatise" *On the Origin of the World*, which is a polemic against traditional cosmogonies (Rudolph, p. 73). In the traditional biblical account, there is nothing before Chaos. But in Gnosticism there is something, which is no thing, but which can best be expressed as light or energy and which is neither male nor female but has male/female (androgynous) aspects. The Highest God, who is not a creator god, has his consort or feminine aspect. She is called the World Soul, Anima Mundi, or Shekhinah (in the Jewish mystical tradition), or more often by the Gnostics, the holy Sophia. Since this Highest God was rather passive and was disinterested in creation, the Sophia thought about creating a work alone, without her consort. Her thought became a work, an image of heaven, a curtain between heaven and the lower regions, called aeons. Then a shadow was cast forth, and the origin of matter is described in what may be called archetypal symbology.

> Thereupon the shadow took note that there was something stronger than itself. It became envious and immediately it gave birth to envy, after it had become pregnant from itself. From that day on, the beginning (*arche*) of envy made its appearance in all the regions (aeons) and their worlds. But that envy was found to be an abortion in which there was no [divine] spirit. (Rudolph, p. 73)

It is said in some versions of the myth that this spiritless being, this Golem, lacked spirit because Sophia's consort had not concurred with her. Then the hatred (envy) that originated from the shadow was cast into a part of chaos. Matter thus originated from a negative action on the part of the "shadow," therefore it was discounted from the beginning. Close upon the origin of matter, there follows that of the world creator, the Demiurge, who bears the name Jaldabaoth. He is evidently an esoteric interpretation of the biblical creator-God, called the "accursed God" because he created the visible world and withheld knowledge from men, beginning with his warning to Adam and Eve not to eat of the Tree of Knowledge (Rudolph, p. 73). Knowing this, we can appreciate what Jung felt when he saw in Gnostic mythology corroboration of his own belief that the stern god of his parson father was, in many respects, evil.

To continue the creation story, when the Sophia saw that through her error the matter of chaos was like an abortion because there was no spirit in it, she was sorely troubled. Out of her compassion, she descended into the world of matter to breathe into its face in the abyss. There she encountered out of the depths of matter the "ruler" (archon), which was in the form of a lion and bisexual and full of power in himself. Jaldabaoth had embarked upon his creative activity, and through his word were created the lower heavens and the earth and all the hierarchies of heaven (archons), each of whom have their own heavens and thrones, glories, temples, and chariots. There are innumerable versions of this story in Gnostic literature. But the important episode that follows is common to many of them.

When the heavens and earth had been established and all the gods and angels praised Jaldabaoth, he exalted himself and boasted continually, saying to them, "I have need of no one." And further, "I am God and there is no other apart from me." In another version the Sophia cries out to him, "You are mistaken, Samael" (which means the blind god). And again, he exalts himself saying, "I am a jealous God; apart from me there is none." And it is written, "Thereby he indicated to the angels under him that there is another God; for if there were no other, of whom should he be jealous?"

The narrative now returns to Sophia. In the world of matter to which she has descended, she is overcome and defiled by the archons and becomes blind. In her suffering she repents, recognizing her deficiency and the loss of her perfection. She understands that the abortion of darkness was imperfect because her consort had not concurred with her. She weeps bitterly, and the Spirit hears her prayer and her repentance and sends the Christ down to her in order to put right her deficiency and make her whole again.

In commemoration of this, it is read today in the ritual of the Gnostic Church:

> And Jesus answered: "They say I came for all, but in truth I came for Her Who came for all. For it had come to pass that there were those who had lost their way and, lacking in spark, could not return unto the Father, and seeing this, She came unto them, giving her life to the depths of matter. And in truth She did suffer and became blind. But our Father, sensing her anguish, sent Me forth, being of Him, so that She might see and We be as One again. Though they see it not, it is She, the tender Mother of Mercy, Who is the great redeemer."[2]

We can recognize the archetype of anima in the figure of Sophia, the willful, creative, compassionate, suffering, redemptive feminine principle. As anima, she also has the dual role that is characteristic of an archetypal figure: she is Barbelo, the female aspect of the Father that is a kind of Gnostic mother-goddess; and she is the higher, incorruptible Sophia. One Gnostic document suggests that it is not even the holy Sophia who is violated by the archons, but that she leaves her body and they violate only her likeness. Still another Gnostic document from Nag Hammadi, called *The Thunder, Perfect Mind*, expresses the dual nature or, rather, the pluralistic nature of the anima:

> For I am the first and the last.
> I am the honored one and the scorned one.
> I am the whore and the holy one.
> I am the wife and the virgin.
> I am the mother and the daughter.
> I am the barren one and many are her sons. . . .

For I am knowledge and ignorance.
I am shame and boldness.
I am shameless; I am ashamed.
I am strength and I am fear. . . .

Why then have you hated me, you Greeks?
    Because I am a barbarian among the barbarians?
For I am the wisdom of the Greeks
    and the knowledge of the barbarians. . . .
I am the one who has been hated everywhere
    and who has been loved everywhere.
I am the one whom they call life,
    and you have called death.

Thus the feminine wisdom figure of the Gnostics is a many-sided phenomenon who unites in herself many aspects of the Gnostic view of the world, both negative and positive.

The narrative moves from creation to the Garden of Eden. In the primal history of Adam and Eve, emanations of the Ineffable Light in the highest heaven move through successive stages, with the light becoming more dense with each transformation. The Tree of Knowledge in the garden is the Tree of Gnosis. There is a heavenly God-man or *Urmench* or Anthropos, a Primal Man who is, or emanates from, or has a close relationship with the Highest God. This is Anthropos, the "first Adam." He is earlier and superior to the Demiurge (creator-god). The Heavenly Eve is an emanation of the Sophia. The first Eve is Mother, Wife, and Virgin in one person, and thus represents the female aspect of the kingdom of light. A drop of light passes from the Sophia to the Heavenly Eve, from which the "Instructor of Life" is born. Later he is the serpent in Paradise, the wise one who instructs Adam.

The creator-god creates a man, the second Adam, after the image of the first Adam who is the God-man, or the Man of Light. But the second Adam has no real life in him until he is imbued with the Divine Spirit, which is the pneuma substance. This comes about either through the intervention of the Highest God or of the Heavenly Eve, who is the prototype for the earthly Eve. So this places the second Adam above the creator-god in the Gnostic hierarchy, and bestows upon the first man the capacity for redemption. The powers of darkness see that Adam is alive. They see Eve speaking to him, and they are confused. They do not wish Adam to have power over them, so they fall upon Eve in order to cast their seed into her so that they, and not Adam, shall have control over her children. But the Heavenly Eve has turned herself into the Tree of Gnosis, and only her likeness has remained with Adam. The archons make the sleep of forgetfulness fall upon Adam, and they say to him in his sleep that she (Eve) originated from his rib, that the woman may be subject to him and he be lord over her. But Eve laughed at their purpose and made them blind. She left her likeness with Adam and entered into the Tree. The archons defiled the likeness, but they became thoroughly confused (as you must be, and as I was when I read all these many and conflicting versions of the story). The archons took counsel together and went in fear to Adam and Eve and said to him(!), "All the trees which are in paradise are created for you, to eat their fruit, but the Tree of Knowledge (Gnosis) do not eat. If you should eat of it you will die."

The serpent in Gnosticism plays a thoroughly positive role. He appears at this point, and asks Eve what the archon has told her. When she replies, he says, "Know that if you eat of it your understanding will become sober and you will be like gods, since you will know the difference between evil and good. He, the creator-god, said this to you because he is envious, that you should not eat of it." Eve eats the fruit and gives it to her husband, who eats also. Then their understanding (nous) is opened, for when they had eaten, the light of knowledge (Gnosis) was opened to them.

The archons see what has happened, and in their dismay they curse Adam and Eve and all their children, and cast them out of Paradise and out into the world. And as if what they had done is not sufficient, they go to the Tree of Life. They surround it with great terror, with fiery creatures that are called cherubim, and set a fiery sword into its midst, which turns about so that no one can ever return to that place. The Sophia, seeing that the archons have cursed her likeness, is enraged. She drives the archons out of their heavens and casts them down into the sinful cosmos, and so they become like wicked demons on the earth.

One can imagine Jung poring over these Gnostic legends late into the night, and reflecting that here are the myths that deal with the troubling questions of the sick psyche. Here are the demons who inhabit people's dreams and fantasies, who give rise to unwelcome suspicions, compulsions, and complexes of all kinds. Here is the mischief out of which psychosis is fashioned, for all these "powers" still exist as the stuff of psyche, to give rise to all manner of human suffering.

But this Gnostic parable is not just a story of how evil came to be in this world. Gnosticism is only in part the mythology of the fall from grace—from a higher, more subtle form of existence to one that is lower and gross. Gnosticism also offers a message of redemption. Here, I believe, was its great fascination for Jung. The act of self-recognition introduces the possibility of deliverance from suffering in the world and guarantees salvation. It is little wonder that Jung would find an affinity with Gnostic mythology, for in the analytic process, the whole objective is to discover who you are. We all tend to be what I call "prisoners of the mind." We are enslaved by our thoughts, our projections, our preconceptions, and our prejudices. They blind us, and because of this we become lost in the snares of our own ignorance. So knowing (Gnosis) is all. The task of individuation is to free ourselves from what William Blake so aptly calls "the mind-forged manacles." Know thyself, in the language of Gnosticism, means to gain knowledge of the divine spirit (nous) which forms the true human nature, thus our divine nature. Poimandres says, "God, the Father, from whom man (Anthropos) came, is light and life. If you therefore learn that he consists of life and light, and you derive from him, you will again attain to life and light" (Rudolph, p. 113).

II

What prompted me to begin to explore the Gnostic tradition more deeply was an invitation to co-lead a workshop with Elaine Pagels on the subject of "Little-known Stories about Adam and Eve." Probably I had been asked to do this because I had included a chapter on Gnosticism in my book *Androgyny*, and it was assumed that therefore I must know something about Gnosticism. True, I had done some research, but compared with Dr. Pagel's distinguished work, my own was minimal. Nevertheless the subject intrigued me. I accepted the invitation. Then I plunged into a season of reading and rereading much of the *Nag Hammadi Library* (Robinson 1978), Mead's classic works *Fragments of a Faith Forgotten* (1931) and *Pistis Sophia* (1921), Stephen Hoeller's *The Gnostic Jung* (1982), and other recent books on Gnosticism, as well as those works of Jung in which Gnosticism is a major theme. Still, I felt that I had only scratched the surface. It was all so theoretical, so philosophical, so often "dry bones." I wanted to touch the life of gnosis if, indeed, gnosis were alive today.

I recalled having heard that there existed a Gnostic Church in Palo Alto, California, where I live. Although something in me was fascinated by that bit of news, I had never gone there because I had made a judgment that it must belong to some California cult-group using an historic name to conjure up a sense of mystery, something like the Rosicrucians in nearby San José. Still, I wanted to have something to say about Gnosticism that possibly Elaine Pagels would not be saying. So one Sunday morning I decided to take myself to the Ecclesia Gnostica Mysteriorum. Interestingly enough, it turned out to be less than a mile from my home. I walked up the stairs of an office building that was part of a small shopping center. I entered the anteroom, where the faint fragrance of incense was present, and then I entered the sanctuary itself. I was totally unprepared for what I found.

The room was softly lit. Exterior light filtered through a rose, mauve, and blue stained-glass window patterned with forms of sun and moon and abstract shapes. What especially impressed me was the silence. As people entered, there was hardly a sound, no handling of pages or shuffling of feet or looking around, but a sense of people perfectly composed, turning inward. I saw delicate flowers beautifully arranged behind the altar, not as a florist would arrange them, but as someone who was creating a very personal work of art would have done. In the center was the statue of a Black Madonna seated with great dignity, her Child in her lap. I fell into my own reflection, and the image of the first Black Madonna I had ever seen came to me. She was the Lady of Einsiedeln, and I had made a pilgrimage to see her when I was a student at the Jung Institute in Zurich.

I was startled out of my reverie to see a woman clothed in a black cassock and white surplice slowly walking from the rear of the sanctuary up the aisle toward the altar. She bowed before the statue, turned to the audience, and began to preach. There was a simple teaching story about a little boy who was walking with his grandfather. He asked the old man about whether he needed to do what his parents and teachers told him to do when he didn't understand why, or when something didn't make any sense to him. He had been told, "Do it just because I say so," and this had troubled him. The grandfather said that it was not necessary to follow blindly the people in charge, but that it was all right for him to sit quietly with his own thoughts and to listen to what might come up in him. And he was to understand that God did not only speak to parents and teachers or priests and rabbis, but that God spoke to everyone, to children and adults, and even to animals and plants. It is more important to discover the truth within ourselves than to look for it out in the world, Grandfather told the little boy. This was a very different message than any I had learned in Sunday School.

I heard, too, that wisdom comes from self-examination and from the Self, in which our innate wisdom is lodged. This Self of the Gnostics sounded very much like the description of the Self as Jung has conceptualized it. After preaching, the priest withdrew, and an acolyte lit the candles to signify the beginning of the rite. I found it interesting that the sermon was not a part of the service itself. That was the "teaching." Now the priest returned, this time wearing a deep blue embroidered chausable and holding the aspergilum. Sprinkling holy water on the people assembled, she said,

> In Thy strength, O Lord, do we command the powers of chaos to wither into nothingness, that they shall not abide, and that our temples within and our temples without may be so purified as to receive the blessing of those who come in Thy name.

The phrase "temples within and temples without" showed me clearly that this service was not to be based entirely upon the wisdom of the collective. The liturgy was to be very different, not something to be grasped with the intellect but to be entered into, a different space, an archetypal space, unbounded by time as we know it in ordinary life. There, everything that was said and done would be symbolic of the inner life, of the psyche, the temple within.

In this ritual there was no creed. No one was told what to believe, nor did anyone need to profess any collective belief. There was no mention of "sin" or of "guilt." I was to learn that Gnostics feel that ignorance, not sin, is responsible for the unhappy condition of many human beings. Ignorance is an intoxication, a drunkenness, a sleep. The soul's ignorance of itself, its origin, and its situation is the cause of much of human misery.

The mystery of the Eucharist is celebrated as a *hieros gamos*, a sacred marriage, of the Sophia, radiant Mother of the World, and her consort, the Christ. Indeed, the chalice that holds the host is covered by a veil of white lace that resembles a bridal veil. The priest says the following words: "Come enter the Bridal Chamber and receive the most holy mystery of the Three-in-One. As the Logos and the Holy Spirit are united in the Father, so may ye attain to this divine union."

It entered my mind that this offers, in symbolic form, what Jung has given us with his idea of the Divine Syzygy, the union with the soul. Then I was suddenly startled to hear the priest utter these words: "Ye are all welcome to partake of holy communion, regardless of your religious backgrounds."

It's hard to express the power this had for me. Perhaps it evoked in me a time when I was about seven years old and lived for a year in a Roman Catholic convent boarding school. Being Jewish, I did not take communion, nor was I ever asked to. I was excluded. I felt excluded. I was the outcast, the one who was different. Unacceptable. Now I was hearing "Ye are all welcome to partake of holy communion, regardless of your religious backgrounds." What this meant to me was that here was a religion (if you could call it that) that was not exclusive. Nothing was asked of you. It didn't matter what your past was, or what you believed. You were welcomed. It is there for you. You have only to make your own choice whether to accept it or not.

I wish that I could convey to you the richness of that ritual, but you would have to experience it to feel its impact. I can only say that it was conducted with exquisite feminine grace, not in any sense contrived, but with a radiance of spirit flowing forth in abundance, guiding the psyche toward its origin and its fulfillment.

Later, reflecting on all that had transpired, I found myself of two minds. One of them wanted to enter into that ritual over and over; the other wanted to study the documents relating to Gnosticism, and especially to an understanding of contemporary Gnosis. Fortunately, I have been able to do some of both. My perspective is that of an analyst, not a theologian. I find in Gnosticism, as I explore it further, an approach to real-life issues that is psychologically sound and, in most cases, quite consistent with Jung's approach to spirituality. I would like to share with you some of my observations, sometimes comparing and sometimes contrasting what I understand to be the traditional Judeo-Christian stance with the Gnosticism of today. One caveat first: Since Gnosticism has no creed, and each person seeks the truth from inner wisdom, Gnostics do not always agree on what Gnosticism is. In that respect, Gnostics are like Jungians; so please understand that my comparisons are rather broad generalities that need not be too concretely taken. I hope they will serve to indicate the "spirit" of Gnosticism, as compared with that of the more traditional religious forms.

Christianity closed the canon, implying that revelation happened at a certain time in history, for all time. Gnosticism recognizes many books contemporary with the New Testament and later, and sees revelation as an ongoing progression.

Orthodox Christianity (and here I mean especially the Roman Catholic Church) places authority within the Church establishment, with the Pope as final authority on certain important issues. Gnosticism stresses the authority of the inner voice, sometimes referred to as the voice of God, within each person. Authority, then, becomes a function of the person's experiential perception of Divine Will.

The Judeo-Christian God is referred to as "a jealous god, having no other gods before him," thereby recognizing by this statement that there are other gods, but that they are somehow "inferior." Gnosticism sees the creator-god, the Christ, Yahweh, as well as the gods of all other cultures, as manifestations—in this world of manifestation—of something pointing toward, but not equivalent to, an Unknown God. All other gods who can be described in any way are but attempts to approximate the Unknown God.

The Mass, for the orthodox Christian, is celebrated in commemoration of a past event, with vicarious benefits to those who partake of it. In the Gnostic celebration of the Eucharist, the participant enters into the immediate experience of the death of the personal ego, and the resurrection that follows is that of an integrated ego-self union.

In traditional Christianity, the Trinity consists of Father, Son, and Holy Spirit. Notable by its absence is the fourth element, which could include the "material," the "feminine principle," or the "demonic" element. The Three-in-One "is now and ever shall be." In Gnosticism, the principle of Source is the Mother-Father element; the second in the Trinity is the Logos or Christ-figure, who represents the personal ego; and the third is the Sophia, Holy Spirit or wisdom figure (also known in Judaism as the Shekhinah, in Hinduism as Shakti), the aspect of psyche that provides the dynamism that leads to individuation. Gnosticism restores to a vitally important place in the world the material, in the form of body; the feminine principle, in the form of Sophia; and the demonic, in the form of the archons. These archons represent the non-creative powers in this world, who must be recognized for what they are and must be confronted.

Christianity sees God as Father, and as Creator through the power of Logos, the word. Gnosticism sees the Father-Mother principle as an ongoing creative power emanating light or energy in the universe, and in the human spirit as the *principium individuationis.*

In Christianity the feminine power is subdued, as nature and body are subdued. Where woman is recognized, it is in her biological function as Mother and bearer of the Divine Child, or as virgin, as in religious orders. But as a fully independent and sexual woman, she has little status. In Gnosticism the feminine is redeemed from the depths of matter and returned to co-equal status with the masculine. In Gnosticism, from its very beginnings, women as well as men have been priests.

Christianity regards as a high virtue the *Imitatio Dei*, the imitation of God, with the words, "Be ye perfect." Not so in Gnosticism, where what is sought is not perfection, but wholeness. This wholeness is to be sought in the sacred books as well as in the individual person, and it implies a recognition and an integration of the dark side, the shadow.

With its litany of "Thou shalt nots," Christianity encourages the repression of the "shadow," the part of oneself that is unacceptable to the collective. Gnosticism urges the integration of the shadow by progressively recognizing and bringing to the light of consciousness the ignorant and destructive parts of one's own nature. Its goal is the "bringing together of the fragments," as we read near the conclusion of the service:

> I have recognized myself and gathered myself together from all sides. I have sown no children to the ruler of this world, but have torn up his roots. I have gathered together my limbs that were scattered abroad, and I know thee who thou art.

Jung saw in Gnosticism a necessary heresy—necessary to correct some of the one-sided positions of the Christian Church—with which he had carried on a lifelong struggle. He hoped, through his studies of Gnosticism, to find some way to bring together the opposites, and to find in Gnosticism a sort of fertilizer for a contemporary religion that for him seemed to be losing its energy. Jung said in his essay "Transformation Symbolism in the Mass": "Disparagement and vilification of Gnosticism are an anachronism. Its obviously psychological symbolism could serve many people today as a bridge to a more living appreciation of the Christian tradition" (1969, par. 144).

Some Christian theologians also have hoped that Gnosis might provide the leaven that they feel is lacking in Christianity. John P. Dourley, analyst and priest, in his Jungian critique of Christianity titled *The Illness That We Are*, attempts to use what he calls a "Gnostic-Christian perspective" to patch up the ailing Christian spirit. He writes:

> Instead of considering revelation to be somehow over and done with, ending with the historical closing of the canon, a psychological perspective would un-

derstand revelation to continue in the individual dialogue between the ego and the unconscious. The New Testament or Covenant would cease to be a once-upon-a-time contract whose terms are spelled out in sacred texts. Rather, a genuinely *new* testament would be struck every time the individual was led by the Self into dialogue with it, in the interest of its (the Self's) more conscious incarnation. As this process developed, one would be able to relate one's own testament to the biblical New Testament. (1984, p. 96)

I wish I could share Father Dourley's optimism, but I cannot imagine the Gnostic heresy ever being incorporated into the main body of Christianity. By its very nature, Gnosticism is opposed to the institutionalizing of a religion. Furthermore, the commitment to the inner search in the darkest corners of the psyche will never, in my view, become a popular movement. We who have found our way to the inner path, through the inspiration of such unconventional people as Jung and the early and contemporary Gnostics, are a pitiful few in comparison to the multitudes of Christendom. Nor do I believe that contemporary Gnosis is for everyone—nor should it be. If it were, it would lose the mystery and awesomeness that is its essence. Soon people would be cutting it down to fit the size of weekend workshops. No, Gnosticism is a perspective slowly gained and difficult to sustain in our materialistic world.

I believe, with Gnostic Bishop Rosa Miller, that Gnosticism will remain what it has always been, "an antibody in the bloodstream of traditional religions." Actually, that may not be insignificant. After all, were not Jesus and his disciples in some way also antibodies in the bloodstream of the traditional Judaism of their time?

Notes

1. The phrase is borrowed from the Most Reverend Rosa Miller, Presiding Bishop, Church of the Gnosis, Palo Alto, California.

2. This and other quotations from the service of The Gnostic Holy Eucharist are used by permission of Bishop Rosa Miller.

References

Barnstone, W., ed. 1984. The thunder, perfect mind. In *The other Bible*. San Francisco: Harper and Row.

Blake, W. 1957. The marriage of Heaven and Hell. In G. Keynes, ed., *Complete writings of William Blake*. New York: Random House.

Dourley, J. 1984. *The Illness That We Are: A Jungian Critique of Christianity*. Toronto: Inner City Books.

Hoeller, S. 1982. *The Gnostic Jung and the Seven Sermons to the Dead*. Wheaton, Ill.: Theosophical Publishing House.

Jaffé, A. 1984. Jung's last years. *Spring.* Dallas: Spring Publications.

Jung, C. G. 1961. *Memories, Dreams, Reflections.* New York: Random House.

_____. 1942. Transformation Symbolism in the mass. In *Collected Works,* 11:201–98. Princeton: Princeton University Press, 1958.

Lao Tsu. 1972. *Tao Te Ching.* Gia-Fu Feng and J. English, tr. New York: Random House.

Mead, G. 1921. *Pistis Sophia.* London: John M. Watkins.

_____. 1931. *Fragments of a Faith Forgotten.* London: John M. Watkins.

Miller, R. 1984. *Gnostic Holy Eucharist Service.*

Ponce, C. 1972. *Kabbalah.* San Francisco: Straight Arrow Press.

Robinson, J., ed. 1978. *The Nag Hammadi library.* San Francisco: Harper & Row.

Rudolph, K. 1985. *Gnosis, the Nature and History of Gnosticism.* San Francisco: Harper & Row.

Singer, J. 1970. *The Unholy Bible.* New York: G. P. Putnam's Sons. Reprinted 1986, Boston: Sigo Press.

_____. 1972. *Boundaries of the Soul.* New York: Doubleday.

_____. 1976. *Androgyny.* New York: Doubleday/Anchor Press.

Beyond the Anima:
The Female Self
in the Image of God

Joan Chamberlain Engelsman

One of the most treasured passages of scripture relates how God created the world. On the last day

> God said, Let us make man in our image, after our likeness. . . . So God created man in his own image, in the image of God created he him; male and female created he them. And God blessed them . . . and saw everything that he had made, and behold it was very good. (Genesis 1:27–31)

Male rabbis, churchmen, scholars, and psychotherapists have always interpreted this text from the point of view of men. However, I would like to test its implications for women. How does the female self resemble the divine?

This undertaking, even asking this question, would have been unthinkable before the current feminist revival. The exponential growth of religious feminism that has occurred in the past fifteen years would certainly have interested Carl Jung. He, Eric Neumann, and, of course, Esther Harding first began talking about the Goddess and the feminine decades before this new movement began. They are the ones who originally proposed the necessity of recovering the feminine, which they saw as vital for the psychic health of the world.

Despite this delight in the world of feminine archetypes, the initial promise of support for women that many women detected in Jungian writings never materialized however.

I believe there is a reason for this failure. Although Jung and his followers have been able to see how imperative it is for the feminine to find an honored place in the world and in a man's psyche, they have remained trapped in a patriarchal culture that could only define the world in terms of men.

Many feminists have responded to this situation with anger. I assume many readers are familiar with Naomi Goldenberg's critiques of Jung's work (1979). As you may recall, she denounces his theory because she believes the feminine archetypes are indistinguishable from patriarchal stereotypes of women. This opinion is shared by others. For example, in her most recent book, *Sexism and God-Talk*, Rosemary Ruether attacks Jungian psychology because it provides the intellectual base for men who "in their identification of their suppressed self with the 'feminine' . . . think they have a handle on women's true 'nature' " (1983).

To some extent, I agree with these feminist criticisms. Certainly Jung and Eric Neumann created and defined the feminine archetypes in a patriarchal way. Using Jung's own insights, however, it is possible to see that whenever he talks about the feminine, Jung is actually talking about his personal anima which, of course, represents the inferior part of a man's psyche. Once I adopted this interpretation, it became obvious that the feminine archetypes reveal only how and what men think about women. They are not relevant or valid for women *qua* women.

Because Jung lived in a period when patriarchy went unnoticed and unchallenged, he could easily mistake these two positions. By expecting real women to conform to his archetypal projections, he actually minimized the fact that women had their own psychic agenda that differed from his. There is, however, at least one place in his corpus where he does highlight the differences. When he describes the Demeter-Kore myth as one that "exists on the plane of mother-daughter experience, which is alien to man and shuts him out," I believe Jung is trying to acknowledge a difference between the way men and women evaluate the same material (1966, p. 203).

Since Jung's thought is heavily affected by patriarchy, is there any way it can help women to understand themselves or God? I believe that Jung's understanding of the connections between the human psyche and the realm of the divine provide an approach that can be useful.

Today women are setting aside Jung's description of the anima and are beginning to explore female images for themselves. Not only has this work progressed quite rapidly, but the energy and excitement generated by the exploration of the female face of God seem to indicate that this is the aspect of the divine that is turning toward us today.

I do not think Jung would be surprised. I believe his interest in the anima and in feminine images indicates his belief that these are the images that will vivify and bring life to people in the 20th and 21st centuries. Certainly he deplored the classic Protestant tradition that, devoid of icons, especially that of the Virgin Mary, had become sterile and bankrupt for him.

Now that women have begun examining female images for themselves, they are finding *not only* that the anima does not reflect a woman's self, but also that there are more appropriate archetypes. One of these is the female self; another is the Goddess. Thus, getting beyond patriarchy means more than getting beyond the anima. It also requires setting aside masculine images of God.

Because the Goddess is not present in Judaism and Christianity, the search for a divine female figure begins elsewhere. For example, although most people consider Goddess religion a dead tradition, it has been revived. Closely aligned with feminism, Wicca (or the Craft) not only supplies images and liturgies, but also embodies a tradition for Goddess worship.

Although I am personally grateful to witches such as Starhawk for their contributions to women's spirituality, those of us who are strongly identified with Christianity still need to find our own female images for the divine.[1] This is the realm of the Christian Goddess that is, theologically, just as valid as that of the male God. Because of the recent emergence of this icon, the functions of the Christian Goddess have been more defined than her content. At this point most Christian feminists would probably agree that She has two major tasks.

The first is to shatter the old values of patriarchy, hierarchy, dualism, and triumphalism. Since these norms have dominated Western culture for 5,000 years, this will be a formidable task. Nevertheless, as Edward Whitmont observes, the survival of the planet may depend on our ability to assist the Goddess in this task (1982). Her second function will be to usher in a new reality that can replace the one we find to be so destructive.

The content of this archetypal image, along with a description of the female self, will probably come initially from feminists and from woman-identified women. I think it is obvious what I mean by feminist; what I mean by woman-identified women may need further clarification. The latter will certainly include lesbians, but I am trying to indicate a wider group of women who neither identify with male values nor try to live out male anima projections. Alice Walker probably captures my meaning best with her definition of a "Womanist":

> A woman who loves other women, sexually and/or nonsexually. Appreciates and prefers women's culture, women's emotional flexibility . . . women's strength. Sometimes loves individual men, sexually and/or nonsexually. Committed to survival and wholeness of entire people, male *and* female. Not a separatist, except periodically, for health. (1984)

In order to be specific about this Goddess, I am going to share with you a portion of Nelle Morton's encounters with this divine figure, which she records in her book *The Journey is Home.*[2] Consider them, if you will, as verbal slides or pictures in words that illustrate certain characteristics of the Christian Goddess. For those of you who don't know her, Morton is a distinguished feminist theologian, whose respect for Jungian psychology probably dates from her days in therapy with Esther Harding. It is, therefore, especially fitting to share these stories with you.

Morton's first encounter with the Goddess occurred during a worship service where only female words were used. When the leader said, "Now *She* is a new creation," Morton felt as if an intimate, infinite, and transcending power had enfolded her, as if great wings had spread themselves around the seated women and gathered them into a oneness. This was not something she heard or reasoned. It was something she knew.

Her next experience happened while on board a plane flying through turbulent weather. Never comfortable in the air, Morton had always called on the male God for protection. She would make promises, confess her sins, pray for others, and thank God when the flight was over. This time she envoked the Goddess. Closing her eyes, Morton felt someone sit down beside her and put a hand on her arm. The Goddess told her to relax and feel the rhythm of the waves in the air, to trust the experience of the pilot. When Morton did what the Goddess directed, the fear vanished, and she enjoyed the flight. The Goddess left before Morton could thank her, and Morton did not feel guilty.

Another encounter took place at a Goddess celebration led by Z. Budapest at her shop in Santa Monica. As the service progressed, Morton felt lifted into the air, up to the ceiling, until her eyes were level with the names of the Goddesses that were printed around the top of the four walls. Suddenly the Goddesses began to take form, clothed in garb appropriate to their country and era, while Morton floated in and out among them. She was at home with them. After the Goddesses became their names again, Morton returned to the floor. When she opened her eyes and looked at the women in the room, she thought, "These women are Goddesses, and maybe I am also!"

The fourth encounter is notable because the Divine Female does not appear in her usual form. Morton describes the occasion as a secular event. Two women open an ice cream shop in San Diego. What makes it special was the number and diversity of people who are involved. Despite the mixture of nationalities, races, ages, and sexes, Morton and her friends believe they have something important in common. Strangers become unstrange as they talk of a new humanity envisioned on the basis of what is taking place between them and within them. Once again, female names are written on the walls. In this case they do not represent Goddesses per se, but are names of friends, and of the mothers, grandmothers, and foresisters of the ice cream shop's owners. Morton says this secular event, repeated annually, has taken on profound spiritual overtones.

In the last encounter, Morton struggles to overcome a depression. As she opens herself to the Goddess, the Goddess sweeps in, then steps aside and bows Morton's mother into the room. "My mother floated in on a river of blood. It seemed all the blood in front of her was blood she had shed in her lifetime, and behind her, all the blood I had shed."

Then she speaks, telling Morton she had made a mistake by teaching her that menstruation was an illness. Her mother recognizes that she passed her negative ideas on to all her daughters, but only Morton internalized them so deeply that they caused her to suffer severe menstrual pain and to fear menopause. Now her negative input has gone into her bone marrow, causing sideroblastic anemia, a disease of the red blood cells that has no cure. Morton's mother tells her to forget visualizing whole red blood cells, but to be thankful for the wild and bizarre ones that are keeping her alive.

Morton says her depression lifted immediately as she received this beautiful gift from her mother. "I jumped up from my chair and kissed her on the mouth." After her mother disappeared, an enormous spider came into the room. She handed Morton some woven material and said, "Your mother spun this for you. . . . As I took the material, the spider dissolved into me, as did the Goddess and then my mother. When I opened my eyes, my entire attitude toward my illness had changed."

Encounters such as these increase our knowledge of the Goddess; they also illustrate a number of Her qualities. Although Rosemary Ruether and others use the word "God/ess" to indicate the bisexual nature of the deity, experiences of the divine female move the discussion to an entirely different level. The Goddess is no longer an academic concept, but a spiritual and psychological reality that shatters the old patriarchal order and provides new insights into the divine nature.

As Christian feminists and others meet the Goddess, our picture of the female image of the divine will grow. However, I believe there is enough material from old and new sources to begin describing Her and to make some comments about the female self created in her image.

First, I believe it is important to note that the process that modern women undergo may not differ substantially from previous spiritual journeys or quests, except for the important fact that the aspect of the deity that is revealed is specifically female. Thus as knowledge and faith in the Goddess increase, intimate revelations of the divine move from without to within. This pattern, which characterizes religious experience in many traditions, has begun to provide an undeniable credibility for both the Goddess and those who speak of her.

The process is a gradual one that continually transforms the people who experience it. For example, although some people believe the conversion of a Saint Augustine or Saint Teresa happens in a moment, those who have studied their lives pay close attention to what happened before the moment, as well as to the later experiences that deepen their faith. Thus, the process occurs over a lifetime, with each stage revealing a different and more profound concept of the divine. Although we can plot each encounter on a continuum, those who have been and are going through it note that each step is sufficient to itself. Furthermore, each step incorporates the preceding level into itself, so there is increased fluidity in and among the various levels. This is not ladder-climbing. Rather, each stage is more inclusive; it widens the circle. Therefore, it is not necessary for everyone to experience all the stages. Indeed, it would be naive to assume that most people could, because the majority of us lack the spiritual sensitivity, the energy, and the time to make a full commitment to the journey.

Although every encounter is personal, the Goddess initially approaches us through language. We hear Her; She hears us to speech, into being (Morton 1985, pp. 54 and 60). The primary qualities the Goddess reveals at this point are those of transcendence and power. She appears as a cosmic advocate or as a universal other who cares about women.

Although there is still substantial distance between the human being and the divine, women react strongly to this aspect of the deity. In patriarchy, men may experience this interaction with the divine and not find it particularly earth-shaking. For women, however, this initial meeting is always a shock. To know the divine as female is to know something radically new. Thus, although language may not be the most intimate vehicle of the divine, it is often the first. Christian feminists are therefore right to insist on linguistic changes in scripture and liturgy. To be sure, no one can compel the divine to appear, but Her way can be eased by the use of female terms.

Next the Goddess comes closer. She is still outside, but She is no longer remote or primarily intellectual. As She nears, She becomes more intimate, perhaps even physical. The Goddess may touch and speak as She guides and encourages women to use their adult, intelligent capabilities. This stage marks the first occasion in which a woman may personally appropriate the wisdom of the divine. As a student in seminary and graduate school, I always looked for usable truth, that is, for truths that had the power to change my life. Unfortunately, most of the theologies and philosophies I heard could not survive my kitchen sink. Although they seemed impressive in the rarefied atmosphere of academe, they could not survive the rigors of real life. In other words, they didn't wash.

This second level of encounter with the divine provides insights that the deity Herself makes viable. In Morton's case, for example, she overcame her life-long fear of flying because the Goddess made it possible for her to use her own intelligence. Clearly this is not a case of mind over matter. Who among us has not tried to believe six impossible things before breakfast in order to save our own souls? This is not how the divine operates. The Goddess responds, She comforts, She leads a woman in a new direction, and She enables it all to happen.

This experience changes the relationship between a human being and the deity. The person has been raised to maturity. As a result, instead of propitiating the divine with prayers of supplication and thanksgiving in the manner of a child, a woman is encouraged to use her intelligence and power for herself and for others, and to do so freely, without guilt. Since most women can't remember a time when they didn't feel guilty, they find this encouragement to be remarkable. One of the most difficult tasks a woman faces involves being an adult and breaking the claims of dependency on her mother.

The price of this adulthood is almost always guilt—sometimes specific, sometimes free-floating. Thus to encounter a Goddess who helps us attain what Esther Harding describes as a "virginal state," in which a woman is one-in-herself, without demanding a guilty conscience, seems like a miracle (1972, pp. 125–126). It allows women to remake their relationships with family and friends, with the environment, and with the divine.

As radical as this change may be, the next stage in the process signals something even more far-reaching. Whereas previously the Goddess has been external to the person, now a process begins which can only be described as the internalization of the divine. At this point, a woman is able to see herself and her friends as Goddesses, or, if I may be blunt, to see that they are divine.

Those of us who come out of a Christian tradition should not be shocked, as this can seem like a form of incarnation in which the individual is lifted up to the divine level. Certainly part of our theological heritage teaches that God became human so that human beings could become divine. Unfortunately, most Christians do not believe those words, or they interpret them to signify a condition after death. The Goddess, however, restates them in a forceful way so it is possible to understand that She is not only within us now, but She *is us*.

As the process continues, the power of the Goddess becomes more obvious. First, when we know that the divine is us or is within us, then we can function as the Goddess to our neighbor. This is similar to Luther's expectation that people could be Christ to their neighbor. At this point the Goddess does not have to appear externally, or even internally. She can empower people to find Her face in different people, as well as enable human beings to function as the divine for others.

The ox-herding pictures of Zen Buddhism, which reflect the life of the sage, make a similar point about the wise person returning to the world. Here is the sage walking through town, utterly unremarkable except for her contentment and openness. Clearly, the Zen woman or man of the "highest spiritual development lives in the mundane world of form and diversity," mingling with the utmost freedom (Kapleau 1967, p. 301). One poem that describes this phenomenon puts the miracle this way:

> Barechested, barefooted, he comes into the market place.
> Muddied and dust-covered, how broadly he grins!
> Without recourse to mystic powers,
> > withered trees he swiftly brings to bloom. (*Ibid.*, p. 311)

This is the level of religious development that follows the internalization of the divine.

True ethical commitment begins *after* a profound encounter with the divine. Usually people behave ethically in order to get God's attention, to please him, and to get God to give them what they want. True ethics, however, flows from spirituality. Once a person experiences oneness, acceptance, or incarnation, then she can truly give to others. Now the spiritual process involves community and relationship; this is where ethical behavior and the wider vision of justice and peace for all people should arise.

Although it is tempting to end the spiritual quest here, there is yet another stage that reveals God is All. This is a point reached only by people of the greatest spiritual sensitivity. I believe the profound healing brought about by this final encounter brings an understanding and acceptance of life and death, which creates an entirely new consciousness. Certainly it is totally unlike the current patriarchal one that many feminists hold responsible for shaping what Mary Daly identifies as a sado-society in love with death.[3]

In the case of the Goddess, this final part of the process involves meeting Her in Her triune form. In ancient Catal Huyuk, She could appear as the one who gives birth, as a young virgin, and as a vulture who cleans the bones of the dead. At Eleusis, She was Demeter, Persephone, *and* Hecate. The Goddess manifests herself to Nelle Morton as her personal mother, as a virginal woman who is one-in-herself, and as a spider who, stepping on the darkness, brings her a shroud—a reminder of death.

This triple nature of the divine indicates that throughout life, as well as before it and after it, the Goddess is there. Saint Paul describes a similar awareness when he says that he knows nothing can separate us from the love of God. I believe the mystery of the Goddess incorporates death even more radically. Discussing it like this, however, makes the experience seem abstract. In reality, the Goddess experience conveys a total affirmation of the uniqueness of the individual, who cannot be lost in death nor in some uroboric concept of the divine. Thus, by restoring the part of our lives that is wasted by fear, the Goddess gives back life and helps us to live it fully.

This process of revelation provides an image of the Goddess that can form a basis for describing the female image of God and of the female self, which scripture tells us has been constructed in that image. The appearances of the Goddess reveal that although She functions as a cosmic advocate, exuding qualities of transcendence and power, She also manifests Herself in the immanental structures of this world. When She chooses to present Herself through relationship and community, for example, She might not appear in the form of a divine woman, but only in the interaction of human beings.

Thus, in addition to Her presence at sacred liturgies, the Goddess can be found in secular events. Secular occasions are especially interesting, because rather than shunning the mundane, the Goddess transforms it into the sacred. Her presence in the world and ordinary life underscores a quality of rootedness that is also conveyed by the fact that, in some cases, the Goddess touches people in a physical way. A hand on the arm or a kiss convey a certain sensual quality that patriarchal deities do not exhibit.

The Goddess does not appear to have a jealous nature. By facilitating relationships among women, for example, the Goddess displays Her comfort with others and in community. This is especially noteworthy because the jealousy of the patriarchal Gods of Christianity and Judaism are so well known and so basic to their worship. The New Testament dictum that one must give up mother, father, sister, and brother in order to follow Jesus apparently does not apply to the Goddess at all.

There are several less surprising qualities of the Goddess. Clearly, She encourages women to use their intelligence and wisdom. In order for that to happen, however, the Goddess also enables women to appropriate what they know in a saving way. Anyone who has ever been the beneficiary of "good advice" knows the difference between these two situations. It is the difference between knowing in the gut and knowing in the brain. Only the former allows a person to transform her life. In this mode the Goddess resembles Sophia, but with an added component—She facilitates the understanding of Her own Wisdom.

A second quality is Her multiform nature. The Goddess appears in many guises. She has many faces, forms, and names. Not only does She assume the form of Goddesses already known, but She also can appear in friends, or as one's own mother. This historic diversity of individual Goddesses has been widely documented.

In Her aspect as three-in-one, however, She has not been sufficiently appreciated. Since the meaning of this trinity has not been adequately probed by women, as a Christian I am looking forward to learning what this image of the Goddess will disclose about the nature of the divine.

If these are some of the qualities that constitute the nature of the Goddess, then—to return to the original question—what is the nature of the female self?

First, *the female self knows the sacredness of woman's personal existence*, that women are indeed made in the image of the divine, and carry that image into the world. With a sense of being one-in-herself, which Esther Harding once indicated was the hallmark of the Goddess, the female self exudes self-esteem.

Since the female self is estimable in herself, *she can have a strong sense of community*. Under these circumstances, her relationship with others is not governed by guilt or inappropriate dependency. Thus, it is possible for her to share herself and her wisdom and her maturity.

The female self is rooted in the world. There is a sensual side to her nature that allows her to be both erotic and practical.

This sensual side is not divorced from her intellect. The dualism that permeates patriarchal society is alien to the female self, which does not separate mind and body. This wholistic vision also governs her relations with others and is reflected in her ethical actions. She can be at one with other people and stand in solidarity with them.

Because of the various qualities of the female self, she can be described as *both independent and inter-related.* Patriarchal society promotes dependency in women, but the female self does not accept that condition. Depending on others for one's self-esteem is an intolerable and infuriating experience. It also promotes infantile relationships. When it comes to other people, therefore, the female self gives up dependency in order to have a mature relationship. The difference between these two situations reflects the consensus of most therapists, who believe that a person must be independent before she can truly relate to another. I believe the female self promotes this kind of independence.

Finally, *these qualities of independence and interrelationship redeem the relationshp with one's own mother, as well as with the divine Mother.* Neumann believes that the central message of the Eleusinian Mysteries is the unification and identification of mother and daughter. In my opinion, this view is more compatible with a patriarchal understanding of mother and daughter, which for Oedipal reasons may find this blurring of female generations desirable.

As far as I can see, however, the female self has a basic integrity that cannot be breached even in relation to the mother. In other words, the female self is truly one-in-herself. Certainly, mother and daughter may be compatible, but they cannot become identical. Actually, blurring the distinctions between these individual women does not seem to be encouraged by the divine female. On the contrary, one interpretation of the multiplicity of Goddess figures indicates how much the uniqueness of each woman matters on both the divine and the human levels. One-in-themselves women, working in concert and interrelating, seem to define the constituent parts of the archetypal female self.

This focus on the adult nature of the female self also marks a significant change in the divine-human relationship. By focusing on fathers and sons, patriarchal Christianity does not seem to encourage the maturity of the believer. Over forty years ago Dietrich Bonhoeffer began to call for a new Christian faith that would emphasize adult consciousness.

Today, more and more people are finding that a female side of God has turned toward us, and human beings are discovering that the Goddess does not treat us like children. On the contrary, relationship with Her provides divine encouragement and help in our steps toward mature faith and responsibility in the world.

In sum, then, the point of this paper is deceptively simple. I believe the time has come for women to investigate their humanity in the image of God. In order to do this it is necessary to set aside patriarchal divinities and to recognize that the anima projections of men are inappropriate sources of female imagery. Once this has been done, it is possible to begin the enormous task of discovering the divine female, and how She will help women understand themselves.

Notes

1. Starhawk has written two excellent books that cover the history, liturgy and ritual, and ethics of contemporary Wicca. See *The Spiral Dance*, San Francisco: Harper and Row (1979) and *Dreaming the Dark: Magic, Sex, and Politics*, Boston: Beacon Press (1982).

2. Her encounters with the Goddess cover pages 155–64, but I am indebted to her whole discussion. Overall, this is one of the most important books of Christian feminism.

3. Mary Daly's penetrating analysis of contemporary patriarchy can be found in all her books. But see especially *Gyn/ecology: the Metaethics of Radical Feminism* and *Pure Lust: Elemental Feminist Philosophy*.

References

Daly, M. 1978. *Gyn/ecology: The Metaethics of Radical Feminism.* Boston: Beacon Press.
————. 1984. *Pure Lust: Elemental Feminist Philosophy.* Boston: Beacon Press.
Goldenberg, N. 1979. *Changing the Gods: Feminism and the End of Traditional Religions.* Boston: Beacon Press.

Harding, M. E. 1972. *Women's Mysteries, Ancient and Modern*. New York: G. P. Putnam's Sons. This work was originally published in 1935.

Jung, C. G. 1969. *The Archetypes and the Collective Unconscious*. In *Collected Works* 9/i:203. Princeton: Princeton University Press.

Kapleau, P. 1967. *The Three Pillars of Zen: Teaching, Practice, and Enlightenment*. Boston: Beacon Press.

Morton, N. 1985. *The Journey is Home*. Boston: Beacon Press.

Ruether, R. R. 1983. *Sexism and God-Talk: Toward a Feminist Theology*. Boston: Beacon Press.

Walker, A. 1984. *In Search of Our Mothers' Gardens*. San Diego: A Harvest/HBJ Book, Harcourt Brace Jovanovich.

Whitmont, E. C. 1982. *Return of the Goddess*. New York: Crossroad.

Jung's Challenge to Biblical Hermeneutics

Wayne G. Rollins

Queen Victoria once remarked of Lord John Russell that he would be a better man if he knew a third subject; he was interested in nothing but the Constitution of 1688 and himself. Those of us in Biblical studies realize that scriptural scholarship twenty years ago found itself in a comparable fix. We knew two subjects well; historical/archaeological research on the one hand, and literary/linguistic studies on the other. In the last two decades, however, we have come to realize that we need a "third subject."

The number of "third subjects" that Biblical scholars have begun to explore continues to grow. John Dominic Crossan of DePaul University describes the situation aptly. He observes that "Biblical study will no longer be conducted under the exclusive or even dominant hegemony" of any one of the disciplines, but "through a multitude of disciplines interreacting mutually as a field criticism" in which historians and literary critics will be working side by side with structuralists, new literary critics, folklorists, and social anthropologists (Crossan 1977, p. 41). My purpose in this paper is to suggest ways in which insights and data from the field of psychology, particularly the analytical psychology of C. G. Jung, constitute part of this larger "field criticism," challenging the assumptions and practices of earlier approaches to Biblical study and interpretation.[1]

New Questions for Biblical Scholarship

Traditional Biblical scholarship has busied itself for over a century with a standard set of questions about the Bible. Who wrote it? What is really being said? What really happened? When? Where was the author at the time of writing? Who were the audience? What was the author's purpose?

The result of the resolute application of these questions to the Bible by generations of scholars has been impressive. For example, the questions have led to the discovery that the flood story in Genesis is rooted in the Babylonian *Gilgamesh Epic*; that the synoptic gospels (Matthew, Mark, and Luke) are the products of a fascinating history of interwoven oral, literary, and theological components; and that the language of St. Paul was not a literary Greek, but a lively, vibrant street Greek or "camel-driving Greek," which in the original read much more like "news" than it does to some today.

But beyond the range of the "who," "what," and "where" questions is a whole new set of questions that traditional Biblical scholarship has found itself uncomfortable with, not because of a lack of interest in the questions themselves, but because of a lack of satisfactory methods for providing satisfactory answers. The old questions of Biblical scholarship could all be answered with the tools provided by historical and literary criticism. The new questions, however, require tools provided by newer disciplines: structuralism, anthropology, sociology, and psychology. The old questions tended to focus on Biblical backgrounds: where the Bible came from and what produced it. The new questions, however, are shifting the focus to another dimension of Scripture, not to its backward-looking history, but to its forward-facing history; not to its origins, but to its effects; not to what produced the Bible, but to what the Bible has produced.

What are some of these new questions? One would be, Why is it that a text like the Bible can have such a catalytic effect on its readers across the generations? Another is, Why is it that an Augustine finds in one verse in scripture the catalytic occasion for the consolidation of his life as a Christian? There are more. Why does a John Wesley come away from the text with his heart "strangely warmed"? Why did a friend of mine, a German ecumenical fellow whom I met in theological school in 1951, who had fought in one of Hitler's crack tank corps and who had stumbled back from the Russian front lost and disillusioned, who had shifted from one vocational option to another, finally find his calling in a church one day, hearing the words of John 4:35, "I tell you, lift up your eyes, and see how the fields are already white for harvest"? Why has the Biblical text functioned as a catalytic agent in so many lives, bringing together pasts and opening up futures?

Another new question for Biblical scholars is, Why do playwrights, poets, and sculptors, many of whom regard themselves as happy pagans with no lively interest either in religious institutions or theological promulgations, find themselves constantly returning to the Bible for the *prima materia* of their art? The Communist film producer Pasolini, for example, found himself holed up in the city of Pisa one day in a traffic jam precipitated by a visit of Pope John XXIII to that ancient town. Caught in the gridlock, Pasolini retreated to a hotel room where, to pass the time, he picked up the Italian equivalent of a Gideon Bible and for the first time in his life settled down to a reading of Matthew's Gospel. The experience was so primally startling for Pasolini that he was moved to produce his classic film, "The Gospel According to St. Matthew."

Another new question for Biblical scholars has to do with the nature of the transaction between the text and the reader. Is the transaction fundamentally at the level of conscious, rational thought, or are there other parts of the self that come into play that transcend the purely intellectual and operate at a level far deeper than conscious knowledge?

It seemed to me in 1970, when I first started thinking about these questions, that Carl Jung, with his interest in symbol and archetype, folklore and myth, was the person to whom Biblical scholarship might well turn for assistance in addressing these new questions. I tried his notion out on a colleague in the Psychology of Religion, Dr. Leighton McCutchen, and together we offered a graduate seminar on "Jung and the Bible." As a result of the course, it became clear to me that Jung provided a perspective and theoretical structure for approaching these new questions on the role of the Bible in the life of the psyche. Not only that, but as I continued to read in the Jungian corpus, I discovered to my surprise and delight that Jung demonstrated a seasoned familiarity not only with the Biblical text, but with the modern interpretive methods of Biblical scholarship as well.

Jung's Use of the Bible

When one looks for Biblical materials in the Jungian corpus, one thinks immediately of *Answer to Job*,[2] the only essay by Jung devoted exclusively to a Biblical topic. However, when one looks further through the *Collected Works*, one discovers that Jung's references to the Bible are not limited to a single essay, but are found throughout his writings.

Throughout the *Collected Works*, Jung alludes to all but thirteen of the canonical writings of the Hebrew and Christian scriptures. In addition, he demonstrates ample familiarity with the Old Testament Apocrypha and Pseudepigrapha (e.g., Slavonic Enoch, Second Esdras, Tobit) and the New Testament Apocrypha (e.g., the Acts of Peter, Book of the Apostle Bartholomew, Gospel of Phillip). His technical knowledge of the text extends to citations of textual variants, for example, the saying of Jesus recorded in Codex Bezae: "Man, if indeed thou knowest what thou doest, thou art blessed; but if thou knowest not, thou art cursed, and a transgressor of law."[3]

In addition one finds a large cast of primary Biblical figures populating the pages of Jung's work, ranging from Adam and Eve, Elijah, Jacob, Abraham, and Jonah to Uriah the Hittite, Pharisees and publicans, and Lilith. Similarly, Jung's prose is studded with Biblical images and phrases. He cites the well known *"kenosis"* passage in Philippians 2:7 in the original Greek, referring to Christ taking on the *morphēn doulou* ("the form of a servant"). He notes what he identifies as a caveat against projection implicit in the dominical saying about beholding the mote in your brother's eye and not perceiving the beam in your own. He speaks of Paul's intuition of "the Spirit searching the deep things of God," and finds special significance in the question Jesus puts to the rich young ruler, "Why callest thou me good?"

Jung himself seems to live out of the power and significance of the text. One verse in particular that Jung found meaningful throughout his life is Job 5:18: "He wounds but he binds up; he smites, but his hands heal." Morton Kelsey tells us that at one particularly difficult time in Jung's life, he found the words of Isaiah 35:1 meaningful: "The wilderness and the dry land shall be glad; the desert shall rejoice and blossom." (1976, p. 1).

Jung's indebtedness to the text as a source of illumination for his own self-understanding is reflected in the words he inscribed on a stone marker near the family tomb in Küsnacht, a Latinized version of St. Paul's statement to the Corinthians: "Primus homo terrenus de terra; secundus homo coelestis de coelo." "The first man is of earth, a man of dust; the second man is heavenly, from above" (I Corinthians 15:47).

Beyond these explicit allusions to Scripture, it should be noted that in many respects Jung adopts what might be called a Biblical perspective on life. Truths and perceptions central to the Biblical world view occupy a central position in Jung's thought: a sense of the holy pervading all things; an appreciation of the wisdom of visions and dreams, myths and legends; an intuition of "divine" fortuitousness in the causal chain of daily events; a lively sense of personal vocation; a sensitivity to the paradoxical interplay between evil and the good; and an acknowledgement of the fact that where sin is great, grace can abound.

Jung knows Scripture. He mines its riches; and he understands its depths. It is no overstatement when he writes to a correspondent on February 8, 1957, "You can rest assured that having studied the Gospels for a lifetime (I am nearly 83!) I am pretty well acquainted with the foundations of our Christianity" (1975, p. 346).

Jung and Biblical Scholarship

Jung offers an aside in his Terry lectures at Yale in 1937 (perhaps inspired by the scholarly audience in New Haven) on a major shortcoming of Biblical scholarship. He observes: "Nor has the scientific criticism of the New Testament been very helpful in enhancing the divine character of the holy writings. It is also a fact that under the influence of a so-called scientific enlightenment great masses of educated people have either left the church or have become profoundly indifferent to it. If they were all dull rationalists or neurotic intellectuals the loss would not be regrettable. "But," he adds, "many of them are religious people, only incapable of agreeing with the actually existing forms of creed" (Jung 1938, par. 34).

Jung's critique of New Testament criticism, however, is not to be construed as a total repudiation of the achievements of Biblical scholarship over the past century and a half. To the contrary, Jung himself has been tutored in this vintage art and betrays an impressive familiarity with its fine points. He quotes the Fathers in Latin and Greek. He understands (and is critical of) the Bultmannian program of demythologization. He is, as noted earlier, in touch with key textual variants of the New Testament text and is easily at home with the technical jargon of the discipline, e.g., the phrase *hapax legomenon*.[4] Without exaggeration it can be said that Jung shows greater familiarity with Biblical scholarship, its methods and aims, than any of his peers in the field of psychology, past or present.

Jung's seasoned familiarity with Biblical criticism is evident in his response to a letter from Upton Sinclair, an American writer who asked Jung for an opinion on his new novel, A *Personal Jesus*. Sinclair's goal in the novel was to extract a portrait of the real, historical Jesus from the mythopoetic Jesus of the gospels. Referring to earlier attempts by Ernest Renan, David Strauss, and Albert Schweitzer to construct a "life of Jesus", Jung comments that such an enterprise focusing on "the personal Jesus" might "be convincing to a modern American mind," but that

> seen from the standpoint of a European scientist, your *modus procedendi* seems to be a bit too selective; . . . you exclude too many authentic statements for no other reason than that they do not fit in with your premises. They cannot be dismissed as mere interpolations.

Jung continues:

> We can learn from your book what a modern American writer thinks about Jesus . . . we can draw a portrait of Jesus that does not offend our rationalism, but it is done at the expense of our *loyalty* to the textual authority. As a matter of fact, *we can omit nothing* from the authentic text. We cannot create a true picture of Hermetic philosophy in the IVth century if we dismiss half of the *libelli* contained in the *Corpus Hermeticum*. The new Testament as it stands is the 'Corpus Christianum,' which is to be accepted as a whole or not at all. We can dismiss nothing that stands up to a reasonable philological critique. (1975, p. 88)

In the end, Jung wishes to disabuse Sinclair of the presumption that the Biblical text can be expected to provide a "rational" protrait of Jesus. With only slight overstatement, Jung writes, "The Gospels do not give, and do not even intend to give a biography of the Lord." Jung's stance comports well with more recent Biblical criticism that understands the primary function of the Gospels to be kerygmatic and didactic rather than biographical. Their goal is less to provide a portrait of Jesus than it is to testify to the Christological impact of Jesus on the faith, language, belief structures, and behavior patterns of first-century Christians. "We cannot unravel a rational story" from the Gospels, Jung tells us, because the story of the Gospel tells "of the life, fate, and effect of a God-man." To gain insight into such a text, it is necessary to go beyond the methods and assumptions of rationalistic, historicistic criticism, and to grapple with the fundamentally non-rational effect of the historical Jesus upon the earliest Christians, and further to become concerned with the congeries of stories, symbols, and images generated by that experience and eventually gathered as "gospel" (*ibid.*, pp. 89–90).

Thus, although Jung supports scientific criticism of Scripture for its rigor, he faults it for its fundamental misunderstanding of the nature and intention of the text. Commenting analogically on the promulgation of the dogma of the Assumption in 1950 and the uncomprehending response to it both in the popular press and in the critical scholarly community, Jung contends that "arguments based on historical criticism will never do justice to the new dogma," because they are "out of touch with the tremendous archetypal happenings in the psyche of the individual and the masses" that provide what Jung identifies as the psychological occasion or "need" for such a dogma. Here, as in his attitude toward scripture, Jung maintains that an exclusively historical-critical approach renders the interpreter out of touch with the "tremendous archetypal happenings" in the psyche that generated Scripture in the first place, and that continue to provide the need in its readers to attend to its stories and its "word."

Jung anticipates a breed of Biblical scholars who will not be content with studying Scripture (or dogma) simply as history or literature, but who will reflect on it as part of a psychic or soulful process. That is, they will study Scripture as a constellation of legends and genealogies, laws and apocalypses, parables and proverbs, epistles and gospels, psalms and prophetic utterances, that in the first place appeared in written form because of their archetypal significance for the scriptural authors and their communities, and that in the second place continued to be preserved and read because of their archetypal significance for the readers and their communities, in both instances in a manner and following habits of the psyche unperceived and unacknowledged by the Biblical critic whose method is limited to historical-literary inquiry alone.

What is the Bible for Jung?

In *Answer to Job*, published in 1952, Jung offers a glimpse of his understanding of the nature and purpose of Scripture. Referring to a passage in Tertullian that speaks of the soul as "mistress" of God and "diviner for men," Jung ventures the following proposition: "I would go a step further and say that the statements made in the Holy Scriptures are also utterances of the soul." He spells out the implications of this statement for a psychological understanding of the Bible as follows:

Religious statements are psychic confessions which in the last resort are based on unconscious, i.e., on transcendental processes. These processes are not accessible to physical perception but demonstrate their existence through the confessions of the psyche. . . . Whenever we speak of religious contents we move in a world of images that point to something ineffable. We do not know how clear or unclear these images, metaphors, and concepts are in respect of their transcendental object. . . . I am also too well aware of how limited are our powers of conception. . . . But, although our whole world of religious ideas consists of anthropomorphic images that could never stand up to rational criticism, we should never forget that they are based on numinous archetypes, i.e., on . . . [a] foundation which is unassailable by reason. We are dealing with psychic facts which logic can overlook but not eliminate. (1952, pars. 555–557)

For Jung, the subject matter of Scripture is fundamentally *numinous*; its *raison d'être* is rooted in the realm of the psycho-spiritual; and its main business is soul-making. It is with these objective qualities of Scripture in mind that Jung can speak to his scientific colleagues of the "divine character of the holy writings," drawing their attention not only to the special psycho-spiritual genre that Scripture represents, but also to the special hermeneutical approach this reality recommends. In Jung's judgment, the purpose of Scripture is not primarily to inform the mind, but, to borrow a phrase from D. H. Lawrence, "to change the blood."

Limits and Possibilities
for a Psychological Interpretation of Scripture

Although Jung was convinced that "to gain an understanding of religious matters, probably all that is left us today is the psychological approach," he was at the same time fully aware of what he called "a wrinkling of the nose at psychology" among certain clergymen (1975, p. 85). The resistance to "psychology" and things psychological is deep-seated in many clerical, theological, and religious academic circles, as Robin Scroggs, an American New Testament scholar, reports in reflecting on his "first foray into the use of psychoanalytic models for interpretation of the New Testament before a group of scholarly peers" (Scroggs 1982, p. 335). One of his peers later recounted, "The general reaction was that what was true was not new and what was new was not true." Scroggs cites a further experience in the home of a European elder statesman of New Testament studies. The conversation ended with the fiat, "Bultmann taught us years ago to be suspicious of psychology," a caveat I also recall from the lips of one of my own respected mentors, a Bultmann protégé, at Yale in the 1950's.

Jung is not surprised at the "wrinkling of the nose at psychology," whether among clergy or Biblical scholars. With characteristic insight he understands that "even a scientist [in this case, the Biblical scholar] is a human being. So it is natural for him, like others, to hate the things he cannot explain" (1964, p. 92). Jung also realizes the justifiable fear of *reductionism*, that is, the tendency on the part of some psychologists to re- duce the Biblical text to *nothing but* a psychological phenomenon, ruling out any transcendent reference. Jung warns against the abuse of reduction- ism in his essay "On the Relation of Analytical Psychology to Poetry":

> In the realm of religion . . . a psychological approach is permissible only in regard to the emotions and symbols which constitute the phenomenology of re- ligion, but which do not touch upon its essential nature. If the essence of reli- gion and art could be explained, then both of them would become mere subdi- visions of psychology. This is not to say that such violations of their nature have not been attempted. But those who are guilty of them obviously forget that a similar fate might easily befall psychology, since its intrinsic value and specific quality would be destroyed if it were regarded as a mere activity of the brain. (1922, par. 98)

Applying this observation to the psychological study of art, Jung warns, "Art by its very nature is not science, and science by its very nature is not art. . . . If a work of art is explained in the same way as a neurosis, then either the work of art is a neurosis or a neurosis is a work of art . . . ." In summary, Jung acknowledges that "psychology has only a modest contribu- tion to make toward a deeper understanding of the phenomena of life and is no nearer than its sister sciences to absolute knowledge." But, he would insist, it nevertheless has a contribution to make (*ibid.*, pars. 99–100).

Eight Jungian Challenges to Biblical Hermeneutics

What is the contribution that Jungian psychology can make to Bibli- cal interpretation? I would like to answer that in the form of eight chal- lenges that Jungian psychology issues to the Biblical interpreter.

1. The challenge to recognize the Biblical text as part of a psychic process. Above all, Jung challenges the Biblical scholar to recognize that the text is to be perceived not only as part of an historical, literary, social, and lin- guistic process, but also, and perhaps above all, as part of a psychic pro- cess in which unconscious as well as conscious factors are at work, not only in the Biblical author and his community, but in the psyche of the Biblical interpreter and his community as well. Such realization, even prior to spelling out its methodological implications, depends on the readi- ness of Biblical scholarship to take up the difficult task of thinking professionally and consciously about the nature, structure, and dynamics of the human psyche, and specifically about the unconscious dimension of the self. As Jung observes with respect to examining the unconscious element, "No matter how low anyone's opinion of the unconscious may be, he must concede that it is worth investigation; the unconscious is at least on the level with the louse, which, after all, enjoys the honest interest of the entomologist" (1964, p. 32).

2. *The challenge to recognize the meta-rational dimension of hermeneutics.* A second challenge to the Biblical interpreter, from the standpoint of Jungian psychology, is to come to conscious grips with the fact that the hermeneutical event engages not only the intellectual function of the human psyche, but the conative, intuitive, moral, spiritual, sensual, and affective functions as well; in other words, hermeneutics involves more than rationality.

The Biblical interpreter would do well to realize that the *thinking function*, for example, on which the Biblical interpreter has historically put most of his reliance, provides access to certain dimensions of Scripture but not to others. It allows him to comprehend the wisdom of the Proverbs; it sets him to working on a riddle; it helps him thread through a tortuous Rabbinic argument of Paul's; and it will support him in untangling and synchronizing the lists of the kings of Israel and Judah. But there are some truths in Scripture that will not yield to intellection alone.

Without the *sense function*, for example, one cannot "understand" the erotic elements in the Song of Solomon, the allusions to the starry heavens in the Psalms, nor the wine that gladdens the heart. Nor will the realities of the demoniac shrieking among the tombs, the image of three crosses on a hill, or the sparrow lying on the road come through apart from the "knowledge" provided by the experienced senses.

Without the *feeling function* one cannot "comprehend" the point of the prophet Nathan's confrontation of David nor Jesus' rebuke of the circle of men poised to stone an adulteress. And without the *intuitive function*, how can one begin to understand what has touched Isaiah's mind, as well as his lips, when he relates his vision and intones the words, "Holy, holy, holy"?

To fail to appreciate the range of psychological functions out of which an author writes and a reader interprets, is to fail to understand the galaxy of meanings Scripture has spawned and the variety of psychological types it addresses.

3. The challenge to recognize the symbolic polyvalence of the Biblical word.
A third challenge to the Biblical interpreter, aided by the work of structuralist and philosophical hermeneutics, is to rediscover the symbolic metier of the text. Jung saw this as one of his prime hermeneutical objectives, as noted in a letter to a friend in Basel in 1952. Jung writes:

> Recently an elderly Swiss clergyman wrote me a touching letter emphasizing that through my writings I had at last opened the way to the Bible for him. I certainly never expected that. But you can see from this that the figurative language of the Bible is not understood even by a clergyman. (1975, p. 84)

Jung challenges the Biblical scholar to recognize that meaning exceeds language, and that when we deal with scriptural vocabulary we are not dealing with univocal, unambiguous signs aimed at economy of meaning, but with polyvalent images redolent with meaning.

From Jung's standpoint, the language of Scripture has meanings that are fluid and depths that exceed the reach of simple linguistic analysis. Images that on the surface are homely and prosaic are held up to the light to disclose deeper truth. Beginning with the known, the Scriptural symbol invites contemplation of the unknown. And what Jung says about the Roman Catholic Church might also be said of the *corpus scriptorum sanctorum*, that it provides a galactic objectification of symbols representing the stages of the soul, the drama of the human condition and its encounters with the Holy, and it describes the process of individuation with an accuracy that defies simple discursive language.

4. The challenge to understand the archetypal life of Biblical images and stories. Jung would also challenge Biblical scholars to take note of scriptural motifs and figures that are *archetypal* in character, that is, as Walter Wink observes, they appear

> so frequently in widely scattered mythic traditions that we are justified in regarding . . . [them] as a standard component in spiritual development. The very pervasiveness of such stories . . . is evidence that we are dealing with something fundamental to the spiritual journey itself, and not merely with etiological legends invented to "explain the origin of things." (1978, p. 142)

If this is in fact the case, then one of the tasks for psychologically tutored critics will be to expand the already rich collection of comparative archeological, historical, and linguistic data that Biblical scholars have gathered in their lexicons and handbooks, with the addition of comparative mythological and symbolic data recorded in statuary and paintings as well as in texts and inscriptions and collected by anthropologists, myth-

ologists, and historians of religion, toward the end of enhancing our lexi-
cographic understanding of the range of potentiable values that a given
Biblical image can register in the human psyche. As John Dominic Crossan suggests, "The full study of a biblical text . . . will demand in the future as much use, for example, of James Pritchard's magisterial *Ancient
Near Eastern Texts and Pictures* as of Stith Thompson's equally magisterial
Motif Index of Folk-Literature," to which we would want to add, among
others, Erwin R. Goodenough's classical work on *Jewish Symbols in the
Greco-Roman Period* (Crossan 1977, p. 45; Goodenough 1953, p. 68).

As a footnote to the challenge issued to the Biblical scholar by archetypal psychology, two additional questions should be noted. The first has
to do with the puzzling fact of the archetypal attraction of sacred texts
themselves. Why is it that human cultures everywhere seem ineluctably
drawn to the veneration and cultic celebration of sacred texts? Rarely do
we find a gathered people without "scripture": the Quran, Torah, the New
Testament, the Book of Mormon, the sacred writings of the Zoroastrians,
the Mandaeans, Gnostics, and Alchemists, the Vedas, and the vast array
of Buddhist literature.

Why is it that some cultures, lacking *written* scripture, seem to have
"*oral* scripture," standardized versions of tribal tradition, lore, and teaching
passed on orally by priests, prophets, shamans, monks, and medicine men,
sometimes in a "sacred" but forgotten language the transmitters no longer
understand but continue to intone because of the "remembered" and felt
sanctity conveyed in the very utterance of the "text" beyond mere rational
understanding?

And what of the *iconographic* "texts," those at Chartes, for example,
or in the medieval *Biblia Pauperum* filled with pictures for the illiterate but
pious peasant, or in the paintings, stained-glass windows, and statuary in
cathedrals and country churches, temples, and even synagogues, that tell
the "sacred story"? The Biblical scholar might do well to ask himself, why
this fascination with the text? It persists not only among peasants, the pious, and the past, but among Biblical scholars themselves.

A second additional question touching on the challenge archetypal
psychology issues to the Biblical scholar has to do with the perplexing
phenomenon of the sudden and rapid spread of particular religious move-
ments at particular times in history, when other viable religious options
are readily available (e.g., the rapid spread of early Christianity from Jerusalem to Rome within two decades; Islam; the Sabbatai S'vi movement).

With respect to the example of early Christianity, Jung theorizes from the standpoint of archetypal psychology that

> Christ would never have made the impression he did on his followers if he had not expressed something that was alive and at work in their unconscious. Christianity itself would never have spread through the pagan world with such astonishing rapidity had its ideas not found an analogous psychic readiness to receive them. (1952, par. 713)

Whereas historical critics would attribute the rapid spread of early Christianity to historical, economic, political, and social factors, Jung would suggest that a dominant, if not preeminent factor is psychological, i.e., that the spread of Christianity was quintessentially an expression of events that transpired within the "souls" of individuals and communities in the form of latent or archetypal hopes, insights, visions, and expectations awakened, as it were, from a long slumber.

5. *The challenge to recognize the levels of meaning that a text can evoke in a reader.* A fifth challenge Jung presents to the Biblical scholar is to reclaim an understanding of the text recognized for centuries by the Stoics, the Rabbis, and the Church Fathers, but lost to historical-critical literalism. This challenge rests on a method Jung used to assist clients in understanding their dreams and the contents of their unconscious. It is called *active imagination.*

Active imagination is the process of using a mode of expression (e.g., painting, sketching, sculpting, dance, poetry) other than that suggested by the dream itself, to bring to concrete expression in a new and "insightful" form those associations or meanings that the dream may have evoked in the dreamer, and those kinds of "truths" the dream may be expressing. In doing a clay sculpture or a water-color painting while "actively" and consciously attempting to express an aspect of the dream not fully comprehended ("to see what's there"), the dreamer often will "crack the code" of the dream and uncover meanings of which he or she had been previously unaware.

Jung would agree that a text like the Bible has depths of meaning of which the author himself may have been unconscious. By the same token, the Biblical text touches on sides, aspects, and dimensions of the self that may not have been touched or awakened for a long time. One may in fact hear a word from Scripture and be moved by it, but not understand why one has been moved.

In looking at the text humanly and psychologically, so to speak, one looks at it with expectation of the many levels of meaning, intention, insight, and relevance to the various aspects of life that its voice and its word might hold. From this perspective, one does not come to the text expecting a simple, univocal message in words devoid of charm, fascination, or ambiguity; one comes to the text as one comes to a person, expecting to be addressed in ways one cannot entirely predict, and then walking away to sit by one's self to ponder what has been said, what has been meant, and what one has heard.

Active imagination appears at this point, where in response to the text one is moved to make a statement of one's own. If one has heard a *moral* message in the text, one may start a reform movement, a soup kitchen, or a social action discussion group. If one has heard a *literal-historical* report, one may set to work on writing a history of King Solomon's reign or the Mediterranean journeys of Paul. If one has heard a message that suddenly moves one to reverie and reflection on an experience in one's own life or that of one's family or people, one might write a novel, or make a painting to drive home the analogy between the time of the text and our times. And if one is inspired by the text to think new thoughts, to dream new dreams, to rise to new aspirations and aspire to new visions of possibility, purpose, and reality, then one might be moved to preach the most inspiring sermons in one's career, or write a musical composition like Handel's *Messiah*, or choreograph a dance, construct a liturgy—or one might simply fall to one's knees in adoration.

Jung's method of active imagination teaches us that the interpretation of the text is possible in more than one mode, because the text speaks at more than one level and the hearer speaks in many different kinds of tongues. Rabbinic tradition knew this. The Rabbinic fathers would take a text, hold it up to the light of moral, spiritual, and theological imagination, and view if from its various perspectives, observing as in a crystal the various hues and unsuspected colors that might radiate from it. Some of the light would illumine the conscience, some the soul, some the problems of everyday life, and some would supply insight into the origin and destiny of the human journey. One of their approaches they called *peshat*, "to make plain," focusing on the "letter" or literal meaning of the text. A second approach was called *remez* or "hint," fleshing out the allegorical or typological meaning. The third, *derash* (hence, "midrash"), used Hillel's seven interpretive rules to unpack the text; and a fourth method, *sod* or "secret," explored the sacred mysteries intuited in the cavernous context from which the text was sensed to have been born.

In a tradition rooted in Rabbinic exegesis, the "doctors of the Church," from Origen and Clement to Luther, Aquinas, and Albertus Magnus, all employed a fourfold mode of reading Scripture: the allegorical, the moral, the literal, and the anagogical (the "up-leading" or "uplifting"). History tells us the unhappy story that these interpretive modes in time were used in ways so outrageously removed from the intention of the text, and so uncontrolled, that a strong and eventually iron reaction set in against it, crystallized ironically both in the fundamentalist tradition (motivated by doctrinal concerns) and the Biblical-critical tradition (motivated by rationalistic concerns), holding that any meaning other than the "literal" (as defined by either of these camps) was untenable and foreign to the intention of the text.

However, with the help of perspectives like that of Jung's, we have reached a point where we recognize that a strictly literal approach to the text will not suffice, and that the meaning of text calls for amplification at many levels and in many forms, whether in stories, sermons, miracle plays, liturgies, cantatas, stained-glass windows, paintings, or statuary. Active imagination has been a function of Biblical hermeneutics for centuries. It is time for the Biblical critic to recognize consciously that this in fact is and should be the case.

6. *The challenge to develop professional sensitivity to the psychological dynamics at work in the text.* A sixth challenge Jungian psychology issues to the Biblical scholar is to take more seriously the task of identifying the psychological factors or dynamics at work in the content, structure, textual placement, or communal history of the text, whether myth or legend, court history or gospel story, psalm or wisdom saying, apocalyptic vision or epistle. It goes without saying that preparation for such an undertaking does not come easily. Developing sensitivity to the psychological dynamics within a text requires years of training, as many as a literary critic requires to become aware of telling nuances in morphology, style, syntax, and vocabulary in a text, or as many as the art critic requires to distinguish brush strokes and shades, schools and periods, styles and special motifs.

Despite the difficulty of training for the task (along with the perennial temptation to "psychologize," i.e., to interpret a phenomenon *only* in psychological terms and in terms of a single psychological model), it seems clear in terms of work already attempted both by trained psychologists with some knowledge of Scripture and by trained Scriptural scholars with some psychological training, that when a seasoned psychological observer trains his or her experienced eye on the text, fresh and illumining observations are forthcoming that the traditional exegete would never have noted—observations that identify psychological factors at work in the text even though they may have been given a name only in recent times (e.g., transference, projection, repression, suppression, rationalization, complexes, neurosis, compensatory behavior).[5] Most of the work to date has focused on psychological factors at work in specific Biblical stories or in the character structure of certain Biblical figures as they are depicted in the text. However, it is also possible to focus on psychological dynamics within the Scriptural tradition itself, identifying psychological forces that seem to be at work in the production and selection of certain books or motifs for inclusion in the developing canon.

One example of a psychological dynamic operating within Scriptural tradition would be the principle of *enantiodromia*, which Jung identified as the psychological tendency within an individual or community to seek to include within itself (or restore in itself) values that previously had gone unnoticed or excluded. The therapeutic function of this dynamic principle is to protect the individual or community from psychological, spiritual, intellectual, or moral one-sidedness. Jung helps us to see how this principle has been at work in the development of the canon, and that Scripture is in effect a *complexio oppositorum*, a place, as it were, in which conflicting and compensatory perspectives have come to dwell and to be simultaneously entertained. Thus a priestly conservative parochialism is maintained in the same canon with a prophetic, reformative strain; the cultural narrowness of Ezra is paired with the universalism of Ruth and Jonah; and in the New Testament, the Jerusalem-centered church of James receives honors along with the Gentile-oriented church of Paul.

In her essay, "Image and Imago: Jung and the Study of Religion," Ann Ulanov makes a related point (1985 pp. 2–25). Noting that certain clusters of imagery turn up both in the Hebrew Scriptures and in the New Testament, she asks in a way that brings Jung's principle of *enantiodromia* to mind, "What made some of the New Testament authors take up some dominant Old Testament images and Christianize them, while omitting others. . . . This question," Ulanov contends, "does not exclude the valuable research into the literary and the contextual socio-political-economic situation" that current Biblical scholarship would be interested in, but it challenges the scholar to add to his reaearch an inquiry "into the images themselves—their archetypal bases and autonomous propensity to undergo transformation to new levels of differentiation in the human psyche under the influence of Christianity" as they are transmitted from one psychological quarter to another within the Judaeo-Christian tradition and within the pages of Scripture (1985, p. 16).

7. *The challenge to apply psychological insight to the phenomenology of religious experience in the Bible.* Jung also challenges Biblical hermeneutics to come to an understanding of the phenomenology of Biblical religion from the standpoint of analytical psychology, that is, to look with more than linquistic interest at the profound human experiences housed in the "key words" of the Bible: sin, guilt, grace, forgiveness, *enthousiasmos*, inspiration, conversion, glossolalia, visions, and dreams, not to mention the key developmental concepts in Scripture of growth in faith or the moral life. A psychological approach to Scripture promises to put existential meat on the theological bones of Biblical religious language, rescuing it from being mere technical indicators of antique religious experiences, to become symbols of profound psycho-spiritual reality available to humankind everywhere.

One might make special mention of the phenomenon of Biblical dreams which (until recently in modern Biblical criticism) represented a phenomenon totally foreign to the historical interests of the Biblical scholar. Dreams were effectively relegated by Biblical scholarship to the same mythic limbo in which the lurid images of Ezekiel or the Apocalypse were kept, the reporting of which one would never take seriously as evidence of anything but the uncontrolled imagination of a pre-critical mentality. Morton Kelsey, among others, has led the way in urging the scholarly and pastoral communities to take a second look at these visionary dream materials in Scripture as phenomena worthy of serious hermeneutical and even historical attention, ranging from the "big dream" of Pharaoh (Genesis 41:1–8) in the Joseph saga, to the compensatory dreams of Peter and Paul in Acts 10:9–16 and 16:9.

8. *The challenge to study the effect of the Bible on individuals, communities, and cultures, past and present, as part of its history.* Finally, Jung challenges Biblical hermeneutics to analyze with greater precision the impact and effect of Scripture on the psyches and habits of its readers, individu-

ally and corporately, religiously and theologically, morally and culturally, socially and politically.

In his article "The Study of Religion and the Study of the Bible," Wilfred Cantwell Smith calls for a new generation of Biblical scholars specially bred to study the *Nachleben* or post-history (or "continuing history") of the text, identifying not only the forces that have produced Scripture, but also the forces that Scripture has unleashed, and commenting not only on Biblical origins but also on Biblical effects. Such study would entail a closer examination not only of what the text brings to the reader, but of what the reader is moved to bring to the text, and the social, religious, and political policies and institutions that have been erected on the exchange (Smith 1971).

In closing, one can hardly do better in the task of trying to summarize Jung's challenge to Biblical hermeneutics than to quote his words to a certain Frau Schmit-Lohner in a letter dated May 20, 1947:

Dear Frau Schmit-Lohner,

I think I can set your mind at rest in regard to your question whether the days of the gospel are numbered. People will read the gospel again and again and I myself read it again and again. But they will read it with much more profit if they have some insight into their own psyches. Blind are the eyes of anyone who does not know of his own heart, and I always recommend the application of a little psychology so that he can understand things like the gospel still better. (1973, p. 463)

Notes

1. The proposals in this paper represents an amplification of ideas suggested in my book, *Jung and the Bible* (1983), and my article, "Jung on Scripture and Hermeneutics: Retrospect and Prospect" (1985), pp. 81–94.

2. In his October 11, 1985, presentation on "Patriarchy in Transformation: Judaic, Christian, and Clinical Perspectives" (see Schwartz-Salant, pp. 41–71 in this issue) Nathan Schwartz-Salant observed that "Jung liked [*Answer to Job*] better than anything he wrote. In a letter to Aniela Jaffé he said if there is anything like the spirit grabbing one by the scruff of the neck and getting you to do something, it was in *Answer to Job*. It was the only book he was totally satisfied with."

3. Jung 1973, p. 65, referring to a textual variant at Luke 6:4.

4. Jung 1975, p. 75. The phrase means "mentioned only once," referring to a phrase or word that occurs one time only in a given text.

5. Note should be made of the original work of John Sanford, Morton Kelsey, Heinz Westman, Elizabeth Howes, Sheila Moon, and the New Testament scholar Walter Wink, all of whom have contributed substantially to an understanding of the dynamics of the Biblical story with insights from analytical psychology.

References

Crossan, J. D. 1977. Perspectives and methods in contemporary biblical criticism. *Biblical Research* 22:39–49.

Goodenough, E. R. 1953–68. *Jewish symbols in the Greco-Roman period*, vols. 1–13. New York: Pantheon.

Jung, C.G. 1922. On the relation of analytical psychology to poetry. In *Collected works*, 15:65–83. Princeton: Princeton University Press, 1966.

_____. 1938. *Psychology and religion*. In *Collected works*, 11:3–106. Princeton: Princeton University Press, 1958.

_____. 1952. *Answer to Job*. In *Collected works*, 11:357–470. Princeton: Princeton University Press, 1958.

_____. 1964. Approaching the unconscious. In *Man and his symbols*, M.-L. von Franz et al., eds., pp. 18–103. New York: Doubleday.

_____. 1973. C. G. *Jung letters*, vol. 1, 1906–1950. Princeton: Princeton University Press.

_____. 1975. C. G. *Jung letters*, vol. 2, 1951–1961. Princeton: Princeton University Press.

Kelsey, M. 1976. A little child shall lead them. *The Pecos Benedictine*.

Pritchard, J. 1958. *The ancient Near East: An anthology of texts and pictures*. Princeton: Princeton University Press.

Rollins, W. G. 1983. *Jung and the Bible*. Atlanta: John Knox Press.

_____. 1985. Jung on scripture and hermeneutics: Retrospect and prospect. In L. II. Martin and J. Goss, eds., *Essays on Jung and the study of religion*. New York: University Press of America.

Scroggs, R. 1982. Psychology as a tool to interpret the text. *Christian Century*, March 24.

Smith, W. C. 1971. The study of religion and the study of the Bible. *Journal of the American Academy of Religion* 39:131–40.

Thompson, S. 1955–58. *Motif index of folk literature.* Bloomington: Indiana University Press.

Wink, W. 1978. On wrestling with God: Using psychological insights in Biblical study. *Religion in Life* 47:136–47.

Ulanov, A. B. 1985. Image and imago: Jung and the study of religion. In *Essays on Jung and the study of religion*. L. H. Martin and J. Goss, eds. New York: University Press of America.

The Church as Crucible for Transformation

William L. Dols, Jr.

The best kept secret in contemporary church life is a passionate religious yearning hidden within those who sit passively in the pews. It remains concealed because a serious longing for The Word among the words threatens authorities friendly as well as alien to the church. Many ordained and lay leaders of the institutions who share this desire for a deep religious experience assume a burden of orthodoxy that inhibits attempts to search beneath traditional definitions of The Faith. Critical observers of the church are threatened by the likelihood of having to relinquish fond assumptions about the repressive nature of the institution and the regressive quality of its members. The secret, however, is leaking out. The increased restlessness in the churches is spawning a growing number of brave church-goers willing to sacrifice the silence in return for a parish church that may be experienced as a crucible for transformation.

There are those in the pew who desire more than the security provided by the traditional collective. They seek, instead, a transformation of their lives and renewal of all life on the planet. Even if you agree with that general assumption, you may not agree that such an experience is possible within the institutional church—not that it happens all the time, not that it is frequently encouraged, but that it is *possible*. I assert that a parish church can, on occasion, be a crucible in which the prima materia of Christian lives may be transformed into something precious and new.

My interest in the subject arises out of twenty-five years as a parish priest in congregations of the Episcopal Church in Maryland, eastern North Carolina, and northern Virginia. In the discussion that follows, it is important to be mindful of the historic uniqueness of the Episcopal Church. On the one hand, it seeks to be informed by the symbolic and sacramental mysterium of a Catholic heritage, but without the attendant dogmatism. On the other hand, there abides a Protestant longing for truth based upon Scripture, but without the radical iconoclasm and extreme rationalism. What follows is influenced by important work in which I share, done at the Guild for Psychological Studies in San Francisco, as well as my work in a doctoral program at the Graduate Theological Union and the Universiy of California at Berkeley.

Jung's search, like those of countless others, is testimony to the fact that "it is not the prerogative of the Christian church to bring about psychic transformations, but . . . behind the church there is a living primordial image which . . . is capable of enforcing them" (Jung 1917, par. 176). I suggest that the church can be a place to confront these living primordial images in a life-transforming process, and can serve as a "powerful instrument" to do more than "keep the great masses more or less right in the head" (Jung 1973, p. 494).

> [T]he church is simply the latest, and specifically Western, form of an instinctive striving . . . as old as mankind itself. . . . It is a striving . . . found in varied forms among all primitive peoples who are in any ways developed and have not yet become degenerate: I mean the institution or rite of initiation into manhood. (Jung 1928, par. 271)

Though Jung himself did not experience the church in this way, I am of the opinion that the institutional church can be a crucible for transformation that initiates one into personhood.

Dourley describes a process in which

> Christian symbols would no longer be understood as foreign or "revealed" pieces of information about divine realms and realities wholly beyond the human, nor as referents to discrete historical instruments of the divine into human affairs separated from the present by space and time. Rather they could be experienced as expressions of the deepest rhythms and movements of psychic and spiritual life, enabling the individual more easily to enter and more fully to be transformed by these rhythms. In this case the symbols and myths . . . would reveal the powers of transformation of those levels of psychic and spiritual life which transcend the ego, working to heal and make it whole in the here and now. (1984, p.8)

This revelation occurs when one is in touch with, informed, challenged, and guided by the primordial archetypal images of the Self in relationship to a committed ego. I maintain that the biblical text offers access to such archetypes, which are hidden in the evolution of church doctrine and are most readily encountered in liturgy. The critical difference between church as traditional container of the psychic energy and church as crucible for transformation, with the latter engaging the archetypes, entails basic shifts in authority and attitudes.

I want to refresh your memory of that world of primordial images of the Self with the following account of the garden myth found in Genesis 3:1–13, 20–24:

> Now the serpent was more subtle than any other wild creature that the Lord God had made. He said to the woman, "Did God say, 'You shall not eat of any tree of the garden'?" And the woman said to the serpent, "We may eat of the fruit of the trees of the garden; but God said, 'You shall not eat of the fruit of the tree which is in the midst of the garden, neither shall you touch it, lest you die.'" But the serpent said to the woman, "You will not die. For God knows that when you eat of it your eyes will be opened, and you will be like God, knowing good and evil." So when the woman saw that the tree was good for food, and that it was a delight to the eyes, and that the tree was to be desired to make one wise, she took of its fruit and ate; and she also gave some to her husband, and he ate. Then the eyes of both were opened, and they knew that they were naked; and they sewed fig leaves together and made themselves aprons.
>
> And they heard the sound of the Lord God walking in the garden in the cool of the day, and the man and his wife hid themselves from the presence of the Lord God among the trees of the garden. But the Lord God called to the man, and said to him, "Where are you?" And he said, "I heard the sound of thee in the garden, and I was afraid, because I was naked; and I hid myself." He said, "Who told you that you were naked? Have you eaten of the tree of which I commanded you not to eat?" The man said, "The woman whom thou gavest to be with me, she gave me fruit of the tree, and I ate." Then the Lord God said to the woman, "What is this that you have done?" The woman said, "The serpent beguiled me, and I ate."

I propose three modes (or levels or stages or aspects) of involvement with such a sacred text. They surely overlap, they may or may not be sequential, and certainly they are not static.

In the first mode, images of the story are the objects of projection. What we recognize as inner mythical images of tree, Adam and Eve, serpent, and God are historicized and related to externally in a literal manner. As one would expect, the images grip, fascinate, intrigue, and bewilder, since linkage with what we know to be the archetypes is unconscious. The mythical account is mysterious and awesome, encouraging identification with the myth as personal outer history: Adam's sin is my own inherited sin, his guilt taints each of us from the womb, Eve personifies the evil female, and the wrath of God is justifiably visited upon the unredeemed. In Mode I the truth is external. It is lived from the outside and drawn inward as prescribed by the accepted authority, and a profession of belief in it is often required for membership in a church.

The second mode moves from projection to symbol. It differs from Mode I in that some relationship is established with the mysterious inner. The purpose, however, is to comprehend rather than to encounter. In Mode II, the story is a mixture of the mythic and the historic. Consciousness is growing, and the bewilderment resulting from the projections is diminished. Fascination and numinosity are sacrificed in the search for meaning: rather than identifying with images, the response is to develop insight. Images remain largely external; they become the religious data that produce doctrine and dogma. As understood through Mode II relatedness, the story now instructs rather than intrigues. It provides lessons that may, indeed, be theologically and psychologically sophisticated. It is not that in Adam I sinned or that I bear his guilt, but now, in the spirit of Protestant enlightenment, I understand the nature of guilt and how consciousness evolves. For instance, the literal fall downward into sin is now seen as a psychological fall upward into consciousness. The end is a highly honored kind of wisdom, but it is not *sophia*. It is the one-sided kind of cognition that led EST guru Werner Erhard to comment that "understanding is the booby prize." Even though some inner authority is developing at this point, the attitude remains that of the outer informing the passive inner, as it is in Mode I.

The third mode is engagement, wherein the encounter is with what Jacob Needleman calls "a metaphor of life" (1980, p. 80) before (or after) it has evolved (or regressed) into a symbolic expression that is too easily divorced from the inner reality. The images constellate and arouse the archetypes of the Self. Wayne Rollins (see pp. 107–25) referred to them as "catalytic agents"; as they are encountered inwardly, the ego-Self axis shifts, and new energy is born in the psyche. The images are more than a hook for projections or a source of insight. The engagement of image and archetype reflect the mystery beneath Catholic numinosity in Mode I: There is awareness that on the other side, there will be some "Protestant" meaning, i.e., the goal of Mode II will be reached. However, the purpose of the experience is neither to analyze nor to define. The purpose is to be enlivened, rather than to be enlightened. In Mode III the myth is known within. It grows out of the creative matrix of the Self that I call the immanent God, in whom are found the rhythms of life. It may be that Mode III cannot be reached until one has been cured of what Jung calls "a systematic blindness . . . the prejudice that God is outside man" (1937, par. 100).

Emily Dickinson describes Mode III:

> The Bees—became as Butterflies—
> The Butterflies—as Swans—
> Approached—and spurned the narrow Grass—
> And just the meanest Tunes
>
> That Nature murmured to herself
> To keep herself in cheer—
> I took for Giants—practicing
> Titanic Opera—
>
> I could not have defined the change—
> Conversion of the Mind
> Like Sanctifying in the Soul—
> Is witnessed—not explained—
> 'Twas a Divine Insanity. (1957, p. 291)

The three modes of relatedness can be applied to the interpretation of dreams. In Mode I, dreams are mysterious omens from the outer realms of the angels and demons. In Mode II they are owned, written down, and their meaning pondered. In Mode III dreams are engaged, met, and allowed to enter into dialogue with the ego. My assumption is that the creation story of Genesis is a great dream in the psyche of Western people.

Isak Dinesen writes:

> For we have in the dream forsaken our allegiance to the organizing, controlling and rectifying forces of the world, the Universal Conscience. We have sworn fealty to the wild, incalculable, creative forces, the Imagination of the Universe. (1961, p. 110)

G. Van der Leeuw states:

> The myth is not reflective contemplation, but actuality. . . . It is the reiterated presentation of some event replete with power. . . . [It] . . . recalls some powerful event . . . [and] . . . by bestowing form the mythical utterance becomes decisive. It does not kill, like the concept that abstracts from life, but calls forth life, and thus constitutes the most extreme antithesis conceivable to pure theory. (1938, p. 413)

In order to realize their powers of transformation, biblical images as collective symbol must work deep within the core of the Self, rather than function merely as the object of reflective contemplation. It is not recollection of a powerful event; rather, it is *present* and evokes the fantastic archetype in a form that Van de Leeuw calls "decisive." When engaged it is too power-filled to discount or ignore, and requires decision and choice.

To be gripped by the garden story inwardly, rather than to be enlightened by it outwardly, is to know what Martin Buber meant by "our exile from the center." It is to sense the "Cosmic" or "World tree" that Eliade calls "the symbolism of the Center" (1952, p. 45). This familiar image in every religious tradition, and thus by implication embedded in the psyche of the human being, becomes "eternal: it happens now and always, and operates as a type" (1938, p. 414). Hurwitz refers to the medieval "correspondence theory" in which there is a constant reciprocal relationship between inner and outer (1954, p. 4). Egypt, the deliverance, wilderness wanderings, crossing Jordan are seen as historic events, but neither primarily nor exclusively as such. They take on their true meaning only as they are appropriated as an inner drama—a personal, eternal truth, activated and informed by the collective symbols.

The metaphor experienced as inner drama begins as we (not Adam and Eve, and not everyone) stand east of Eden at the garden gate. It is the ego come to itself in a far country, longing for home that is Self. It is, for Nikos Kazantzakis, "a great and merciless Cry . . . blowing through heaven and earth, and in our hearts and the heart of every living thing" (1965, p. 291). When the engagement occurs at the garden gate, the terrible choice of ego is to remain outside among the dead, or to move through a flaming sword that will inflict suffering and a different kind of dying on the way to life. The feeling of one standing at the gate, seeing the Tree in the distance, is, I think, what Jung identifies as:

> a loneliness that cannot be quenched by anything else. . . . That thing in you which should live, is alone; nobody touches it, nobody knows it, you yourself don't know it; but it keeps on stirring, it disturbs you, it makes you restless, and it gives you no peace. (1954, par. 632)

To manage the deep restlessness, Jung notes, Freud "had to invent a system to protect people, and himself . . . by putting a most depreciatory explanation upon these things, an explanation that always begins with 'nothing but'" (1954, par. 633). Freud, the Church, and Jung have good reason to be anxious and seek protection against such stirring of the unconscious. It is more than "nothing but"; once awakened, it will allow no peace. Each of us has stood there, known that moment of choice there before the inner gate—staring in the bathroom mirror, or alone in the kitchen at 3:00 a.m. — knowing that to enter the gate and meet the sword will require dismemberment, a chopping up and taking apart that is necessary before the new can be born.

It is when one "reaches the inmost depths," James Martineau writes, "remembering how short a time and he was not at all; how short a time, again, and he will not be here; opens his window and looks upon the night, how still its breath, how solemn its march, how ancient its forms" (1885, p. 213).

The words of T. S. Eliot echo the familiar moment:

> We shall not cease from exploration
> And the end of all our exploring
> Will be to arrive where we started
> And know the place for the first time.
> Through the unknown, remembered gate
> When the last of earth left to discover
> Is that which was the beginning. . . . (1930, p. 145)

Now we move from Hebrew scripture to Jesus. If the church is to be a crucible for transformation, the critical issue illustrated in the application of the three modes to the garden myth is central in terms of Jesus. Essentially, the process will challenge orthodoxy's 2000 years of Jesus Christology as savior, and confront the idea that the mythic dimension is only in him and is unavailable to anyone else. The elucidations of the historical-critical method of biblical scholarship and the insights of depth psychology are needed to explore the religious experience of Jesus and to face its implications for us. Mode III is unavailable without a bridge between both disciplines of enquiry, such as has been built in the pioneering work of Elizabeth Boyden Howes of the Guild for Psychological Studies.

My exploration of Jesus the Jew assumes that the *Genesis* creation story was also within his psyche, and that he had something akin to the experience that Eliot describes of arrival at the remembered gate in the Self. The primordial inner cry draws him to John, and his initial and seminal struggle involves the garden images and a way to return to the Tree of Life. Jesus lives the garden myth within himself in Mode III, and his stunning response to that engagement is his spiritual and physical passage through the flaming sword on his unique mythic journey.

The second biblical text I will discuss is from Mark 8:27–33:

> And Jesus went on with his disciples, to the villages of Caesarea Philippi; and on the way he asked his disciples, "Who do men say that I am?" And they told him, "John the Baptist; and others say, Eli'jah; and others one of the proph-

ets." And he asked them, "But who do you say that I am?" Peter answered
him, "You are the Christ." And he charged them to tell no one about him.

And he began to teach them that the Son of man must suffer many things, and
be rejected by the elders and the chief priests and the scribes, and be killed,
and after three days rise again. And he said this plainly. And Peter took him,
and began to rebuke him. But turning and seeing his disciples, he rebuked
Peter, and said, "Get behind me, Satan! For you are not on the side of God,
but of men."

I want to apply the three modes of relatedness to the Jesus text, as we did
with Genesis. Mode I experiences Jesus as the projection of the Christ archetype that we know as a representation of the image of every Self. As
Jesus the Christ, he is the mysterious but external human/divine one of orthodoxy, who grips and fascinates. Jesus is welcomed as the Christ, the
fulfillment of the historical messianic longing that persisted throughout
nearly 500 years of Jewish history. As the one to come who is now arrived, he carried power that is to be revered, feared, bargained for, and
manipulated.

In the Markan text is the account of Peter's identification of Jesus as
the Christ. I join with those scholars who believe that Jesus rebukes Peter,
commanding silence, as an indication that Peter's answer is off the mark.
Jesus scolds Peter, but in a way that neither accepts his projection (a
Mode I attitude) nor rejects it, sending him to seek another to serve that
purpose. Jesus' answer of neither yes nor no becomes important in his attempt to have Peter discover a messiah, but a different kind than ever before, i.e., an inner Christ as manifestation of the Self.

The Mode II perception is of the great man Jesus of Protestantism,
who is teacher and one to be emulated and imitated. In Mode II, we "understand" a great deal about Jesus. The Christ archetype projected on the
Catholic Jesus Christ goes unconscious, and the loss of an external absolv-
ing one leads to ever greater repression of the dark side. Once the saviour
aspect behind the Christ image is withdrawn from Jesus the good man, its
unconscious projection continues upon people, parties, and prejudices that
promise salvation.

In our text Jesus attempts to save Peter from this trap by not an-
swering "no" to his projection, and sending him away after another. The
projection upon him has been challenged. Jesus seeks to redefine the messianic role in terms of "son of man," but at the same time he wants to
keep it alive in Peter in hopes that Peter will yet encounter his own inner
messiah.

Mode III sees Jesus as the paradigm of one living responsively to the mythic messiah within himself—going through the gate and the flaming sword, empowered and enlivened by the Christ image hidden in the messianic longings of his people. In Mode III we discover the Christ, the messiah, the saving one within ourselves, just as Jesus did. What results is a new and radical kind of Christology, in touch with the divine rhythms of God as Jesus was, but heretical to orthodoxy.

Jung describes Mode III-type people as:

> people who, not satisfied with the dominants of conscious life, set forth— under cover and by devious paths, to their destruction or salvation—to seek direct experience of the eternal roots, and, following the lure of the restless unconscious psyche, find themselves in the wilderness where, like Jesus, they come up against the son of darkness. (1944b, par. 41)

"The reason why Jesus' words have such great suggestive power," Jung writes, "is that they express the symbolic truths which are rooted in the very structure of the human psyche" (1912, par. 335). This is what Jesus personifies in the committed life he lives in Mode III. I believe it was made possible by his awareness at the baptism of his connectedness to the transcendent God—the enlivening of his ego-Self axis in what Teilhard might have called a "sporting" new way. How this is a turning point in the evolution of humankind and in that of God, I leave unanswered.

John Middleton Murry writes:

> Nineteen hundred years of Christianity have left Jesus . . . in our bones. . . . If we try to push him out of our midst, he is busily at work in our instincts. Our duty is to get him out of our bones, and into our consciousness. (1929, p. 160)

The crucial alternative is between identification with the Jesus journey and consciousness of our own journey: the challenge is to ensure that what he was historically in terms of his mythic process not be substituted for the very same struggle that uniquely confronts us. The critical distinction is implicit in the words of Jim Pike, the late Episcopal Bishop of California: "[W]e are called to live our lives as authentically as Jesus lived his." We cannot live his life nor ape his response to his inner mythic urging, but we must do our own work to live our own peculiar destinies.

To meet Jesus in this way faces us abruptly with the confusion of myth and history. There is a tendency to historicize the myth, making it only about Jesus, and thus to rob us of the opportunity to engage within ourselves the same kind of mythic archetypes represented in him. There is a corresponding tendency to mythologize the historic, which categorically removes his journey from ours, putting him outside our experience. The inclination to historicize the myth can best be seen in the birth narratives and resurrection-appearance stories that present eternal mythic motifs such as virginal birthing and death-rebirth as unique Jesus experiences. The inclination to mythologize the historic is illustrated by a Christology of Jesus as a divine-human being whose very human mythic journey becomes separated from our experience.

The task is to become conscious of and engaged by these same mythic motifs, i.e., virginal birthing, death-rebirth, as well as by archetypes of the wounded healer, the messianic saving element—essentially the archetype of the Self as Christ image. The question is not whether the mythic archetypes are present and active, but whether or not we are conscious of them and how that awareness or lack of awareness affects our choices.

Jung describes "the eternal images," with their "archetypal power," as meant to "attract, to convince, to fascinate, and to overpower. They are created out of the primal stuff of revelation, and reflect the ever-unique experience of divinity. That is why they always give man a premonition of the divine." He adds that by "a comprehensive system of thought" bearing the authority of the church, "they always give man a premonition of the divine while at the same time safeguarding him from immediate experience of it" (1934, par. 11).

The church as crucible for transformation must do more than give assent. It must liberate the eternal images embedded in systems of thought, i.e., in doctrine. Rather than deny or angrily desert ancient doctrine, the church should seek to go beneath the "sacrosanct unintelligibility" (Jung 1942, par. 170) of the words to reach the energy that, when short-circuited, is experienced as alienation, guilt, longing, restlessness, and woundedness. The deep inner mythic motifs are disguised in that complex and rich tapestry of doctrine, the result of efforts to put into unambiguous words the inexpressible poetics of the religious journey. Taken seriously, doctrine is seen as part of an inevitable, natural, essential, and even sacred process by which church people can be guided to the heart of the Self as readily as one might follow the thread of daily projections in human relationships.

Doctrine is the hiding place of the longing for, necessity of, and experience of the mythic motifs within. What doctrine confines to words can be met in action in the liturgy. Ironically, it is at the heart of orthodoxy that the transformation implied in Mode III of my schema becomes a possibility. Although as Jung points out (1939, par. 903), orthodoxy cannot tolerate original experience, the church as crucible can. It happens in liturgy. As Jung observes: "The ritual is the cult performance of . . . basic psychological facts" (1954, par. 617).

Anthropology provides new insight (Turner 1969; VanGennep 1908) into the meaning of ritual as numinous world of the liminal—an in-between place and crack in time bordered on the one side by the ordinary and on the other by the holy, where outer and inner meet. The ritual is the waking avenue to the liminal world of unconscious archetypes. Surrounded by icons and objects of the sacred, with the careful and supportive guidance of the priest or shaman, the fabric and web of the sacred text is encountered.

Liturgy is the liminal anti-structure world of the symbolic. One is invited to share in the deconstruction of the symbolic universe (Berger and Luckmann 1967) and the reconstruction of a new reality. In apocalyptic New Testament symbology, this experience is reflected in images of the sun darkening and stars falling, a description of a liminal experience that grips us in ritual (Herzog 1984). It is the mysterious world of upside down, inside out, experienced as chaos. "We must not," Jung writes, "underestimate the devastating effect of getting lost in the chaos, even if we know that it is the *sine qua non* of any regeneration of the spirit and the personality" (1944a, par. 96).

Jesus accuses the dogmatic priests of the Jerusalem temple of being robbers. He refers to robbery of the possible encounter with the holy, and in its place the substitution of a safe, secure, predictable, rational, patriarchal, sacrifical system. Externalized mythic images discourage any engagement of the worshipper with the inner archetypes. They are explained, observed, and even venerated. So many church people are bored because an impervious shield safeguards them from the dangerous liminal experience of ritual, a shield held in place by well-meaning and dedicated priests who have lost touch with their own mythic dimension and any sense of the shamanistic task. The liminal experience is sacrificed to a super-enlightened, rationalistic, demythologizing theology that robs symbols of their power and even denies their capacity "to keep the masses more or less right in the head" (Jung 1973, p. 494).

Biblical texts, doctrine, and ritual pose the ultimate questions about inner psychological and outer social realities. The sad alternative to them being a part of a process of transformation is the security they provide in a

limited consciousness supported by collective definitions and norms anti-
thetical to change.

When, however, transformation is being effected, the encounter with
archetypes of the Self hidden in biblical texts, doctrine, and liturgy is

> always numinous, for it unites all aspects of totality. . . . But the action of the
> Holy Spirit does not meet us in the atmosphere of a normal, bourgeois (or pro-
> letarian!), sheltered, regular life, but only in the insecurity outside the human
> economy, in the infinite spaces where one is alone with *providentia Dei*. We
> must never forget that Christ was an innovator and revolutionary, executed
> with criminals. The reformers and great religious geniuses were heretics. It is
> there that you find the footprints of the Holy Spirit, and no one asks for him
> or receives him without having to pay a high price. (Jung 1955, par. 1539)

It is to such heretical activity within the crucible of the church that
we now turn. There is a high price that must be paid by the church if
there is to be any likelihood of this kind of transformation taking place.
The highest possible price would be paid by a church that demanded that
its postulants for ordination be consciously engaged by God on their own
mythic journey.

Years ago a good friend shocked me by suggesting that the first step
in seminary training should be at least one year of psychoanalysis, to enable the aspirant to priesthood to understand the urge to serve as priest.
It's a heretical idea, but not a bad idea. Today, however, I am more interested in the intersection of such personal complexes with an emerging
God of the Self. Seminarians need to recognize the process of projection
in human relationships, but, what is much more threatening, they must
learn to identify it in their attitudes towards Jesus and God. Ordinands
must discover this royal road to the unconscious in order to identify
and be able to follow those same threads leading to God that are woven
through biblical images, doctrine, and liturgy.

A comprehensive theological preparation for parish ministry would
include training in the skills needed to minister to people in each of the
three modes of relatedness to the sacred, and an appreciation of the oscil-
lation between the modes in both parishioner and priest. The parish curé
then has hopes of becoming a sacred precinct where healing is available,
as the psychological process of projection leads one to the indefinable God
beyond at the very center of the Self.

I do not know if theological education for the clergy is up to this . . .
or even whether the seminary is the appropriate starting place. Perhaps it

is a more likely possibility for some clergy who are ten, fifteen, or twenty years out of seminary, who are no longer sustained by a morning theology, but are moving into an afternoon theology. That is, the dominants that once nourished them are decaying. They experience increased restlessness from the center, and painful symptoms of depression, alcoholism, and marriage problems discounted as midlife crises, to be weathered or solved by sabbaticals, additional staff, or the call to a new parish. What is ignored is an archetypal shift occurring in the Self—a theological and psychological matter. For those who respond to such pleas for health originating in the Self, there is the surprise of meeting lay people who have been patiently biding their time. With two or three participants taking part in a bag-lunch bible study meeting or an early morning discussion group in the rector's office, the underground church of Mode III is born in the most ordinary and nondescript parish church.

Once the shift has been accomplished, the parish is experienced differently by the few. The high price paid by the church includes reordering priorities for the long list of tasks for the priest, such as preacher, teacher, and liturgist. Nothing will come of the new possibility unless lay people with whom the priest can be open and honest support and share in this initial movement.

To the degree that the shift takes place, a different kind of preaching evolves. Not new, it reclaims the old. A recovery of the power of the sacred text produces a style of sermon storytelling that is faithful to the unique biblical literary style that Auerbach identifies in *Mimesis* (1953). The preacher's task is no longer to embellish or flesh out or fill in the blanks of narratives because they are sparse; rather, seeing that they are precisely designed in that manner, the task is to draw the hearer into the intervals. A sermon of insight is supplanted by images that engage and enable the listener to find his or her own meaning. The dialogue between preacher and listener is replaced by one between listener and text (really Self in disguise, the immanent Thou). The preacher vacates the center and lets go of the impossible but jealously guarded mantle of authority to define meaning for the others.

After sitting through three hours of sermons by a guest preacher on Good Friday, an angry parishioner said to me at the door: "I already knew the story. I came here to find out what it *means*!" Now, years later, when I really know the story, not only with the head but in the heart, I say to myself that when I am engaged with the achetypes I will know the mean-

ing. Clergy need not so often fall into the trap of having to please by being that external authority waylaying honest seekers. It is not the job of
the clergy to give the meaning.

Robert Alter, the literary critic who teaches in Berkeley, suggests that
the dual but contradictory accounts of the creation of the female/feminine
in Genesis—the one telling of Adam and Eve created of the same likeness
and the other the rib affair—are no mistake. It is neither needless dupli-
cation nor stutter. Rather than determining the oldest or most authentic
account, the primary task of the exegete is instead to present both stories
simultaneously, just as the biblical editor linked them to express two ways
the feminine is experienced—as opposite but equivalent to the masculine
value, and as submissive and out of balance. The meaning and message is
discovered not by the preacher resolving the dilemma, but when such contradictory truths are held in tension and new meaning emerges at a third
point Alter terms "the intersection of the incompatibles" (1981, p. 154).
The archetypal images are enlivened in the Self, and the ego in dialogue
with them is energized and moved to choice concerning the same opposites encountered in the world.

A different kind of teaching evolves. The priest begins to sacrifice
the projection of being the one who knows, being that outer authority
whose apostolic responsibility is to explain, provide meaning, and give answers. The lay person also must sacrifice that same projection. For both
the task becomes infinitely more difficult. Augustine writes: "Go not outside, return into thyself: truth dwells in the inner man" (Jung 1973, p.
466). Priest and lay person become midwives for one another. The locus
shifts. No longer is there a passive waiting for revelation from the outside,
or the expectation that another is able to supply it.

A different kind of liturgy evolves. The priest sacrifices the security of
a worship that is predictable, safe, contained, manageable, and that costs
little in terms of time or energy. Priest and laity together create a different
kind of ritual that carefully encourages entrance into a liminal world
where archetype can speak to archetype—an experience of sacred images
engaging the immanent holy at the core of the Self. Since parishioners are
in all three modes of involvement and in movement between the three, a
variety of liturgical expressions is called for that affirms where people are,
but at the same time challenges their movement toward more consciousness and depth.

Touching the imagination in this way requires more planning and guidance if it is to unravel doctrine by identifying its projective quality. Liturgy should include more, not less, of traditional Catholic symbology, with diminished reliance on liturgical revisions in contemporary language. The problem is not semantic, but theological-psychological. The purpose of the liturgy is to convey, engage, and stir the mythic motifs that from the beginning has been at the heart of ritual. Drama, music, silence, movement, art, dance, and imaginal meditation become valuable means to that end. In a gap or pause in the Sunday service, there is an opportunity to limn a feeling or complete a sentence or write a brief dialogue between inner biblical figures on the back of the service leaflet.

The back of the service leaflet is blank because the former manic activities in the parish have ceased. This means that old ideas of community change also. *Being* starts to take precedence over *doing*, and new appreciation develops for the essential movement between the solitude of the Jesus "closet" and fellowship. With the psychotherapist, the congregation affirms in new ways that "the patient [parishioner] must be alone if he is to find out what it is that supports him when he can no longer support himself. Only this experience can give him an indestructible foundation" (Jung 1944, par. 32).

> As experience unfortunately shows, the inner man remains unchanged however much community he has. His environment cannot give as a gift something which he can win for himself only with effort and suffering. On the contrary, a favorable environment merely strengthens the dangerous tendency to expect everything from outside—a metamorphosis which external reality cannot provide . . . [when what is required is] a new process of self-reflection. (Jung 1957, par. 537)

One result of "a new process of self-reflection" that is possible in Mode III is a growing sense of inner authority that alters the nature of the community. Members place more value on assisting one another to become conscious of the religious nature of their projections rather than living into unconscious expectations of helping that often inhibit transformation by reinforcing feelings of impotence and neurotic dependency.

Because projections are honored, the attitude toward conflict changes. Painful conflicts about the ordination of women and Prayer Book revision and deciding about joining the Sanctuary movement and picking the color of the parish-house carpet are no longer seen as difficulties to get past so that we can be the church; rather, as Dittes suggests, they are "the church in the way" (1967). Conflict is baptized and welcomed as the occasion for consciousness and growth. There is a parallel to the blockage that Murray Stein suggests results in symptoms of neurosis in the individual. It may be that the corporate/congregational pathology that infects and sickens the entire process "is created by the patient's [parish's] incapacity to suffer the present conflict consciously . . . [and the] consequent unconsciousness of fantasies" (Stein 1985, p. 38). The great hymn by William Alexander Percy is frequently forgotten by the time the singer has walked from the sanctuary to the parish hall for the coffee hour:

> The peace of God, it is no peace,
> But strife closed in the sod.
> Yet, brothers, pray for but one thing—
> The marvelous peace of God. (1924)

Management skills adapted from business school seminars are not used simply to get the organization running smoothly; they can also provide tools with which to explore conflict and identify the violence being done among community members. The congregation becomes a laboratory—a loving, supportive, testing, pushing, consciousness-seeking place. Being aware of such projections, and honoring them within the collective in a Mode III attitude, are ways of going through the gate and finding new life on the other side of the dismembering sword. It requires the sacrifice of some old ideas of a soft and easy community.

My concentration on the role of priest comes from personal and professional bias, but it is also born of the conviction that despite the current emphasis on "the ministry of the laity," nothing changes in the church until the priest changes. The others have learned to wait, or they simply leave. Ultimately what I have described is the healing of the priest-person. Only as this healing takes place can the collective be renewed and become a place of healing. The wound to be addressed is deep within the psyche of the priest where, in Guggenbuhl-Craig's terms, the archetypes have been split and a terrible price has been paid for the unconscious one-sidedness (1971). It is incumbent upon the priest to reclaim the shadow side that longs for absolution—an inner penitent who is so often projected out and identified with the parishioner. Ardent ministering to the penitent parishioner is what is so desperately needed by the priest's own repressed penitent.

Part of the high cost of restoring the split archetype is having to contend with and finally sacrifice a kind of egocentricity that becomes horrendously inflated when one is trained for and lives out the priestly role in the church. No one gets far in the ordination process until the institution is assured that one has been "called." The illness born of that feeling of being special is reinforced by seminary, parish, and even family until, from deep within, God's wrath erupts. The cry is to come to Self and return home to reality and healing. Only when the priest-person experiences transformation can a call by God be discerned in a new way as a call to a deeper ministry. The split archetype of priest and penitent-within is united; this facilitates in others an inclination to withdraw projection of the priest-absolver back into themselves and thus introduce the penitent within themselves to the priest-absolver hidden in their shadow, which was previously projected out onto the ordained one.

Such a redefinition of priesthood in both priest and lay person does not happen by changing titles or learning more or moving the sanctuary furniture or building a new cathedral. It happens inside. When it does, people have the vision and power to change the world, for the goal is not to renew or save the church—the agenda is the human soul and even life on this planet. I think the stakes are that high. The choice remains ours. I am reminded of the Gospel of Thomas:

> If you bring forth that within yourselves, that which you have will save you. If you do not have that within yourselves, that which you do not have within you will kill you. (Guillaumont 1959, p. 40)

Such is the high price in heretical activity if the church is to be a crucible for transformation. It will most often happen off in a corner of the collective, out of the mainstream, in unexpected places among unlikely people. When it occurs, the church becomes a different kind of home, and things that used to be crucial aren't any more, and some essentials get overlooked. Knowing less becomes more important than believing more. One of the highest costs of all is never really being completely in step again and forever feeling like an outsider. It is like being a heretic and wishing someone cared. Most people don't. Old temptations to regression persist but, finally, there is no going back. It is never the same again.

In his novel, A Chain Of Voices, the South African writer Andre Brink speaks of archetypal images within a different tradition from ours, but a tradition that embraces the same mythic motifs of death and rebirth, of woundedness and healing, of the search for a messianic one, of the birthing of the new. He speaks of the madness of the liminal, of life lived at the level of engagement from the inside out.

The story takes place in South Africa 100 years ago—or this morning. The people are them, or any one of us in exile. It is about the gate, the sword, the Jesus path back to The Tree—transformation through analysis and even in the church.

A wise old black woman speaks:

> There is one kind of lightning that one sees with one's eyes, the lightning that announces the storm which lays waste the wheat but which also brings forth new life to the earth for the next year's harvest. But there is another kind of lightning, invisible, and inside you, leaving its mark on your heart; it lies there waiting for years, curled up, as patient as the egg of the Lightning Bird in the darkness of the earth; and suddenly one day it breaks out to burn and scorch you inside, driving you into a madness until it has destroyed you; and only then, perhaps, can you be fertile again for a different kind of harvest. (1982, p. 439)

References

Alter, R. 1981. *The Art of Biblical Narrative*. New York: Basic Books.

Auerbach, E. 1953. *Mimesis*. Princeton: Princeton University Press.

Berger, P. and Luckmann, T. 1967. *The Social Construction of Reality*. Garden City, New York: Doubleday.

Brink, A. 1982. *A Chain of Voices*. New York: Penguin Books.

Dickinson, E. 1957. *The Complete Poems of Emily Dickinson*. T. H. Johnson, ed. Boston: Little, Brown and Co.

Dinesen, I. 1961. *Shadows on the Grass*. New York: Random House.

Dittes, J. 1967. *The Church in the Way*. New York: Scribners.

Dourley, J. 1984. *The Illness That We Are*. Toronto: Inner City Books.

Eliade, M. 1952. *Images and Symbols*. London: Harvill Press, 1961.

Eliot, T. S. 1930. *The Complete Poems and Plays*. New York: Harcourt, Brace, and Co.

Guggenbuhl-Craig, A. 1971. *Power in the Helping Professions*. Zurich: Spring Publications.

Guillaumont, A., Peuch, H.-Ch. et al. 1959. *The Gospel According to Thomas*. New York and Evanston: Harper & Row.

Herzog, W. R. 1984. Apocalyptic and the Historical Jesus. *Pacific Theological Review* 19/1:17–25.

Hurwitz, Siegm. 1954. The God Image in the Cabbala. *Spring*.

Jung, C. G. 1912. *Symbols of Transformation*. In *Collected Works*, vol. 5. Princeton: Princeton University Press, 1956.

—————. 1917. *On the Psychology of the Unconscious*. In *Collected Works*, vol. 7. Princeton: Princeton University Press, 1966.

—————. 1928. *The Significance of the Unconscious in Individual Education*. In *Collected Works*, vol. 17, Princeton: Princeton University Press, 1954.

—————. 1934. *Archetypes of the Collective Unconscious*. In *Collected Works*, vol. 9, pt. 1. Princeton: Princeton University Press, 1969.

—————. 1937. *Psychology and Religion*. In *Collected Works*, vol. 11. Princeton: Princeton University Press, 1969.

—————. 1939. *Forward to Suzuki's "Introduction to Zen Buddhism."* In *Collected Works*, vol. 11. Princeton: Princeton University Press, 1969.

—————. 1942. *A Psychological Approach to the Dogma of the Trinity*. In *Collected Works*, vol. 11. Princeton: Princeton University Press, 1969.

—————. 1944a. *Individual Dream Symbolism in Relation to Alchemy*. In *Collected Works*, vol. 12. Princeton: Princeton University Press, 1968.

_____. 1944b. *Introduction to the Religious and Psychological Problems of Alchemy.* In *Collected Works,* vol. 12. Princeton: Princeton University Press, 1968.

_____. 1954. *The Symbolic Life.* In *Collected Works,* vol. 18. Princeton: Princeton University Press, 1955.

_____. 1955. *Letter to Père Lachat.* In *Collected Works,* vol. 18. Princeton: Princeton University Press, 1955.

_____. 1957. *The Undiscovered Self.* In *Collected Works,* vol. 10. Princeton: Princeton University Press, 1970.

_____. 1973. *C.G. Jung Letters,* vol. 1. G. Adler and A. Jaffé, eds. Princeton: Princeton University Press.

Kazantzakis, N. 1965. *Report to Greco.* New York: Simon and Schuster.

Martineau, J. 1885. From quotation in *The Choice is Always Ours.* D. B. Phillips, E. B. Howes, and L. M. Nixon, eds. Wheaton, Ill.: Re-Quest Books, 1977.

Murry, J. M. 1929. *God.* New York and London: Harper Bros.

Needleman, J. 1980. *Lost Christianity.* Toronto: Bantam Books.

Percy, W. A. 1924. *The 1940 Hymnal.* New York: The Church Pension Fund.

Stein, M. 1985. *Jung's Treatment of Christianity.* Wilmette, Ill.: Chiron Publications.

Turner, V. 1969. *The Ritual Process.* Ithaca: Cornell University Press, 1977.

Van der Leeuw, G. 1938. *Religion in Essence and Manifestation,* vol. 2. Gloucester, Mass.: Peter Smith.

VanGennep, A. 1908. *The Rites of Passage.* Chicago: The University of Chicago Press, 1960.

Ritual Process, Initiation, and Contemporary Religion

Robert L. Moore

The untimely death of Victor Turner was a tragic loss, not just to his field of cultural anthropology, but to those of us in other fields who found his seminal work to be an increasingly important resource for revisioning fundamental approaches within and between disciplines. There is scarcely a single humanistic or social scientific field that has not been touched by the power of his mind and the breadth of his concerns. At the time of his death in December 1983 he was continuing to broaden and deepen his *processual symbolic analysis* in its scope and in its applications to the pluralistic, global challenges that face us on this troubled planet.[1]

I had the privilege for several years of being his collaborator in attempts to rethink the role of ritual process in human adaptation—especially for a postmodern, planetary culture. This collaboration, under the auspices of the Institute for Religion in an Age of Science, culminated in a conference held in Chicago to examine findings from disciplines ranging from neurobiology to theology as they illuminate the task of rethinking the role of ritual process and ritual leadership in our contemporary cultural context. In his keynote address at that conference, entitled "Body, Brain, and Culture" (Turner, 1983) Turner surprised his interdisciplinary audience by emphasizing the importance of Jung's theory of archetypes for understanding the relationship between human biology and the continuing human need for the experience of transformative ritual. At the time of his death, Turner and I were planning another conference, which was to focus on archetype and ritual in analysis and religion, emphasizing the radical nature of Jung's challenge to both psychotherapy and religious practice.

That elaboration of the archetypal basis for the necessity of transformative ritual process never came to fruition. The following reflections are an attempt to survey some of the insights that manifest when perspectives from Jungian analysis encounter Victor Turner's work on ritual process.

I. Protestantism, Modernization, and the Eclipse of Sacred Space

In a recent article in *The Christian Ministry* (1983), I reflected on the strange way in which theological education has lost the sense of ministry as uniquely *religious* leadership. I noted the way in which most seminaries now fail to draw on cultural anthropology and the history of religions for insights into what makes ministry unique among its cognate professions. I discussed the tendency to deemphasize symbolic forms, myth, and ritual, and the resultant growing hegemony of secularized models of ministry issuing either from the culture of professionalism or from Marxist pietism. Cut off from an understanding of the nature of *homo religiosus* and the archetypal foundation of religious leadership, ministry and theological education have suffered increasingly from an identity crisis of serious proportions. In that article I touched briefly on a number of issues that must be addressed if we are to recapture a vision of theological education as education for religious leadership. In this essay I have narrowed my focus to one significant issue through which we can see the importance of the archetypal basis of ritual process for contemporary religion: that of the importance of an understanding of sacred, transformative space for religious practice.

In this context the name of Mircea Eliade will immediately come to the reader's mind. Eliade's entire corpus of writings on the human religious experience is based on the central role played by his distinction between the sacred and the profane in the religious experience of archaic *homo religiosus*.[2] For Eliade, the key experience in archaic religious life was that of *the heterogeneity of space and time in religious experience*. Profane space and time was characterized by duration, disorientation, and deterioration. Sacred space and time, on the other hand, manifested an encounter with the eternal, the orienting center, and regeneration. Sacred space, in short, was the locus of regeneration, creativity, and transformation. The capacity to locate and utilize appropriately such transformative space was the special province of the religious leader in human culture.

In Eliade's view, modernization brought with it a fall for human culture, in that it marked a loss of the capacity to experience space and time as heterogeneous. In effect, *for moderns, all space and time is profane*—the experiences of space and time are homogeneous. This meant, for Eliade, that moderns living under the conditions of contemporary industrial culture and technical rationalism *could not have an experience of sacred space*.

It is easy to see why Eliade concluded that modernization had brought an end to people's ability to exerience sacred space. The iconoclastic influences of the Reformation were the beginnings of what has proven to be a sustained movement toward the depreciation of the importance of ritual process in religious life. With the impact of the Enlightenment and subsequent trends in secularization, this decline in understanding of and appreciation for the importance of ritual process and ritual leadership has continued. Today it is difficult to find either religious leaders or psychotherapists who have much of a grasp of the power of ritual process and the way in which the effectiveness of ministry and therapy depend upon the adequacy of ritual leadership.

In contemporary industrial culture, the human need for ritualization in many areas of life has not diminished. What has diminished, however, is the availability of knowledgeable "ritual elders" who understand the archetypal needs of humans for ritualization throughout the life cycle and who are prepared to respond competently and effectively by providing ritual leadership to those in need of it. Failures in ritual leadership in contemporary culture are manifested in many ways. Among the most important of these failures are inadequate provision for initiatory process in transition states, whether life-cycle based or precipitates of life crises; rituals of conflict resolution, both intrapersonal and interpersonal; and bonding rituals to facilitate species identification.

It is not difficult to discern the effects of inadequate attention to initiatory process. The archetype of initiation is constellated in these situations [see Table 1], but the psychosocial containment and leadership that are necessary components of effective initiatory process are absent. This social and cultural failure is having devastating results in our time. The increasing anomie that we observe among youth and young adults is a distressing case in point. We lack images of mature masculinity and femininity, and we seem to believe that development into mature adulthood "just happens." In our practice of analysis we see, day after day, the human tragedies that occur because we have not attended to the seriousness of the crisis in failed initiations which currently afflicts our culture. We discuss "midlife crises" without any genuine realization of the ritual dimensions in-

Table 1
The Archetype of Initiation

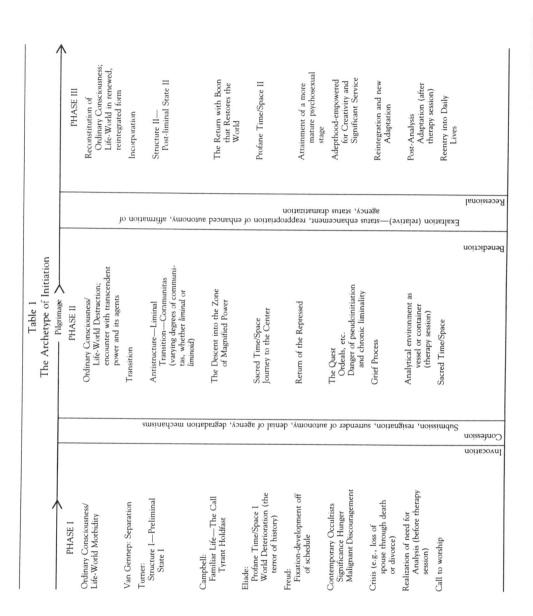

PHASE I	Invocation / Confession	PHASE II (Pilgrimage)	Benediction / Recessional	PHASE III
Ordinary Consciousness/Life-World Morbidity		Ordinary Consciousness/Life-World Destruction; encounter with transcendent power and its agents		Reconstitution of Ordinary Consciousness; Life-World in renewed, reintegrated form
Van Gennep: Separation		Transition		Incorporation
Turner: Structure 1—Preliminal State 1		Antistructure—Liminal Transition—Communitas (varying degrees of communitas, whether *liminal* or *liminoid*)		Structure II—Post-liminal State II
Campbell: Familiar Life—The Call / Tyrant Holdfast		The Descent into the Zone of Magnified Power		The Return with Boon that Restores the World
Eliade: Profane Time/Space I / World Deterioration (the terror of history)		Sacred Time/Space / Journey to the Center		Profane Time/Space II
Freud: Fixation-development off of schedule		Return of the Repressed		Attainment of a more mature psychosexual stage
Contemporary Occultists / Significance Hunger / Malignant Discouragement		The Quest / Ordeals, etc. / Danger of pseudoinitiation and chronic liminality		Adepthood-empowered for Creativity and Significant Service
Crisis (e.g., loss of spouse through death or divorce)		Grief Process		Reintegration and new Adaptation
Realization of need for Analysis (before therapy session)		Analytical environment as vessel or container (therapy session)		Post-Analysis Adaptation (after therapy session)
Call to worship		Sacred Time/Space		Reentry into Daily Lives

Confession band: Submission, resignation, surrender of autonomy, denial of agency, degradation mechanisms

Benediction band: Exaltation (relative)—status enhancement, reappropriation of enhanced autonomy, affirmation of agency, status dramatization volved in such critical junctures in life—and we usually view such crises as merely personal challenges to the individual involved. In fact, such crises are biosocial in nature. They invoke the archetype of initiation and demand by their very nature a response that can only be seen as social ritualization. When adequate ritual leadership is absent—as is usually the case in our culture—the individual seeks out partners in ritualization wherever they may be found.

In terms of conflict resolution, the magnitude of our crisis in ritual leadership is enormous. In tribal cultures ritual processes existed to deal with the potent emotional residues of intrapersonal, interpersonal, and intertribal conflicts. That which Jungian analysts call the shadow side of both individual and group life was honestly faced and processed through ritual means. While in premodern culture these ritual techniques were often brutal and involved the liberal use of scapegoating and other mechanisms based in intrapsychic splitting phenomena, they did, nevertheless, honestly address the seriousness and depth of the emotional problems issuing from the cauldron of human social existence.

Ritual techniques in tribal cultures were effective in maintaining and enhancing group identification and mediating conflict while reducing the residual toxic effects of the narcissistic rage elicited by such conflict. In our cultural context, the challenge is much greater and the ritual responses far less adequate. Cultural and religious pluralism in a planetary context complicate the structure and dynamics of conflict and call for a sophistication in ritualization which has not been forthcoming. Perhaps the most dangerous and least understood contemporary crisis in ritualization lies in the psychocultural dynamics that underlie the arms race and the nuclear posturing of the superpowers. In particular, Russia and the United States are currently in the grasp of an archetypally grounded, unconscious ritual dance organized around apocalyptic initiatory imagery and fueled by malignant, untransmuted narcissistic rage. No national leader, whether political or religious, has demonstrated any understanding of the ritual dimensions of the conflict—much less leadership in responding to the depth dimensions involved in it.

Finally, we must face the realities that the revolutions in technology have thrust upon us in collapsing social distance on the planet. The need for species identification and species bonding has never before been so critical. Those of us who have studied bonding dynamics in human culture and personality are certain that bonding and identification are complex ritual processes—*and that they do not occur without adequate ritualization.*

We are, therefore, faced with a situation in which the need for ritual leadership is greater than it has ever been before. Yet the culture of Protestantism and the subsequent modernization process has rendered us "ritually tone-deaf." We try to live as if—as Eliade supposed—moderns cannot locate and utilize transformative space. Jungian analysts often speak of the "heroic ego" that is characteristic of modern consciousness. This is a psychological way of talking about the view of consciousness and perception which is characteristic of the Enlightenment and modern culture. The perception of the Enlightenment ego is considered to be "immaculate perception," untainted by shadow dynamics and not requiring inquiry into the possible falsification of perception by the influence of deep structures unavailable to consciousness. The notion that time is homogeneous is acceptable because there is little sense of a need for the relativization of the ego, its dissolution and reconstitution, its death and rebirth through initiatory process. Since a fundamental transformation of consciousness is not believed to be needed, there is no awareness of any need for an understanding of the role of the heterogeneity of space in human transformation, both personal and social.

It is ironic that this same Enlightenment consciousness gave birth to two interpretive traditions, critical sociology and psychoanalysis, which have turned a revolutionary hermeneutics of suspicion on their predecessor. Both traditions have exposed and criticized the fantasy of immaculate perception and the atomistic, isolated individual ego. However, in recent years depth psychology has begun to recapture an awareness of the importance of ritualization in modern life. Psychoanalysis, and thus psychoanalytic psychotherapy, has gained much of its influence in contemporary life precisely because of psychoanalytic attention to depth ritual dimensions which religious communities and religious leaders no longer felt the need to address. I will discuss this further in analyzing the significance of the rise of pastoral counseling and psychotherapy within the specialized ministries of the contemporary church. Here I want to emphasize that the uncritical attitudes with regard to Enlightenment theories of change are presently being challenged at their foundation—in the naive theory of consciousness so characteristic of the modern mind.

II. The Archetype of Initiation
and the Necessity of Transformative Space

It is precisely here, in our understanding of how change takes place in human culture and personality, that we can see the critical importance of the eclipse of the understanding of sacred transformative space—the necessity of the heterogeneity of space in human transformation—in our contemporary cultural and religious situation. The culture of Protestantism and subsequent modernization gave rise to a dangerous naiveté with regard to the nature and dynamics of human consciousness. While the emphasis on the isolated individual psyche and the values of autonomy have had their positive impact in the humanization process, the heroic ego of modernity has proven to have a fatal flaw—a flaw grounded in its fantasy of mastery, control, unfalsified perception, and moral superiority. In theological terms, modern culture and consciousness have forgotten the truth embodied in traditional concepts of sin as bondage of the will and depravity of the mind. Given this view of an ego which is free of its biosocial matrix and which, once formed, is not in need of metamorphosis—and therefore has no need of ritual means of transformation—change is believed to occur primarily through education and realpolitik. World Wars I and II struck a blow at the naive acceptance of the validity of the consciousness of modernity. The inability of the modern mind to grasp the depth dimensions of the Holocaust, however, manifests the tenacity of the appeal of Enlightenment consciousness. The dragons that lurk beneath the repression barrier of modern consciousness are the same realities that archaic *homo religiosus* confronted honestly and dealt with via ritual technologies.

The legacy of Victor Turner is most important because of his challenge to Eliade's assumption that contemporary moderns cannot experience the heterogeneity of space, cannot experience deep initiatory process involving fundamental psychological and spiritual transformations. For Turner, *all* human cultures—preindustrial *and* contemporary—manifest a cultural metabolic process that includes experiences of the heterogeneity of space. It was his view that new ways could be found to facilitate experiences of *liminality* and *communitas* which are appropriate to and adequate for the challenges of a postmodern planetary culture. He was working on the development of this concept at the time of his death. By helping us to look again at the biocultural matrix of consciousness, at the ritual processes through which it is formed and transformed, he has helped us to realize some of the reasons why the optimistic vision of the progressive era in social thought has gone unrealized. The stark realities of the Holocaust and the threat of nuclear war become more comprehensible and yet more terrifying because of the humiliation of the heroic modern ego which results when we begin to see clearly the biocultural embeddedness of human consciousness. The ineffectiveness of modern theories of change based in education, persuasion, and political "enlightenment" becomes increasingly understandable as we realize the fundamental necessity for ritual leadership which can locate, consecrate, steward, and make use of transformative space in the task of changing personality and cultural systems.

Before we turn to an examination of the challenges that a rediscovery of initiatory process and ritual leadership will bring to contemporary ministry, let me first summarize some of the implications of Turner's *processual symbolic analysis* as they affect our understanding of how change occurs in human personality and culture. No approach to ministry or religious leadership can be understood without an awareness of how it takes into account the nature and dynamics of change in human psychocultural processes. To understand Turner, we must understand his view that in human personality and in culture, ongoing processes of structurization and destructurization, of construction and deconstruction, inevitably operate. These processes function through root metaphors and symbolic paradigms that are not arbitrarily fabricated but are grounded in the neurophysiology of the human organism. They are variously elaborated in symbolic forms in different cultures. Creativity and innovation are built into the very foundations of this psychocultural metabolic process. There is always a dialectic between *structure* and *communitas*, between structure and transformation in both personality and society. Like Eliade, Turner maintains that the fabric of human space/time is not homogenous, but is characterized in all cultures by heterogeneity. He distinguished between the social functions of *ceremonial* and deep transformative *ritual*. Ceremonial in human culture serves to confirm, consolidate, and legitimate the organization, values, and behaviors of existing *structure*. From a Jungian perspective, we might call this a "persona-restoring" process. Ritual, on the other hand, involves a process of deconstruction and reconstruction in a ritually contructed "space/time pod" or, as the British psychoanalyst D. W. Winnicott would put it, *holding environment.*[3] From a Jungian perspective, this process is constellated by the Self and is an expression of the archetype of initiation. Together, the Jungian and Turnerian perspectives enable us to see more clearly the integrated biosocial nature of transformative initiatory process and the role that sacred space plays in personal and social change.

It is here, in his understanding of the importance of transitional space in all human cultures, that Turner has given us his greatest gift. Unlike Eliade, he understood that such space/time pods can and do exist in contemporary culture. The ritual construction of such sacred space and its appropriate use are not mere vestiges of archaic religious forms, unrelated to and unimportant to more "real" secular psychosocial processes; rather, such transitional, transformative space is integral to *all* human personal and social transformation.

Turner has given us, for the first time, an elaborate phenomenology of the radically different human experience of space within the transformative vessel or container. His elaboration of the concepts of *structure*, *communitas*, *liminal*, and *liminoid* have given us conceptual tools through which we can discern the subtleties of the nature and dynamics of deep structural change in both personality and society.

Before turning to some of the implications of these theoretical perspectives for contemporary ministry and theological education, it is important that I elaborate further on the importance of *containment* during processes of deep change in human personality and society. The word *containment* is not Turner's, but is one that I use to describe the significance of *liminal space*, Turner's space/time pod. In my view, there is no more important issue that confronts those of us who are concerned with human transformation. *It is evident to me that apparent personal or social changes that occur outside a context of containment are usually, if not always, superficial in nature or abortive in consequences.* Deep structural change requires a reliable psychosocial *framing*, the facilitation of a *holding environment* that can help individuals and groups to tolerate the terrors of change, with its attendant painful truths and emotions. From an analytical point of view, we would say that outside of a holding environment the repressed can return, often issuing in destructive unconscious "acting-out" or irreversible fragmentation of the personality. In depth psychotherapy, however, the destructuring that occurs in truly liminal states is not fragmentation but rather a dissolution of inner organizations based on early structuring, which has maintained pathological dynamics in the personality. In the analytical holding environment, this deconstruction clears the way for an integrating, healing movement in the personality toward wholeness and consolidation.

We should emphasize here that parallel processes can and should occur at all levels of systems in our psychosocial life-world. Analysts did not need Turner to teach them about the *existence* of transformative space. We have needed his help, however, to deepen our understanding of the ritual processes involved in our work. We now can see that analysts are functioning in our culture as ritual elders for a small part of the population. More importantly, Turner has helped us to see how our work relates to dynamic processes in other settings and at the macrosystemic level of cultural metabolism. In other words, Turner's concepts have assisted us in locating and placing analytical theory and technique in the context of a more comprehensive theory of cultural and personality processes. Let us turn now to an examination of the significance of these ideas for contemporary ministry and theological education.

III. Ministry, Sacred Space, and Theological Education

It is difficult today to find clergy, theological educators, or seminarians who have any sense whatever of the depth dimensions of ministry as ritual leadership. This is not to say that many do not exercise fairly effective ritual leadership. Like many psychotherapists, however, many clergy are so uninformed as to the nature and dynamics of ritual process, transformative space, etc., that they would be insulted—or at least confused —if told that they were performing an important role as ritual elders. The decline of ritual (as Turner uses the term) is at least as complete in American churches and synagogues as it is anywhere else in our contemporary culture. One could hardly call what passes for worship in most American churches transformative space/time in a Turnerian sense. Liturgy in much contemporary worship more closely resembles what Turner called ceremonial.

There are many ways in which this assertion could be argued convincingly. Here, however, I will limit myself to pointing out one telling factor that illustrates this point. If transformative space is indeed constituted in a given setting, that which has been the source of conflict in a person or group is invited to appear in a context of containment. In effect, the repressed is invited to return. This is, of course, the intentionality behind the Christian understanding of the confessional; the decline of the confessional in Christian worship should be understood in this context. In Jungian terms we would say that Christian worship has become *persona restoring*, and not a place for the personal or congregational shadow to return, to be confronted, to be wrestled with in an intense and committed way.

It is ironic that the pastoral counseling and psychotherapy movement within the Christian community has been disparaged as being a secular deviant, too individualistic, and not really an integral part of the life of the church. As I noted above, we owe much of our current awareness of the depth dimensions of ritualization in personality and culture to the Freudian and Jungian psychoanalytic traditions. I have argued that psychotherapists and analysts of various schools are providing ritual leadership in more depth than many overtly "religious" leaders (Moore, 1983). The most significant aspect of the rise of specialized ministries in pastoral psychotherapy and counseling has been the return to the church of a capacity to offer healing ritualization through the provision of true "sanctuaries" where the personal and group shadow *can* manifest and be dealt with effectively—where deep structural transformations can occur. Pastoral psychotherapists are notorious for not being capable of articulating clearly why their ministry is in fact deeply religious in nature and central to the work of the church and its ministry. In recent positive developments, a few leading pastoral psychotherapists are now using Turner's conceptual framework to help them articulate effectively their understanding of the deep foundations of their ministry, which perviously they could only intuit. The pastoral counseling and psychotherapy movement has only just begun to grow and to take its place as an integral ministry of the church. We must welcome and facilitate this growth as a manifestation of one way in which the churches can respond to the need for ritual leadership in our culture.

In recent years those of us in theological education have witnessed an increasing depreciation of the ministry of counseling and more emphasis on the importance of the congregation as an entity in itself. The power of Turner's conceptuality lies in its capacity to help us see the dynamic internal relatedness between the counseling ministries and the congregation as a system in itself. It is interesting to note that, in spite of all the recent attention to the local church and congregational life, there has been very little progress at the theoretical level in understanding the foundational archetypal and religious dynamics that lie at the heart of congregational life. *We must ask foundational questions about the ritual significance of the congregation.* Should it serve, for example, as a holding environment in its own right?[4] Should it provide, both in its liturgical life and in other associational forms, the kind of sacred space that we have been describing in this essay? From my point of view, the congregation already serves as a sacred space—*without the leadership understanding the nature of the processes that are fundamental to the effectiveness of the congregation in the spiritual life of its members.* If we could become much more conscious of the ritual dynamics in the congregation, we could facilitate far better what Charles Winquist has called a *communion of possibility* within the local church. The congregation as "container" or "space/time pod" has many potentials for human transformation that remain untapped and await our creative revisioning of congregational life.

However, it is not merely life within the congregation which we must consider in the face of the current challenge to global religious leadership. I have noted above that in preindustrial culture, ritual techniques were used to resolve conflicts beyond the group—to negotiate intergroup conflict and to facilitate intergroup reconciliation. Certainly the task of confronting the destructive implications of pseudospeciation at the national and international level cannot be ignored. Do we have any examples of ritual leadership in social transformation that we can examine for evidence of how ritual leadership might provide alternatives to current trends in leadership in this area? It is instructive to reflect on the religious leadership of Martin Luther King, viewed as ritual leadership in *social initiatory process.* King did not reduce his leadership to moral posturing; he did not dehumanize those he wished to change by directing massive shadow projections onto them. Neither did he allow his leadership to deteriorate into one more expression of realpolitik. One can examine the dramatic forms of his leadership and tactics and interpret them as ritual leadership on a national scale. Through the power of his personality and *ritual genius,* he was able to turn the streets of racist cities into sacred geography, containing powerful emotions, allowing the social shadow to become manifest, and facilitating deep structural changes in the psyches of both his supporters and his opponents. Social structure was transformed in the same ritually created alchemical vessel that elicited these changes in psyche. King's role, then, was that of a *cultural innovator* in the Eriksonian sense and should be understood as having deep roots in psychocultural ritual process.

Scholars are only now beginning to examine King's leadership from an interpretive perspective similar to the one sketched here. It should be clear to us at this point that many social problems and social justice ministries need to be examined from this perspective. Take, for example, the problem of gang violence in urban life. Multidisciplinary studies of this phenomenon abound. None, however, addresses the significant initiatory role of gang life in the lives of many young Americans. The "belly of the beast"—the inner world of the American prison—is clearly one of the most powerful manifestations of sacred space in contemporary culture. Yet the stewards of that space—criminologists, wardens, guards, even prison chaplains—do not understand the nature of the space created by barbed wire and turreted walls. Since the stewards do not understand the space they have created, the initiatory process carried out inside leads only to pseudo-initiation and pushes its wards deeper into the underworld. Young men of promise *are* transformed into warriors, but since the larger society and its representatives do not understand the space/time pods they have created, these young warriors blindly turn their powerful energies against their own people rather than using them to confront the demonic realities of urban life.

We cannot, then, begin to fathom the tragedy of American urban life without facing the ways in which we fail to provide our youth with knowledgeable ritual leadership in initiatory process. Lacking this leadership, youth turn to those who cloak themselves in the trappings of ritual elders, but who in fact are the agents of chronic liminality. If religious leaders do not deepen their reflection to include these archetypal realities, then they will continue to function chiefly as ceremonial leaders in persona religion—and not as agents of significant social transformation. From this perspective, social action based on an Enlightenment theory of consciousness is doomed to failure because of its naiveté with regard to the requirements of transformative process.

In conclusion, it is time we faced the fact that contemporary theological education has failed and continues to fail miserably in the task of preparing seminarians for ritual leadership. Confronted with the task of re-visioning an approach to religious leadership appropriate for a 21st-century global village, most seminaries still function as if clergy have no need of preparation in cultural anthropology, history of religions, or archetypal psychology. Without the training in comparative symbology which these disciplines provide, clergy will continue to use the Judeo-Christian symbolic in a "tribal" way, contributing to pseudospeciation rather than making progress toward alleviating it. For the most part, theological educators have not made sufficient use of these resources for understanding ritual processes to be able to assist seminarians in understanding the depth dimensions of ritual process in ministry. I have argued in this essay that the most serious omission has been the neglect of the significance of the archetype of initiation and the necessity of the heterogeneity of space in human transformation. Neglecting the concept of transformative space and its role in a postmodern theory of change, seminarians can hardly be expected to see any depth relationships among their liturgical leadership, their pastoral counseling, and their activism in social-justice arenas. A serious encounter with the work of Victor Turner and contemporary Jungian psychology would go far toward enabling contemporary theological education to address the critical need for ritual leadership as we approach the 21st century.

Notes

1. The best introduction to Turner's work is his book, *The ritual process: Structure and anti-structure* (1969).

An earlier version of these reflections on the significance of Turner's work was my article, "Ministry, sacred space, and theological education: The legacy of Victor Turner" (1984a).

2. For an extensive discussion of the nature and dynamics of sacred space in the thought of Eliade and Turner, see my chapter, "Space and transformation in human experience" (1984b).

3. The influence of D. W. Winnicott has been a key factor in recent attention to the nature and dynamics of transformative space. See Davis and Wallbridge (1981).

4. I am indebted to Professor Sharon Parks of the Harvard Divinity School for her insights into the nature of the congregation as a holding environment.

References

Davis, M., and Wallbridge, D. 1981. *Boundary and space: An introduction to the work of D. W. Winnicott.* New York: Brunner/Mazel.

Moore, R. L. 1983. Contemporary psychotherapy as ritual process: An initial reconnaissance. *Zygon: Journal of Religion and Science* 18:283–94.

———. 1983. Ministry as religious leadership: Resource for a revisioning. *The Christian Ministry*, vol. 14, 5:8–10.

———. 1984a. Ministry, sacred space, and theological education: The legacy of Victor Turner. *Theological Education*, pp. 87–100.

———. 1984b. Space and transformation in human experience. In *Anthropology and the study of religion.* R. L. Moore and F. E. Reynolds, eds., pp. 126–43. Chicago: Center for the Scientific Study of Religion.

Turner, V. 1969. *The ritual process: Structure and anti-structure.* Ithaca: Cornell University Press.

———. 1983. Body, brain, and culture. *Zygon: Journal of Religion and Science* 18:221–45.

Womansoul:
A Feminine Corrective
to Christian Imagery

Julia Jewett

In a paper delivered to the Analytical Psychology Club of Los Angeles, Israeli analyst Dr. Rivkah Schaerf Kluger stated: "Looking into history, it is interesting to see that at times when religions are really alive, there are no theories about it" (p. 1). Today theories abound, but the focus of this exploration is the lived and living experience of women vis-à-vis images of the feminine aspect of the Divine. Theology has been defined as *reflection on the experience of God.* To stay relatively grounded in experience seems a particularly female way; it is the more male "logos" that has gotten lofty as *spirit* and *mind*, setting them in value over lived experience in body. As we know, that is one of the historical problems of the Church. This paper will look at women's dreams and meditative vision, linked to the process of development of the Feminine Self expressed archetypally in Grimms' tale, "The Girl Without Hands" (Manheim 1977, pp. 113–18).

This paper began with a piece of synchronicity. At a time when I was pondering the plight of the handless maiden, a woman brought me the gift of just such an image. She is a primitive Guatemalan statue of the Virgin, carved in wood, not quite a foot tall. She is an arresting presence, grotesquely beautiful, with hollow eye sockets and empty holes in her cape where her hands should be.

It is thought that her eyes were semiprecious stones and her hands ivory, and likely thieved for their value. This avaricious mutilation finds a parallel in Grimms' tale and evolves in a fourfold process of individuation.

A naive girl, living dependently in her father's poor home, is mistakenly given over to the devil in exchange for riches. The process once under way, her parents' belated awareness is insufficient to undo the pact with the devil. The girl ritually protects herself with water, by drawing the magic circle around herself against the evil one, and again by the purification of her own tears' bathing her hands. In a rage, the power of darkness orders that her hands be cut off, or her father must forfeit his own life. In the face of this choice her hands are sacrificed, but her profound outpouring of tears cleanses the remaining stumps, causing the dark one to lose all power over her.

She then leaves home and begins her journey, attended by positive archetypal forces. An angel aids her in entering a king's protected garden, where she is able to eat, directly from the tree, a pear which sustains her for one night. Discovering this "miracle," as described by the gardener, the king and his priest watch her on the second night. Finding her both beautiful and devout, the king weds her and has silver hands made for her.

In time, the king is called away to battle and leaves his bride to bear their child in the company of his mother. The joyous news is sent, but as the messenger naps, the devil replaces the message with one that names the child a changeling. Still, the king replies that his wife should be well cared for; but once again, while the messenger sleeps, the devil exchanges the letter with a false command that the wife and child be killed and her tongue and eyes preserved as proof of the deed. The king's mother, taking pity on the young woman, instead cuts out the tongue and eyes of a doe, and sends the queen and her child out into the world.

Once again on her own and faced with a wild forest, the queen prays to God. Again an angel appears and leads her to a small house; over the door is inscribed: "Here may all dwell freely." For seven years she remains in the company of the angel and, because of her devotion and through God's grace, her own hands grow back again. In time, the king appears, having learned the story of the multiple deceptions and vowed to find his wife and child. Finally, all are joyfully reunited.

Now what I want to suggest, first, is that the Church fathers have done to women something like what the miller in this story did to his daughter. In an attempt to mollify dark forces following the institutionalization of Christianity, the early Church fathers cut off the hands, tore out the eyes, and removed the tongues of women. That's pretty strong, and of course I am speaking metaphorically—although the Salem witch hunts are one remembrance of actual brutalities in the past. But the Church has been a chief contributor to the reality that women have been "dis-abled" to do their own creative work. It has caused us not to *see* who we are by removing most female images and sanitizing what remained; and it has removed our *tongues* by obliterating our history, by commanding that women be silent in church, and by refusing to ordain many.

The historical misuse of women by the patriarchy of whatever religious persuasion begins to find a corrective in broadening our scope to think archetypally in terms of the Feminine *principle* . . . to see images of women representing *soul, psyche, the movement of energy in body.* Just about all we have left in Christianity is the image of the Virgin. We need to bend our minds to think of the Virgin not as a person called Mary but as a representation of soul. We then see that soul is feminine, and that it is in the *soul* that the Christ, representative of love and human suffering, is conceived and both born and borne. In the Christian story Mary represents the human capacity to receive the divine spirit, and that is a *psychological* experience. *Psyche, soul,* is the place of incarnation. The Virgin is an *outer* representation of an *inner* reality. The stable, that representation of the most humble and ordinary of places, is each human's earthy body that becomes the dwelling place of soul, the resting place on the journey where miracles of divine and human interaction take place. Psyche permeates every cell of the body. I believe psyche and body are two images of the same reality, just as energy and matter transform back and forth to one another, just as light is seen as both a wave and a particle. My grandmother used to exclaim, "My soul and my body!" She was right; they go together.

We have a condition in the Church in which *soul, soul in body*, has been devalued in the interest of the dominance of the masculine energies of spirit and mind—of *logos*, of logical thinking, rational separations and sequences, of science and technology; and all of that in a proportion that currently threatens our world with catastrophe. Look what the removal of appreciation for the grounded body/psyche has done. For men have a soul, too, but it is all but gone from contemporary religion. Much of contemporary religious belief, doctrine, practice, seems to me to be sterile—pro forma. Churches too often seem to be (and there are always exceptions) sources of support for societal norms. The living Spirit brings change, and that is difficult for humans. In the religious publications, the chief issues are secular/political . . . or they are overly interested in people's sexuality and how they choose to express it . . . or there is nitpicking about who may bless or distribute or receive the sacraments, when the *real* tragedy is that hardly anyone is being fed in their souls by communion any more.

In the summer of 1985, on the south side of Chicago, at St. John of God Church, a statue of the Virgin Mary wept. The news articles calling the priest a charlatan may be true; but the statue weeps, and I weep with her. The people who have seen her weep may have projected their own souls' tears *upon* her, but there is no question that the soul of persons and of the human collectivity has reason to weep.

In the early centuries of institutional Christianity, every trace of prior religions which expressed devotion to images of a female divinity was obliterated. It took five hundred years, but the statues were tumbled until nothing remained. That was effective as a political move to gain control. The word *image* comes from the root word *imitate* . . . to imitate. And without an image to guide, to revere, to imitate, a person is much weakened. Jung has observed that the person who has the living symbol is the one who will be able to make the journey. Without a living symbol, without a representation of the Feminine Divine, a woman was lost. There has to be a *conjunctio*, a strengthening connection, in order for the individual not to stand alone. But there was no feminine image to have a connection to. And so the patriarchy with their masculine Jesus figure moved into dominance. And that means that mind and spirit took precedence over body and psyche. Such exclusive power can't have been what the man, Jesus had in mind! As far as we can tell, he spent most of his time outside the establishment; and, certainly, in the book of John, he points not to himself as the end-all, but rather to the event of Pentecost that would follow him—the time when each and every voice would be heard, when the spirit would dwell in each soul, and every voice would be understood and included.

Some of us have questioned the need for a gendered image of the archetype of the Self and of God. Some argue that it is absolutely necesary for such a figure to exist in order to create a transformative bridge between the individual person and God who encompasses all. Others prefer to speak of a variety of *energies*—why get caught in gendered figures, in anthropomorphic representations? Can't we transcend genitalia? But I am persuaded that, since we are human, we imagine in human physiological terms. Our souls speak to us in dream, active imagination, fantasy . . . *in images*. We need the image to make the bridge between the personal and that which is so much greater. A *concept* backed with an *image* is finally persuasive. The concepts of Christianity, backed with congruent images, have set up a world in which male dominance and male viewpoints are normative. But the psyches of women are now providing images that say otherwise.

Four dreams and a powerful meditative vision show the archetypal feminine at work:

> In the first dream, the dreamer entered the church of her childhood, a mainline Christian church. In a dim and cool room there were row upon row of what looked like cases of the kind one sees in jewelry stores: glass-topped wooden cases, locked against theft. The cases were filled with religious relics and were presided over by crippled men. The dreamer exited by a side door and found herself at the edge of a meadow which was bowl-shaped with sloping sides. As she stood there, all kinds of people—all ages, colors, sexes, styles—ran over the edges and down to the meadow. There they joined hands and danced a circle dance.

This is such a moving dream. The dreamer was her own age and also the child of no more than six who had attended that church. There is no rigid time/space in psyche! The cool, protected setting was devoted to hermetically sealed vestiges of the faith, overseen and guarded by *crippled* men. There was no life in the indoor setting. Outside the church, however, and really just adjacent to it, is where *life* is. We remember that Jung said psyche is *natural*. It is like nature, unfolding in its own time and also inexorable in its requirements. In the natural setting, every aspect of human life was included. All was represented there, and there were no value judgments or ranking. All held hands and danced in a circle, not climbing Jacob's ladder in hierarchical strata, but dancing Sarah's circle. In the church was exclusivity; next-door, outside, was sunshine and an inclusive modality. While there is no specific Goddess figure here, the natural inclusivity seems a very *female* model.

The second dream image is from a woman in seminary training. Deep into this very masculine enterprise, in a world of masculine interpretations, she had just this image and word:

> I am standing in an ordinary street when there is a SWEEP of color: green, purple, gold, go by in a whoosh! Then the message comes: "YOU ARE WORSHIPPING AT THE WRONG TEMPLE."

The dreamer knew about churches, but not about temples. Our forebears worshipped at temples. The Jewish people, whose history does honor the feminine with Old Testament figures such as Ruth, Naomi, and the Apocryphal Judith, also passes down its culture through the female who presides over Shabbat. But this dream figure was the *Shekinah*, or wisdom figure, an aspect/consort in the Divine Order. Anciently, there was Goddess worship, the Feminine Mysteries at Eleusis and other places. The colors in this dream were extraordinary. Those who have had visions specifically report the intensity of color and its other-worldliness. In this dream it seems that the Goddess emerged, in part as compensation for the over-development of the masculine, but also to claim her daughter—Demeter gone to seek Persephone, who had been hauled off to the netherland.

There is a good deal being written today about the emerging Feminine principle in the world. Books on the Goddess proliferate. But the greatest impact comes from the accumulating images being expressed through psyche. It needs to be noted that this sampling is simply representative of what appears to be a resurgence, in our culture, of an ancient archetypal reality. No matter how much is obliterated from consciousness and history, the archetype remains, ready for a renascence under certain conditions—chiefly, the compensation of a potentially one-sided point of view. The archetypes do set the pace, and our task is to discern what's afoot and try to get conscious about it.

The third dream is mine, and it arrived about five months after beginning a supervisory relationship with a woman whose style was indeed feminine: relational, collaborative, collegial. Too often this style is devalued, considered not rigorous, not confrontational. Our experience, and the assessment of more objective others, was that our separate work in counseling individuals became more fully human (Haight & Jewett).

> As the dream began, I was leaving the neighborhood of my childhood. I was driving the car, and my supervisor was the passenger. At the crest of a hill I saw that the road fell sharply downward and there were no guard rails or shoulder; however, the road was straight, and the car would stay on the road. As we proceeded, I saw that the road went between two opposite landscapes: on the left were woods and mountains, on the right water and beach. Then she and I, not in the car but on foot, were walking one on each side of a cart, pulling it up a path. In the cart sat an infant with a jewelled necklace; she is the Infant Goddess, or Feminine Self. My friend held up an orb, a small marble-like object with a DNA-serpentine scroll in it, and the words connected with this were "Matter is Time Unfolding." Also, there was an accompanying sense that humans were more relative, in the cosmic sense, than we care to believe.

In my childhood I was related to the natural universe; but natural as that relationship was, it also was unconscious. As this dream suggests, that starting place is acknowledged but is departed from, and (as in my life's experience) I risked travelling a road that descends between two opposite landscapes. I take this to mean that the journey requires that I travel a path that does not get caught in either the masculine principle (spirit, symbolized by mountains with their lofty heights) or the feminine (the unconscious, symbolized by the water), but cleave to a median line. The road then becomes an earthen path and my friend and I are on foot, pulling between us a cart with the Infant Goddess in it. This is such a grounded image, as earthy and ordinary as the infant Jesus being born in a stable; who would know that anything unusual is happening? But in fact, the collaborative nature of our work together had indeed brought forward in me a new psychological birth. Through the intimacy of mutual valuing and collaborative work, the deep Feminine was emerging to consciousness. My place in the universe, unconsciously assumed as a child, was being consciously regained.

Knowledge of archetypal rites and rituals sheds light on this image also: in countries where the Virgin is celebrated, her image is often pulled along in a religious procession, carried—in honor—in a cart. This is not an earth-shaking image, it seems—and yet it is. It was quite an event for me personally, and seems to be among those that Jung called "great dreams," having implications for the culture as well. The phrase "Matter is Time Unfolding" has many possibilities. But surely we can say that it has about it, at least, a real sense of the inevitability of the unfolding process of life. There is an inexorable quality to that reality, and that reality is basic to the Goddess, a primary quality of the Feminine Principle now appearing in the conscious life of the culture. The Goddess is a psychological reality: She is present in the life of psychologically mature women; *she is crucial to woman's Selfhood.* The dream's reminder that humans are relativized when placed in a cosmic scheme is, I think, a corrective to our current cultural overemphasis on ego. Our idea that if we could just process enough information we would gain control of things is simply overweening pride, and a *logos,* notion.

> In the fourth dream, the dreamer approached a park-like garden in the center of which stood a gazebo. In the gazebo an innocent girl with baby's-breath braided in her hair played a baroque organ. In contradistinction, above the organ hung a crucifix with the lifeless image of the Virgin superimposed. As the dreamer watched, the Virgin transformed into a living, crucified Virgin in a linen-like garb with blood spattered on it where her hands would have been. And she said to the dreamer, "Make Something."

This image and the command to make something have had a powerful impact on the dreamer. She now has that crucial factor, the living
symbol that will guide her and keep her on the path of individuation.
Some weeks earlier, in a meditation, this woman had had a vision of Jesus, garbed in exactly the same fabric that the Virgin wore in her dream.
Details of this sort need to be noticed, and are too often overlooked in
getting the general sense of the dream. In that meditation, as he stretched
out his arms to her, she had beaten on Jesus' chest, crying out, "Where is
your mother?" and "Why have you no sister?" Now, the curious thing is
that Joan Englesman, in her book *The Feminine Dimension of the Divine*,
describes the interchangeability of Sophia and Jesus in the early days of
Christianity. Jesus and Sophia were equivalent. Then, in forming their
Christology, the early Church fathers assimilated her characteristics to
Jesus, and the Christ figure then became exclusively masculine. The
dreamer did not consciously know that history, yet she had a handle on
the truth by clothing Jesus and the Virgin identically. They are inter-
changeable, and we do not have one without the other; one reality, two
guises.

Months later, the following amplification appeared in the Harvard
Divinity Bulletin, from a reprinted lecture by Rosemary Ruether (1986):

A third way of telling new stories plumbs the dimension of primary religious
experience which I would call "revelation." This way goes beyond simply re-
telling old stories through study and discussion. It assumes that revelation, in
the sense of primary religious vision, happens today and is not confined to
some privileged period of the past. In other words, the Holy Spirit is present
and is not simply the tool of historical institutional structures. Most of these
primary visions remain private, and only occasionally are they shared in such a
way as to take on the function of a communal paradigm that expresses a new
consciousness among a community that is being born. Religious feminism is
generating many new visions of this kind today, some of which are taking hold
as new communal pardigms.

One such new paradigm that is in the process of being born is the image of the
Christa, or the crucified woman. There has been a remarkable proliferation of
such images of crucified women as statues and paintings recently. Whenever
they have been publicized in the Christian community, a storm of hostile protest has risen. The usual argument is to say that Jesus was a male, and so one
cannot represent the crucified as a woman. But the vicious level of the protest
clearly goes beyond a mere statement of historical fact. What is being challenged is the concept that the suffering of a male God is redemptive for both
men and women, while the sufferings of women are regarded not only as non-

redemptive, but as pornographic. Images of tortured women abound in male sexual fantasy as objects of sadism. Thus to suggest that the image of a tortured woman represents the presence of redemptive divine power jars the patriarchal mentality deeply and is experienced as blasphemy against the sacred.

It is not at all clear how salutary it is for women to claim this image of the cru-cified to interpret their own sufferings under patriarchy. The image of Christ's crucifixion has for so long functioned as a tool of passive acceptance of victimi-zation that for most people, women especially, it has lost its meaning as divine presence in human suffering that empowers the explosive protest against and overthrow of unjust powers that proliferate violence and victimization. (p. 7)

I appreciate Ruether's concern over the historical glorification of vic-timization and the passive acceptance of suffering. The figure which she names the 'Christa' is far from a romantic Pietà; she is, rather, powerfully commanding in her insistence on life in the midst of suffering.

A different perspective on the Feminine Divine came to a woman in meditation. Her prayer group had been reading the epilogue to the Gospel of John, in which Jesus reveals himself to his disciples for the third time following his death and resurrection. Following the fishing theme of the scripture pasage, she suggested that each woman meditatively put out to sea with Jesus accompanying her in a fishing boat.

At this point, Jesus said, "Put your net down, and what you bring up is what I want you to give me." She lowered her net for the catch, and when she raised it, it contained a large wooden statue, about two feet high. A bit of blue remained on the skirt, indicating that this was a figure of the Virgin. She offered it to Jesus, saying, "Here is your mother." He held up his hands, refusing the gift. Looking at the statue she saw that it had no face. Again she offered the gift, saying, "I can't be sure this is Mary because she has no face, but the robes look like Mary's robes." Again he re-fused the gift. She dropped it and it smashed utterly.

At this point, Jesus had removed to the shore, where he stood beckoning to her. She began rowing, but the more she rowed the further away she drew. In desperation, she flung herself onto the shore. He embraced her three times, tears running down his cheeks.

The meditator was startled by this vision, and puzzled by several aspects. In working on it, she recalled that the context was a personal struggle with her own ministry, and her sense of frustration and futility as a woman in the Roman Catholic Church. In this crisis of trying to contrib-ute yet feeling unseen, she sought direction. Deep in the unconscious of most women, and perhaps especially so for Roman Catholic women, resides this self-effacing figure, so lauded by the patriarchy for her acceptance of anonymity. But she is not embraced by the Head of the Church. He refuses this featureless and passively fixed statue in favor of the struggling, live woman. His compassion is not earned by her frantic "rowing"; it is the passionate humanness of her struggle that is thrice blessed.

Returning to the handless maiden motif, I want to articulate a simple four-fold pattern of women's development. First, she is obedient to the personal father as head of the household. Next, she moves out into the world with the King as protector. (The King takes many forms today.) Then, she enters a deep introversion in which she goes into her own soul-space for transpersonal guidance. Finally, following naturally from a woman's centering in her own soul, there is a reconciliation of the masculine and feminine in an appropriate balance.

The poet Robert Bly uses this tale in talking about the need for "transformers," transformative figures who initiate us or help us prepare for and cross over into a new phase of life. They intensify the energy needed to make the shifts. He suggests three major transition points for a woman. The first energy transformer is usually the mother or mother substitute. That person takes the girlish energy and concentrates it in the feeling area, also teaching her how to make babies, how to do all the feminine arts—cooking, sewing, weaving, whatever, depending on the time and culture—but it's an *"in-the-house"* kind of energy. The second transformer helps the woman into the culture, but the third transformer needs to be a transpersonal one. Bly talks about Eros, relatedness, as transformative, and uses this story to illustrate what happens when there is inadequate Eros, which surely is the case with these parents. But he concludes that there is, as well, too little for either women *or* men to relate to at the transpersonal level: ". . . to some extent all of us have lost our hands because of the loss of ancient transformers. Men kept Christ, but in so doing lost Dionysius, and my hands are cut off. . . . The problem is that we, even men, are left with only one transformer in the third level and that is Christ." (p.33)

Jean Shinoda Bolen echoes Bly in singling out Aphrodite, the Goddess of Eros, as the transformer. She calls her "the alchemical goddess," and alchemy surely is about transformation in its several stages. But to whom do we look today for reliable relatedness in our process?

At the second level, the energy has to be gotten out into the world to serve the culture. In our time the transformer who helps to constellate that energy may be a mentor, a senior member of one's profession, one's therapist or analyst, or an old, wise relative, if one is lucky enough to have such a one.

The third transformer needs to be a transpersonal one. The task at this stage is to connect with the deepest feminine Self. A woman at this level is discovering her depths, and she may find a rough, dark energy there that will provide her with enormous strength, such as the image in the fourth dream. This is no lightweight, sweet and simple Virgin, a docile handmaiden of the Lord; this is a crucified and bloody woman. This is a woman who has been *through* it, and this is a woman who says, get on with it . . . make something. And what is to be made? At this stage, what is to be made is a Self. At this stage we realize that everything we are about is *not* to gratify the ego—*not* to look good in the world or to make money or something, but the life work of creating the Self that we are, that we will be, and that ultimately needs to be of the durability that will get it across the threshold called death. That is the great transition.

In the handless maiden tale I find a story for our times. The first stage is assumed in the opening image of the miller's daughter, sweeping out behind the house. She has learned from her mother the household tasks, and so forth. But then look how she has to go into the second stage: handless, not knowing how to make her way because her parents have sent her out unequipped. Her father has sold her off and her mother has not protected her from that. What she does have is the sense to get out, and piety; and she is protected, guided and aided by an archetypal spiritual level, represented by the angel. With inadequate personal parents, she has to connect to a different level of things. She's having a rough time of it; how long can she survive, eating pears off trees in other people's gardens at midnight?! And so she gets her second transformer, the King. Now, he loves her and does what he can for her, giving her silver hands. But to live in the masculine world, for a woman, *feels* artificial and only partially adequate. It feels like operating with hands that are not truly yours. Many women have been helped by men, and also have been aided by their own ego needs and *logos* thinking, all represented by the King . . . but finally, to be protected by the reigning powers is to have silver hands. The third transformer in this story is the snow-white maiden who lives in the house inscribed with the words, "Here everyone may live freely." This is an image of the feminine Self, the feminine Divine, and I take the house as a representation of soul. Here indeed is the place where everyone may live freely. This seven-year stretch in the woods is a period of deep introversion which is absolutely necessary to really get to the bottom of things, to really know oneself. And then she grows her own hands. She will have her own ground, her own standpoint, her own style, her own Self.

There is a variation on this tale that would have her child fall into a pool of water and, in reaching in to save him from drowning, her hands grow back. This is nice too, because the pool would image the depths of the unconscious and the child is so often a Self figure and contains all possibility, and of course it is to those deep places that we must attend.

What I am suggesting, then, is that the transformers at the third level, the transpersonal or religious level, have been inadequate or missing, but at the archetypal level *She* still lives. What is needed is a new sense of what piety means. Look to the story. For the handless maiden, piety first meant being dutiful to parents. Then it shifted and meant a reliance on a distant God and established male authority. But when all is gone and she feels utterly abandoned, piety takes a new form. This form of devotion to the discovery of her deepest Self ultimately brings about the reclamation of her handedness, and finally the balance of feminine and masculine aspects within her soul.

This, it seems to me, is what Jung has offered to us: the reality that at one time religion was an experience of the Divine energy, but the accompanying reality that that experience gets codified, dogmatized and institutionalized. If we would be in touch with living religion, with the still-pulsing life energy, we must go inside, turn ego's attention toward the Self in order to reconnect to our Source.

There are now many women in the outer world who have provided a model and given courage to other women. These are women who have found their own voice and expressed it creatively; I think particularly of Georgia O'Keeffe and Adrienne Rich, in art and letters. But each woman of this depth has struggled to find her own rhythm. For this may truly be the essential feature of a reliance on Her: that we develop a religious attitude, attending to the rhythm of the inner life of psyche, which sustains us on the path, is the path, and unfolds the path.

References

Bly, R. 1978. On the great mother and the new father. *East West Journal.* pp. 25–33 (Aug. 1978).

Bolen, J. S. 1984. *Goddesses in everywoman*. San Francisco: Harper and Row.

Englesman, J. C. 1979. *The feminine dimension of the divine*. Philadelphia: Westminster Press.

Kluger, R. S. 1960. Psychology and religion. Paper No. 8, The Analytical Psychology Club of Los Angeles.

Manheim, R., trans. 1983. *Grimms' tales for young and old*. Garden City, N.Y.: Anchor Press/Doubleday.

Ruether, R. R. 1986. Renewal or new creation: Feminist spirituality and historical religion. *Harvard Divinity Bulletin*, Feb./Mar. 1986, pp. 5–11.

"Images of Immortality": Jung and the Archetype of Death and Rebirth

David J. Dalrymple

Jung challenged modern men and women to take conscious account of their non-rational experiences. Jung's challenge specifically names the belief in immortality as a locus for religious imagination:

> A man should be able to say he has done his best to form a conception of life after death, or to create some image of it—even if he must confess his failure. Not to have done so is a vital loss. For the question that is posed to him is the age-old heritage of humanity . . . which seeks to add itself to our own individual life in order to make it whole. (Jung, 1961, p. 302)

A person goes beyond the "known framework" or "bounds of consciousness" set by reason when reflecting upon the archetype of immortality. Jung believed this endeavor was therapeutic for the soul's health and nourishment. Do contemporary men and women heed Jung's challenge? If not, where might individuals in modern times recognize such images of immortality?

An Intrinsic Concern of the Soul

My interest in this theme began as a boy when I became conscious of the reality of death. I took a bus ride with my father. My father's body was warm, secure, smelling of tobacco; he wore a red and black checked wool shirt. He felt like the Rock of Gibraltar—dependable, continuous, and eternal. His presence conveyed a feeling of immortality. Suddenly I realized, "This man will die one day!" I felt a profound recognition that "even the most dependable will die." This was my first conscious recognition of death. Not long after, I was listening to a radio preacher talk about afterlife. He spoke metaphorically about life beyond death, using an image which I remember to this day. He invited the listener to imagine a fetus in the womb as having consciousness. Its amniotic world would be its experience of "life," and its experience of "birth" would be perceived as "death"—the ending of an accustomed world. He asked, "Might this be an image for immortality? What is experienced as death might really be a birth into a new experience?" This was my first experience of eschatology, a reflection on endings; it shows how religious conceptions use images to convey non-rational insights and intuitions. The boy's questioning whether death might not be a final and unambiguous event illustrates how intrinsic the idea of immortality is in human experience once there is an awareness of the reality of death.

A Difficult Belief in Contemporary Life

The theme of immortality has fallen into neglect in modern times. Death has often come to be seen as the final annihilation of the individual personality, the absolute and irrevocable end of personal existence. Belief in an afterlife is often dismissed as having little significance, as being an anachronism. Even Shirley MacLaine's recent writing about her belief in reincarnation is entitled, *Out On a Limb*, suggesting it is a bit risky or lonely to share one's belief in immortality.

As a hospital chaplain, I sat with men and women preparing for death. Many individuals do not inwardly trust that personal awareness will continue after death. Public polls say the majority of Americans believe in a life after death; however, this may be a statement about "explicit faith" imposed from collective consciousness rather than an "implicit faith" unfolding from personal experience. Many "good Christians" are overwhelmed in their sick beds: although they have said, "Yes," to catechismic questions, they have little heartfelt trust that death might not be the final event of their experience. Why is this ancient belief so "lifeless" in contemporary religion?

Others (Grof and Grof, 1980; Kelsey, 1979) suggest that dehumanization and alienation of "the soul" in Western culture is the shadow side of our materialistic and scientific bias. Industrialized society has alienated people from the "biological basics" of life—birth, sex, death, and spirituality. Many individuals are taught that a belief in immortality is incompatible with modern science. The Cartesian-Newtonian world view suggests that consciousness is the product of the biological brain and that it ceases at the time of biological death. Until the past decade, science has avoided discussions of life after death. The possibility of consciousness after death was rejected because it was not compatible with existing scientific theories—not because it was contradicted by any clinical observations. A news article recently suggested, "Near-death experiences deemed worthy of serious research," but still highlighted the tendency of the scientific/medical community to dismiss these experiences as "made-up fantasy," "biochemical or neurophysiological states caused by lack of oxygen or drugs," "the result of religious programming," or a defensive "denial of unpleasant experience" (Jan Ziegler, *Chicago Tribune*, Oct. 5, 1985).

Another reason why belief in immortality has lost its vitality is religious orthodoxy. Religion is often externalized: religious teachings have become creedal and dogmatic rather than existential and inward. The authority in religious matters becomes external—the Bible, the Pope, the creeds and dogmas. People do not look within personal experience for that inner connection to belief. They look outwardly for cues as to belief rather than reflecting inwardly to imaginative processes.

Psychoanalytic Thoughts on Immortality

Similar biases were reflected in psychoanalytic tradition. Sigmund Freud (1949, 1961) suggested the aim of life was death, that there was an innate tendency for human life to return to an inanimate state. Freud stressed the biological truth about death—the absolute destruction of the organism. Freud believed people should be educated to accept reality; he slighted religion as the chief supporter of humanity's illusions. Spiritual comfort was a neurotic support for people who could not outgrow childish illusions. People needed to face the hard realities of life and death with no false hopes. A belief in immortality was compensation for the reality of death which was hard to face: to see death as not being total and final was a false hope. The only real hope was "the rational pursuit of truth." Death was final—the total annihilation of individual. Freud may be admired for his impatience with humanity's ability for self-delusion and for his recognition that facing death could heighten the vitality of living. However, Freud did not value the emotional impact of symbolic experience upon the psyche whether or not a spiritual reality exists behind the "illusions" associated with religious belief.

Recent psychoanalytic thought has acknowledged this limitation in Freud's thinking. R. J. Lifton and E. Olson (1974) recognized that Freud "did not grasp the symbolic significance of images of immortality. In this he underestimated the human need for images of connection beyond the life span of each individual" (*ibid.*, p. 58). Freud did not do justice to the human tendency to continually create and re-create images which could symbolically connect an individual beyond one's own life span. Lifton and Olson conclude that our images of immortality are "psychologically extremely powerful" (*ibid.*, p. 55). The writings of Ernest Becker (1973, 1975) articulate a theory of human nature compatible with Lifton's revaluation of images of immortality. Becker concluded that humanity's innate fear of death underlies modern collective madness: The fear of death and desperate need for symbolic immortality create the dependencies behind authoritarian states.

Jung's Appreciation for the Belief in Immortality

Jung was struck by the fact that myths of all cultures and ages contain beliefs about life after death. Reflections on the unknown mysteries of birth, life, death, fate, and immortality are needed emotional experiences:

> The belief in immortality gives life that untroubled flow into the future so necessary if stoppages and regressions are to be avoided. Although we like to use the word "doctrine" for these—psychologically speaking—extremely important ideas, it would be a great mistake to think that they are just arbitrary intellectual theories. Psychologically regarded, they are emotional experiences whose nature cannot be discussed. . . . To experience them is a charisma which no human art can compel. Only unreserved surrender can hope to reach such a goal. (Jung, 1966, par. 186)

The belief in immortality was "hygienic" in that it added to the meaning, animation, and quality of life. Life could be lived most fully to the end when we had viable images of immortality. As Jung admitted, "When I live in a house that I know will fall about my head within the next two weeks, all my vital functions will be impaired by this thought, but if, on the contrary, I feel myself to be safe, I can dwell there in a normal comfortable way." This admission could be seen as an argument for illusion. However, Jung's respect for immortality was not an illusory denial of death. He admitted that death was "a cruel reality which we have no right to sidestep" (1961, p. 314). Jung suffered great loss at the time of his wife's death as well as at the deaths of friends. The separation from one's loved ones was painful for him—"a silence that has no answer."

Meditating upon images of immortality helps us sense the eternal timelessness of the soul: "If we understand and feel that here in this life we already have a link with the infinite, desires and attitudes change" (1961, p. 325). Jung recognized he had contributed one important scientific recognition to the problem of life after death—his empirical investigations showed the psyche extends into the realm of timelessness and spacelessness (Jaffé, 1979b). He expressed this in his essay, "The Soul and Death" (1969a). He had highlighted this to a good friend's widow in a letter on December 23, 1950:

> This spectacle of old age would be unendurable did we not know that our psyche reaches into a region held captive neither by change in time nor by limitation of place. In that form of being our birth is a death and our death a birth. The scales of the whole hang together.

Jung pointed out that rebirth was a purely psychic experience which could only be conveyed indirectly through personal statements (1969b). Even though direct, empirical observation of such mysteries was scientifically impossible, Jung valued the personal accounts of death and rebirth. The archetype of death and rebirth is inherent in Jung's theories of the transformation of libido and the symbol-creating processes of regression and progressive renewal (1956). Death and rebirth can be seen in such individuation experiences as working through life transitions or within the analytical process as analysands assimilate aspects of the unconscious. Death and rebirth can be seen in passages through major crises, such as puberty, marriage, illness. In speaking of the archetype of the Self, Jung saw that images of immortality are symbols of "the treasure hard to attain": the water of life, the healing herb, the elixer of immortality, the philosopher's stone, miracle rings, magic hoods, winged cloaks. This "treasure" suggests that immortality corresponds analogously to self-discovery and the individuation process. In all creative acts, there is a liberation of what was held captive and an acquisition of some "treasure" which releases productive energy in the soul.

Archetypal Images of Immortality

Jung alluded to the "age-old heritage of humanity" which still seeks to address us in images of immortality. Burial customs contain ancient images of immortality associated with the myth of Osiris, the Lord of Eternity. Osiris was dismembered, his sacred phallus underwent a descent to the Underworld; ascension and reconstitution followed; then Osiris fathered Horus whose lineage connected to the Sun principle (the Sun descends nightly and ascends each morning so this was an image of immortality). Osiris was shut in a chest whose wood was seen as connected to the enduring life of the earth; the coffin made the corpse everlasting. The preservation of bodily shape through embalming was connected to personal afterlife. In the *Egyptian Book of the Dead*, there is a recurring expression, "Together with Osiris." This was the promise that the Ba Soul (the inner presence animating the body) could travel between the land of the living and the land of the dead. This image suggests the psyche has a connection to an eternal world of timelessness and spacelessness beyond the temporal world of consciousness.

The teachings of Zoroaster had an eschatology expressed in images. The "Wise Lord" was imagined as judging the ethical balance of a person's life through tests of fire or weighing scales. Graphic images suggested accountability in the experience of death. The Chinvat Bridge was the Bridge of Judgment. The upright man approaching the Bridge smelled sweet scents of the Garden of Paradise Beyond. A beautiful maiden was met personifying his conscience. She guided him to the House of Song and reunion with the Wise Lord and his righteous company. However, the evil man was forced to inhale a sickening odor and his conscience was a fat, naked, obnoxious, ugly woman who shoved him off the Bridge and into the abyss of Hell below.

The early Hebrews believed that the human being was a body with breath for his soul and organs, whose functions were both physical and psychical. They were not convinced that a dead person was altogether dead. The early Hebrews felt the soul after death was still a body — shadowy replicas of the flesh called *raphaim* (shadows or ghosts). The Hebrew cosmos was three-storied: the heaven above, the earth beneath, and *Sheol* or the abode of the departed below the earth. To the early Hebrews, there was little hope associated with Sheol. It was pallid, unreal, and undesirable. One of the major factors in redeeming Sheol from its original negativity and in arousing hope of resurrection to full life again was the extension of Yahweh's sovereignty to the underworld. Sheol transformed as an image: it ceased to be a meaningless, non-moral land of darkness. It became ethically significant with reward and punishment.

The Biblical hope of life after death was influenced by the growing experience of personal religion — an inward, intimate relationship between the individual soul and God. This "inner connection" yields an experience of essential timelessness, a kind of fellowship with the numinous which suggests its own continuance. If God cares for the individual and dwells inwardly, it feels impossible that the relationship will be abruptly terminated at death. The first Christians applied inherited images of immortality to the death of Jesus, his stay in Sheol, and his bodily resurrection. Millions of Christians still confess their faith saying, "Jesus died . . . descended into hell . . . and rose again." This was a story echoing Jewish themes and highlighting a physical resurrection to restored vitality on earth. This "resurrected body" was the Christian image of life after death even though there was confusion about what the body meant. For Paul, it was not the corruptible flesh and blood but the incorruptible body of man. It was a raised "spiritual body." Eventually, this was imagined as an interior experience. The Gospel hope was not for resurrection on earth but for an eternal life that was not a post-mortem goal but an inner and present posssession of the soul: ". . . whoever believes in him should not perish but have eternal life" (John 3:16). Jesus was the model of a filial relationship with God, a vital experience carrrying confidence that death is an open door through which the soul's life with God moves onward (Hick, 1976).

Images in Modern Experiences of Life After Death

New accounts (Moody, Osis & Haraldsson, Rawlings, Ring) remind us of these ancient concerns about the soul after death. They challenge Western science's dismissal of enduring consciousness beyond death. The first study of near-death experience was by a Swiss geologist who had a mystical experience in a near fatal fall in the Alps (Grof and Grof, 1980). He became interested in the subjective experiences related to life-threatening experiences. Another investigator, Karlis Osis, analyzed questionnaires from physicians in 1961. Vivid visions and images were experienced by patients the hour before death: images of heaven, paradise, the Eternal City, beautiful landscapes, exotic birds, idyllic gardens; very seldom were there terrifying images of devils, hell, or judgment. In 1971 Russell Noyes, a Professor of Psychiatry, studied accounts of people facing death and the autobiographical accounts of exceptional people, like Jung himself, who had described near-death experiences. He identified three successive stages in the patterns: *resistance* (danger, fear, struggle, acceptance), *life review* (reliving memories of one's life trajectory), and *transcendence* (mystical, religious, cosmic consciousness). A composite model of the typical after-death state has been reconstructed from the accounts of individual experience (Grof and Grof, 1980, pp. 12–13). Characteristic elements occur even though these do not necessarily occur in rigid sequence. The experience is ineffable or hard to put into words. The person hears himself pronounced dead. There is a sense of peacefulness. Noises such as buzzings can be heard. The person is drawn down a tunnel-like space such as a narrow valley or well. There is separation from the body as one is drawn through and out of it. There is a sense of isolation and separation. There is the meeting with friends or family who have already died. There is a coming into the presence of the "being of light" who asks two essential questions—"Have you gained knowledge and wisdom?" and "Have you experienced love with others?" There is a review of the person's entire life. The person feels in touch with all wisdom and knowledge. One sees the city of light or heaven. There are observations of other souls who are caught or cannot make up their minds. There is a rescue from death, or a protective presence, or a point of no return and blockage from going farther. There is frustration in returning to normal life. There are profound changes following this death and revival experience.

A man trapped in a nuclear plant with toxic fumes shared his near-death account. It was like standing on a lake shore being surrounded by fog. He felt joy and freedom as pain was gone—"like a gull floating on air currents"—and was on a definite course guided by something. He saw things, but they were hard to describe; what he saw was good. When the fog cleared, he became aware of his anger with the doctor who resuscitated him since he did not want to leave the serenity and peacefulness. This experience had a qualitative impact upon his life and relationship to death. As he summarized,

> I don't think I will ever be afraid to die because of this experience. It was like being able to open the door to a room just a crack to peek in but not allowed to open it all the way to enter. I have now changed my life style and goals and started to live and grow as a person realizing that there are other things to life than working constantly. Before this experience I never let myself become totally involved with people. I don't know if it was because I feared being rejected or if it was selfishness on my part. Since I have reflected on death, life has become more important to me. I've learned that I don't have to wait until death is at my doorstep before I start to live. I should live the years that I have left, live each day as if it were the only one that I have left and start to live life instead of merely passing through it. "Stop to smell the roses," is an expression I am fond of. But that simple expression can mean so much when I really

start to do it. I want to enjoy what God has provided for me in the limited time that he has given me to live. It's not the quantity of life that a person has but the quality of that life that counts.

In 1944, Jung suffered a heart attack and had a near-death experience with powerful visions: "It is impossible to convey the beauty and intensity of emotion during those visions. They were the most tremendous things I have ever experienced" (1961, p. 295). Jung's visions are vividly described in his autobiography; they are rich with images of immortality which profoundly affected his life and work. These visions had a "quality of absolute objectivity" in which Jung experienced "the ecstasy of a non-temporal state in which present, past, and future are one."

Transpersonal States of Awareness

Altered states of consciousness yield images of immortality. Mystical or transpersonal experiences of "ego death" can be induced by psychoactive drugs or by the evocative breathing facilitated by the Grofs who use hyperventilation and powerful music. The Grofs use the analogy of the birth experience for death and rebirth experiences. There is the initial "good womb" of life's stability and tranquility and then a "no exit" when strong anxieties invade the good womb. This is followed by the "birth/death conflict" as suffering and agony are contained in the womb. Lastly, there is the releasing "birth/death experience" as the cervix of passage opens and birth occurs with its liberating expansion. The archetype of death and rebirth is central to all ecstatic, mystical, or transpersonal experiences whether induced by dance, breathing, music, psychedelic drugs, crisis and spiritual emergencies, or ritual encounters; it is the core of shamanic initiation, rites of passage, and the ancient mystery religions (Eliade, 1958). The Greeks used to say, "For one who is initiated, death is not the worst enemy."

A friend's story illustrates a death and rebirth experience. He was traveling with hippies who shared their psychedelic fare. The driver suggested, "We could hit another car head on." My friend felt physical resistance to suggestions of death. Finally, he yielded to this awareness. He had visions or "transpersonal imagery" of a whirling uroboric serpent, the Garden of Eden, feminine guides, the Egyptian pyramids and vibrating hieroglyphics. He felt currents of "life's eternal energies." There was a beautiful peacock whose heart pulsed vivid, acrylic colors that swirled out through the tail and into concentric, whirling mandalas of color that seemed to spread to the limits of his skull. Then his ego consciousness returned and he could relate to time, space, and the human community. Several days later he synchronously discovered Jung's work, *The Archetypes and the Collective Unconscious*; he found an image of the peacock, a Gnostic and Christian image of the immortality of soul (1969b, p. 375). An ancient image had manifested itself in his ecstatic experience.

Dreams and Death

Dreams present images of immortality. Jung and von Franz observed that dreams respond to the imminence of death no differently than they do to most major life experiences. The unconscious views death with less anxiety, apprehension, and concern than does the conscious ego. It is as if a deep part of the psyche knows life is a conjunction as much as it is a separation. Jungians have written about images of death in dreams. Jung knew that dreams in which the dreamer dies do not suggest physical death but may image a change of consciousness. Herzog (1967) wrote on psyche and death in archaic myths and modern dreams, noting the evolution of the images onto which we project our concepts of death (animal, human, mother, marriage, and fate); he noted how primitive images of death reappear in modern dreams. Jaffé (1979) took an archetypal approach to death dreams and ghosts. James Hall (1977) gives illustrations that the psyche "seems to contain archetypal images of death being something other than annihilation" (p. 310). James Hillman (1979) sees death as a metaphor for the ego's sense of death; he suggests that our living connection to death or the underworld has gone into the unconscious and that, "Depth psychology is where today we find the initiatory mystery, the long journey of psychic learning, ancestor worship, the encounter with demons and shadows, the sufferings of Hell" (*ibid.*, p. 65).

Dreams can be useful with terminally ill patients. The dream can be a bridge over which inner connections are made to feelings, memories, and intuitions of immortality. A woman dying of cancer had the following dream:

> I am on a railway train. I am not sure where I am going. At first, I feel a lot of anxiety and fear since I do not know the destination. There is a helpful man who accompanies and guides me on this journey. We travel through two room-like realms. This space is dark, like nighttime; however, the moon hangs in the sky in this middle realm. At the end of this journey, I meet my father, who welcomes me with an embrace.

This dying woman felt no control over her fate; she was afraid of the unknown. The helpful man reminded her of the calming presence that she had associated with Jesus earlier in her life, "a religious teacher and guide." There is the passage between the familiar realm and the unknown place. The moon hangs symbolically over this journey—an image of immortality since its birth, death, and resurrection phases each month symbolize immortality. The moon symbolizes the dark side of Nature as well as the spiritual light in the darkness as the "eye of the Night." Time is measured in lunar phases. It is the bringer of change, decay, suffering. Moon goddesses were controllers of destiny and weavers of fate. As this patient associated to her father, she began to cry as she remembered his love.

A patient dying of kidney failure shared this dream the day before his death. He was a farmer who was reluctant to give up control and hooked anxieties around his vocation. He dreamed:

> I am in my tractor. A swarm of bees comes across the furrowed field. They seem to drive me out of the cab of my tractor. I walk out onto the field. I realize that I have done all the plowing already. There is nothing more to do now. I feel good about what I have accomplished in the field. The swarm of bees moves down the field. I follow in that direction.

This patient consolidated feelings about his life's labors; he seemed to be letting go, recognizing he had accomplished a great deal in his life and could move on. The bee symbolized the soul in Orphic teachings since honey followed their labors and the migration in swarms from the hive was analogous to human souls "swarming" from the divine unity. The archetype of death and rebirth was central in the Orphic mysteries. The bee is connected to Dionysius, the Lord of Souls who was also a dying and reborn god.

A dying woman had the following dream as she grieved the lost opportunities of watching her young daughter grow up. This dream anticipated reconciliation to her death:

> I am in a house. It is a familiar house. I have explored all of the rooms. However, there is one door which I have not walked through yet. I know there are many corridors and spaces yet to discover on the other side of that door. I stand in front of it. There are animals lying down at my feet—a lion, a lamb, and a deer. An Oriental wise man stands beside this door I have not yet walked through; he has a circular, elaborate gold gong that hangs suspended in front of him. This gong has religious teachings engraved on it in an Oriental script. This holy man holds a stick to strike the gong with. I wonder if the door will open once he strikes the gong.

There was calm expectation as this woman elaborated her dream. She used the dream images to explore beliefs about life and afterlife. She died with trust that her journey would not end with dying. She expressed curiosity about the possibilities on the other side of the dream door.

Death needs to be talked about from "the inside" as much as from the outside. Experiential approaches such as sharing dreams, drawing pictures, symbolic death rituals, and guided fantasies can be used. The Simontons (1978) use active imagination at their Cancer Counseling and Research Center. Using a relaxation technique, patients imagine their deaths and funerals, and what will happen to them after death. They let consciousness go out into the universe until in the presence of whatever they believe to be the source. They review life experiences in detail with this presence. They imagine returning to earth in a new body and creating new life plans. They come to appreciate that the process of death and rebirth is continuous with every change in feelings and beliefs (pp. 225ff). The implications of this "Death and Rebirth Fantasy" suggest that images are different, personal, and unique. The experience is not as painful as people fear; valuable insights are gained to ease the inevitable pain and sadness of death. Old beliefs die as new attitudes unfold from imaginal experience of life after death.

Immortality as an Ex-centric Belief

The belief in immortality is less an anachronistic belief than an eccentric belief. It is ex-centric in nature: it reminds us that human existence is "ex-centric." Several months before his death, Jung wrote:

> It is quite possible that we look at the world from the wrong side and that we might find the right answer by changing our point of view and looking at it from the other side, i.e., not from outside, but from inside. (Letter on August 10, 1960)

Our images of immortality help us see from inside or from outside our circle of consciousness. They remind us that something profoundly "other" walks with us. "Consciousness" means "knowing with another"; a "co-knower" is part of being conscious. There is some other vantage point which makes consciousness possible. We are always living and knowing with "another." We see ourselves, hear ourselves, observe ourselves, know ourselves with this "other." This "other" is not merely in humanity, it seems to make humanity. This "other" is transcendent in constituting life, death, and consciousness. This "co-knower" is indeed a mystery. Quite independent of death, this "companioning other" perceives and in perceiving posits an existence beyond death as witnessed in our images of immortality.

Death reminds us of the ex-centric character of our lives. We live with consciousness between the two great mysteries of birth and death, of the before and of the afterward. The fact that we can speak of a before and an after reminds us that death, like birth, is not fulfilled in our mortal lifetimes. In traditional Jungian understanding, death and immortality help us displace the center of personality from the ego to the deeper Self, to the inmost experience of the individuation process. The personality senses the transitory character of the ego—it is relativized. The individual intuits some partial affinity with the Self. We savor an inner consciousness as the ego experiences the deep, abiding, eternal, and immortal Self. As we attend to the primary phenomenon of images, we are companioned by the specific face of the mystery seeking our attention. We hear something hidden shine through the phenomenon of the images even as their mystery remains veiled. We experience what Jung called "*esse in anima*," a being-in-soul. We feel the animating connection to the deep mysteries of birth, life, death, and afterlife which address us from within the images of immortality.

Jung's observations and challenge help us step beyond the grip of limiting cultural attitudes about death and immortality. Jung affirms the emotional impact of images of immortality:

> To the intellect, all my mythologizing is futile speculation. To the emotions, however, it is a healing and valid activity; it gives existence a glamor which we would not like to do without. Nor is there any good reason why we should. (1961, pp. 300–301).

References

Becker, E. 1973. *The denial of death*. New York: The Free Press.
_____. 1975. *The structure of evil*. New York: The Free Press.
Eliade, M. 1958. *Rites and symbols of initiation: The mysteries of birth and rebirth*. New York: Harper and Row.
Freud, S. 1949. *The future of an illusion*. London: Hogarth Press.
Franz, M.-L. von. "Reflections, questions and answers," Notre Dame Conference, April 1975.
_____. 1959. *Beyond the pleasure principle*. New York: Bantam Books.
_____. 1961. *Civilization and its discontents*. New York: Norton, Inc.
Grof, S. 1976. *Realms of the human unconscious*. New York: E.P. Dutton.
_____. 1977. *The human encounter with death*. New York: E.P. Dutton.
_____. and Grof, C. 1980. *Beyond death: The gates of consciousness*. New York: Thames and Hudson.

Hall, J. 1977. "Dreams about death," in *Clinical uses of Dreams*. New York: Grune and Stratton.

Herzog, E. 1967. *Psyche and death: Archaic myths and modern dreams in analytical psychology.* New York: G. P. Putnam's Sons.

Hick, J. 1976. *Death and eternal life.* New York: Harper and Row.

Hillman, J. 1979. *The dream and the underworld.* New York: Harper and Row.

Jaffé, A. 1979a. *Apparitions: An archetypal approach to death dreams and ghosts.* Dallas: Spring Publications.

——————. 1979b. "Life and death," in *Jung: Word and image.* Princeton: Princeton University Press.

Jung, C. G. 1956. *Symbols of transformation.* In *Collected works*, vol. 5. Princeton: Princeton University Press, 1956.

——————. 1961. *Memories, dreams, reflections.* New York: Random House.

——————. 1966. *The practice of psychotherapy.* In *Collected works*, vol. 13. Princeton: Princeton University Press, 1967.

——————. 1969a. *The structure and dynamics of the psyche.* In *Collected works*, vol. 8. Princeton: Princeton University Press, 1969.

——————. 1969b. *The archetypes and the collective unconscious.* In *Collected works*, vol. 9, part 1. Princeton: Princeton University Press, 1969.

Kelsey, M. 1979. *Afterlife: The other side of dying.* New York: Paulist Press.

Lifton, R. J., and Olson, E. 1974. *Living and dying.* New York: Bantam Books.

Moody, R., Jr. 1975. *Life after life.* Atlanta: Mockingbird Books.

——————. 1977. *Reflections on life after life.* New York: Bantam Books.

Osis, K., and Haraldsson, E. 1977. *At the hour of death.* New York: Avon.

Ring, K. 1980. *Life at death: A scientific investigation of the near-death experience.* New York: Coward, McCann & Geoghegan.

Simontons, O.C., and S. 1978. *Getting well again.* Los Angeles: J. P. Tarcher, Inc.

Notes About the Contributors

David J. Dalrymple is a Jungian analyst in private practice in Rockford, Illinois. He is a member of the Chicago Society of Jungian Analysts.

William Dols, Jr., is at the Graduate Theological Union and the University of California at Berkeley. He is an adjunct faculty member of the Church Divinity School of the Pacific. He is an ordained priest in the Episcopal Church.

Carrin Dunne is an assistant professor of religious studies at Rice University and an instructor at the C. G. Jung Center in Houston. She is the author of *Buddha and Jesus: Conversations* (1975).

Joan Chamberlain Engelsman is the coordinator of community education at Grace Counseling Center in New Jersey and an adjunct assistant professor of religion in the graduate school at Drew University. She is the author of *The Feminine Dimension of the Divine* (1979).

Julia M. Jewett is a pastoral psychotherapist at the First Presbyterian Church in Evanston, Illinois, and has a private practice in Wilmette, Illinois. She is on the adjunct faculty of the Department of Religious Studies at Mundelein College.

David L. Miller is Professor of Religious Studies at Syracuse University and the author of *The New Polytheism* (1981); *Christs: Meditations on Archetypal Images in Christian Theology* (1981); and *Three Faces of God: Traces of the Trinity in Literature and Life* (1986).

189

Robert L. Moore is a professor of psychology and religion at the Chicago Theological Seminary. He is the author of *John Wesley and Authority: A Psychological Perspective* (1979) and co-author of the *The Cult Experience: Responding to the New Religious Pluralism* (1982). He edited *Sources of Vitality in American Church Life* (1978) and co-edited *Anthropology and the Study of Religion* (1984). From 1978 to 1984 he served as Chairman of the Religion and Social Sciences Section of the American Academy of Religion.

Wayne G. Rollins is a professor of religious studies at Assumption College in Worcester, Massachusetts. He is the author of *Jung and the Bible* (1983) and *The Gospels: Portraits of Christ* (1974).

Nathan Schwartz-Salant practices as a Jungian analyst in New York City, where he is on the faculty of the C. G. Jung Training Center and is a member of the training board of the New York Association for Analytical Psychology. He is the author of *Narcissism and Character Transformation: The Psychology of Narcissistic Character Disorders* (1982) and co-editor of *The Chiron Clinical Series.*

June Singer is a Jungian analyst in private practice in Palo Alto, California. She is the author of *The Unholy Bible: Blake, Jung, and the Collective Unconscious* (reprinted 1986); *Boundaries of the Soul: The Practice of Jung's Psychology* (1972); *Androgyny: Toward a New Theory of Sexuality* (1976); and *Energies of Love.*

Murray Stein is a Jungian analyst who has a private practice in Wilmette, Illinois. He is the author of *Jung's Treatment of Christianity* (1985) and *In Midlife* (1983), and the editor of *Jungian Analysis* (1982), as well as co-editor of *The Chiron Clinical Series.*